Studebaker's XH-9350

and Their Involvement with Other Aircraft Engines

Studebaker's XH-9350

and Their Involvement with Other Aircraft Engines

William Pearce

OLD MACHINE PRESS

Old Machine Press
Los Osos, CA
www.oldmachinepress.com

ISBN 978-0-9850353-1-0

Revision 20181111

Front cover:
*Top—Studebaker's Red Ball logo that served the
company from 1936 to around 1950, and a drawing
of the complete XH-9350 engine.*
*Bottom—Waldo Waterman's Studebaker-powered
Arrowbile 1, Studebaker-built Wright R-1820
production, and Studebaker-built GE J47 turbojet
engine.*

Back cover:
Top—Section drawing of the XH-cylinder.
*Bottom—Top view drawing of the XH-9350 engine,
and a complete XH-cylinder.*

Image credits:
A: Author
AC: Author's Collection
AEHS: Aircraft Engine Historical Society
BL: Bill Lewis Collection
Hughes: Hughes Aircraft
LIFE: LIFE Magazine
LoC: Library of Congress
NARA: U.S. National Archives and Records Administration
PM: Paul Matt Collection
SDASM: San Diego Air and Space Museum
USAF: United States Air Force
The ads throughout the book were published 1942–1945 in a number of magazines such as Collier's,
LIFE Magazine, National Geographic, The Saturday Evening Post, and others.

Contents

From the highways of peace to the skyways of war...

The highest honor that could be paid any motor car manufacturer...

Studebaker BUILDS CYCLONE ENGINES FOR THE *Flying Fortress*

Working together for victory—America's oldest builder of airplane engines—Wright! America's oldest manufacturer of highway transportation—Studebaker! The expanded facilities of Studebaker have augmented those of Wright in providing battle-proved Wright engines for the Boeing Flying Fortress, invincible dreadnaught of the skies. Studebaker is proud of its assignments in the arming of our United States. The same skill, the same Studebaker plus, which have gone into every Studebaker car and truck are today going into every implement of war being produced by Studebaker.

★ STUDEBAKER'S 90TH ANNIVERSARY 1852-1942 ★

Preface

The Studebaker XH-9350 engine (MX-232 project) has interested me for many years. Very little has been written about this engine, and it has remained somewhat of a mystery. Why would such a large engine with huge 8.0" cylinders be built, and why did it produce only 5,000 hp from its 9,350 in³ displacement? Most have concluded that it was a poorly-conceived project executed as the jet age dawned.

Some years ago, Kimble McCutcheon (president of the *Aircraft Engine Historical Society*) embarked on a mission to write a book on each of the World War II hyper-engines. When his second book (*Chrysler Aircraft Engines*) was published in 2012, I jokingly asked him when a book on the XH-9350 would be completed. While not a hyper-engine, the XH-9350 was developed in the same World War II time frame. Kim surprised me with his response, basically saying the XH-9350 book would be published when I wrote it. He had around 2,500 scans and photos of MX-232 project data from the National Archives and offered them to me, provided I would try to put together something on the XH-9350.

At first I was a little overwhelmed by the number of digital files Kim had given me. But as I organized the files into chronological order, a clear picture began to emerge of the MX-232 project and its development. The long forgotten files contained information regarding why the engine was so large, its intended purpose, and the people most responsible for the XH-9350.

About this time, something unexpected happened: numerous Studebaker MX-232 files became available on eBay. I was shocked by the coincidence. I began to buy what I could. Some of the files added new and intriguing facets to the story, others were duplicates of what I was given from the National Archives, and some were not relevant. The files all belonged to a man named Tilley, and I couldn't help but wonder why the files were suddenly available and from several different sellers.

Norman Tilley was in charge of the XH-9350's design. The government asked him to join Studebaker and design the engine. He accepted and devoted around four years of his life to the project. Apparently, Tilley kept a huge amount of material, not just on the MX-232 project, but also on his other pursuits during his 40-plus year career in aviation. When Tilley passed away in 1962, his collection went to his son, Norman Tilley Jr., who kept the files until he passed away in 2012. Tilley Jr. had no children and was preceded in death by his wife. After Tilley Jr.'s death, various estate sales offered the files on eBay, with the inevitable consequence of them being scattered in all directions.

I wish I could have met with Tilley Jr. It would have been fascinating to hear his recollections of his father, and perhaps his collection of files could have been preserved intact. Based on the files I was able to acquire, I can only imagine what else he had saved over the years. Sadly, I only learned of Tilley Jr. from his obituary, and it was through his passing that the documents became available. I am sure Tilley Jr. would be pleased to know that the files he saved for so many years helped record the true history of his father's misunderstood and long forgotten engine project. As unfortunate as it may be that the collection is now fragmented, there is no telling how many other people acquired some of the Tilley files for their projects.

Admittedly, I have no idea what additional information on the MX-232 project could exist— maybe something that would add immeasurable depth to the project that I have worked so hard to accurately record, or perhaps nothing at all. Even though the records I have covering the events of late 1942 and early 1943 are sparse, and I am confident I have covered more than 90% of the story.

I know that Tilley Sr. kept these documents for 20 years, and Tilley Jr. kept them for 50 years. I too shall keep them and ensure they get passed to an organization that will continue to preserve them—they contain history worth remembering.

My sincerest thanks go to Kim McCutcheon, William Lewis, and the *Aircraft Engine Historical Society* (www.enginehistory.com) for all of their assistance. Very special thanks to my wife Katie for all her help and encouragement.

William Pearce
wpearce@oldmachinepress.com
November 2018

1. Studebaker History

H & C Studebaker

With $68, some tools, and a lot of talent inherited from their forefathers, Henry and Clement Studebaker founded H & C Studebaker on 16 February 1852 in South Bend, Indiana. It was a blacksmith business with a forge for making horseshoes, wagon wheels, complete wagons, and miscellaneous parts for just about everything a frontiersman needed. Business was slow at first, but H & C Studebaker grew to meet the needs of people traveling west for the California Gold Rush.

Henry (1826–1895) and Clem (1831–1901) had moved to South Bend in 1850 in search of more opportunities and a better life. They were the oldest of John and Rebecca Studebaker's five sons. The next eldest son was John Mohler (1833–1917), followed by Peter Everest (1836–1897), and Jacob Franklin (1844–1887). John and Rebecca had five daughters too: Sarah (1822–1901), Nancy (1825–1895), Elizabeth (1829–1909), Rebecca (1837–1915), and Maria (1840–1925). The rest of the Studebaker family moved to South Bend in 1851. All of the sons had inherited their father's blacksmithing and wagon building abilities and helped out at H & C Studebaker.

However, John Mohler grew restless and headed to California in 1853 to pick up the gold nuggets that were said to be lying around. He left with $65, and when he arrived in Hangtown (now Placerville), CA, he had only a 50-cent piece in his pocket. John Mohler did not find gold lying around, but he found that people would pay him gold for his services of making wheelbarrows and pick axes, repairing wagons, and other smith work. The demand for equipment during the California Gold Rush made John Mohler a rich man. He made so many wheelbarrows, he was known as "Wheelbarrow Johnny."

John Mohler paid close attention to the repairs that were needed to the wagons after they had made the journey out west. He sent his insights back to H & C Studebaker, where the information was used to make better wagons. These wagons soon became known for their quality and sturdiness. In 1857, H & C Studebaker was subcontracted by another wagon maker to build wagons for the US Army. Although it was good business, Henry, a deeply religious man, wanted to pursue a simple life of farming. Henry and Clem convinced John Mohler to come back home and help out with H & C Studebaker so that Henry could retire.

In April 1858, John Mohler closed up his shop (the site is now California Historic Landmark #142) and returned to South Bend. He took with him the $8,000 he had earned making tools for the prospectors. H & C Studebaker was getting by, but it did not have the resources needed to expand the business. John Mohler bought out Henry with $3,000 and invested the rest of his money into the company. Up until that investment, H & C Studebaker had built wagons by order. Now the company had the capital to build wagons and find customers for them.

Peter had split off from H & C Studebaker and operated a general store in Goshen, Indiana. In 1860, John Mohler arranged to offer Studebaker wagons at Peter's store. Peter built a shed next to his store (Studebaker's first showroom outside of South Bend) and quickly became Studebaker's top salesman, selling wagons as fast as they arrived. The business was doing well.

In 1861, the Civil War started and brought with it a huge demand for wagons. In 1862, purchasing agents from Washington, DC came to H & C Studebaker requesting all the wagons that could be made. The company expanded quickly, and Peter came back to South Bend to help. After the war, in 1868, H & C Studebaker was incorporated and changed its name to the Studebaker Brothers Manufacturing Company. That year the company made 3,395 vehicles and continued to expand. Sales increased to 6,950 vehicles in 1872 and to 11,050 vehicles in 1874. By 1876,

Studebaker was turning out a finished vehicle every seven minutes and claimed to be the largest wagon and carriage works in the world. Jacob, the youngest brother, passed away in 1887. Before his death, he built a Studebaker salesroom and carriage plant (now known as the Fine Arts Building) in Chicago, Illinois. At the Chicago Fair in 1893, Studebaker displayed 30 different vehicles.

Presidents Abraham Lincoln, Benjamin Harrison, and William McKinley were Studebaker customers, and the Studebaker wagon was known around the world. Orders came in from Africa, Australia, China, Europe, and South America. In November 1899, then war correspondent Winston Churchill and his Studebaker wagon were captured in South Africa during the second Boer War. Fortunately for the future fate of the world, Churchill quickly escaped.

The Horseless Carriage

There was change on the horizon. Since their inception, horseless carriages had been steadily gaining in popularity. Studebaker had been discussing horseless carriages since 1895. A major proponent of the idea was John Mohler's son-in-law, Frederick S. Fish (1852–1936). In 1896, the company allocated $4,000 to build and test a "horseless vehicle." When Peter Studebaker passed away in 1897, Fish became chairman of the Executive Committee and began more intensive design and building of experimental electric, battery-powered carriages. Five models of horseless carriages were first offered in 1902, the company's 50th anniversary, and 20 units were sold that year.

Henry, who had continued to farm, passed away in 1895. Clem, who had worked for the company since its first day, passed away in 1901. This left John Mohler, the sole remaining brother, to usher in the new, horseless form of transportation. Battery powered carriages were slow, and their range was limited by the batteries' capacity. Changing to a horseless carriage powered by a gasoline-fueled, internal combustion engine seemed to be a move in the right direction. In 1904, Fish worked out a partnership between Studebaker and the Garford Company of Cleveland, Ohio: Studebaker would provide bodies for the Garford chassis and engines, and the vehicles would be sold under the name Studebaker-Garford.

Fish wanted to continue expanding the "motor car" business and utilizing interchangeable parts, but John Mohler saw that sales of horse-drawn vehicles were still good and getting better. However, things started to change in 1907. Wagon sales began to decline while motor car sales continued to increase. It was a sign of change, and John Mohler knew it.

The Automobile and Expansion

In 1908, Studebaker partnered with the Evertt-Metzger-Flanders Company of Detroit, Michigan to sell the E-M-F motor cars. The next year, 8,132 E-M-F cars were sold through Studebaker's large network of dealers. Studebaker went on to purchase E-M-F in 1910. That same year, 15,300 vehicles were produced, and 22,555 were sold in 1911. Also in 1911, the Studebaker Brothers Manufacturing Company was incorporated with E-M-F to become the Studebaker Corporation. At the same time, Studebaker's relationship with Garford had soured, and the partnership ended. By 1912, "Studebaker" had replaced the E-M-F nameplate on its autos. In 1912, Studebaker ceased production of electric vehicles after 1,841 were built. Automobile production was based in Detroit, and South Bend continued to manufacture wagons, carriages, and other horse-drawn equipment.

The auto was here to stay, and Studebaker was again known around the world. In 1912, 37% of all cars exported by the United States were Studebakers. But all was not well. The Flanders 20, an off-shoot of the E-M-F 20, was poorly assembled with parts of poor quality. Customers were not happy. Since the company's first days, the brothers believed in a philosophy handed down from their father: *give more than you promise*. John Mohler drew upon that belief to resolve the problems with the Flanders 20 and make their customers happy again. Studebaker dispatched a mechanic to visit every Flanders 20 customer to repair or replace whatever was needed. In an age before recalls, Studebaker stood behind its product even if the company technically did not build it. The repair effort cost around $1,000,000 but earned back the business of many customers.

In 1914, at the start of World War I, John Mohler was still involved with Studebaker, but Fish was now its president and Albert R. Erskine (1871–1933) its vice president. South Bend kept busy filling various orders that came in for the British military, while Detroit continued to produce automobiles. In 1915, John Mohler retired to honorary president; Fish became the chairman of the board, and Erskine was promoted to president. Automobile sales reached 46,845 units that year. Erskine brought with him a desire to increase production and lower costs. Backed by increasing auto sales and war contracts, Erskine began an expansion of the Studebaker business and sought to bring auto production to South Bend.

John Mohler Studebaker passed away on 16 March 1917. He was 83 years old and the last of the original company founders. There were only a few people with Studebaker blood still involved in the company. Over the next decade, the Studebaker blood line would slowly sell their Studebaker stock, completely divesting themselves from the company.

With the United States entering World War I in 1917, Studebaker placed its manufacturing abilities at the disposal of the government. The government was quick to capitalize on the offer, ordering 73,000 horse-drawn vehicles.

Erskine's expansion plans continued, and one of the buildings constructed in 1917 was the Motor Machining and Assembly Plant (Building 72) on Sample Street in South Bend. This building (and its additions) would be the epicenter of the XH-9350 engine development during World War II.

During the war years, Studebaker slowed auto production and focused on government contracts. After World War I, Studebaker quickly concentrated on its auto business and began to sell off the horse-drawn vehicle side of the business in 1919. By 1920, Studebaker had liquidated the entire wagon business and had sold 51,474 autos. Manufacturing expansion continued; the goal was to move all auto production to South Bend. In 1923, Studebaker sold 145,167 cars. Customers spent more money on Studebaker products in that one year than in the entire 68-year run of the horse-drawn vehicle business. Unfortunately for Studebaker, 1923 would be its high mark for a long time.

Erskine continued to push for lower retail prices and more innovation. In 1925, Paul G. Hoffman (1891–1974), an experienced car salesman from Los Angeles, California, became the vice president of sales. By 1925, all automobile production had been moved from Detroit to South Bend. That same year, Harold S. Vance (1890–1959), an employee whose roots traced back to E-M-F in 1910, became the vice president of production. Studebaker opened an 840 acre vehicle proving ground (an industry first) west of South Bend. Although Studebaker had the capacity to build 200,000 cars, only 111,315 were sold in 1926.

With the decline in sales, Erskine sought to bring attention to Studebaker's brand by establishing a number of records. Some 160 speed and distance records were set, but perhaps the most impressive was a 30,000 mile run by two stock President Eight Sport Roadsters and two stock President Eight Sedans. The record run occurred from 21 July to 8 August 1928 at the Atlantic City Speedway in New Jersey. The fastest of the vehicles, a Roadster, finished the 30,000 miles in 26,326 minutes, averaging 68.37 mph over the 18.28-day run.

With media exposure achieved, Erskine worked to diversify Studebaker's product line to appeal to a larger customer base. Studebaker created a low-price brand called the Erskine and purchased the luxury brand Pierce-Arrow. With the changes, the Studebaker Corporation offered vehicles from $895 to $10,000 in 1929. This variety, combined with numerous redesigns, could have proven successful had the Great Depression not intervened. By 1930, Studebaker and Pierce-Arrow auto sales had dropped to only 67,269 cars.

Studebaker and Erskine Fall

Erskine believed that an economic recovery was just around the corner. Studebaker had seen many economic slumps in its history, and the economy had always recovered after a few years. Cutbacks were made, and employees were either laid off or had their hours cut. Erskine moved to put Studebaker in a position that it could capitalize on when the economic recovery occurred; the company paid dividends to the stockholders, restyled cars, and released a new vehicle line in 1932 called the Rockne.

The vehicle that became the Rockne was designed for Willys-Overland by Ralph A. Vale and Roy E. Cole (1887–1950). Suffering its own financial hardships, Willys-Overland did not produce the vehicle. On a whim, Vale stopped in to see Erskine and pitched the small and affordable car that he and Cole had designed. It was exactly what Erskine thought would appeal to the masses as the economy recovered. A deal was made on the spot. Named after famed Notre Dame Football coach Knute Rockne, the Rockne auto line was built in the old E-M-F plant in Detroit as a separate brand from Studebaker. Launching the new brand used up much of Studebaker's cash reserves.

Comparatively speaking, the Rockne brand sold well. The 22,223 Rocknes accounted for almost half of the

44,711 cars Studebaker built in 1932. But the Rockne's success was not enough to revitalize the cash-strapped company. Studebaker found itself with more expenses than income; the company was essentially surviving on credit. A potential savior was found in the White Motor Company (WMC). Walter White, founder and head of the company, had passed away in 1929, leaving WMC somewhat adrift and in need of leadership. Studebaker could provide WMC with leadership, and having $22 million in cash, WMC could provide Studebaker the financial infusion it needed.

The Studebaker and WMC merger negotiations were almost complete when President Franklin D. Roosevelt took office and declared a bank holiday. With the banks shut down, Studebaker could not access any cash to keep itself going. In addition, rumors were circulating that Chase Manhattan Bank was going to call Studebaker's $5.6 million loan once business resumed. The WMC deal fell through, and the Studebaker factories were shut down. As protection from larger creditors, Studebaker worked with a local creditor to be declared insolvent. The Studebaker Corporation went into receivership on 18 March 1933, and Erskine and Fish resigned.

Erskine did not take the fall of Studebaker well, and, perhaps for the first time in his life, did not see any opportunities in his future. He had also lost a lot of money in real estate and owed back taxes. Always a numbers man, Erskine saw a way to make one last "deal" and provide for his family, but it would cost him dearly. He invited his wife's family to his house for a visit, but it was really to give his family support for the trying times ahead. Quietly, sometime on the evening of 30 June 1933, he wrapped a gun with a towel and took his own life. His life insurance policy did not have a suicide clause, and the payout was sufficient to pay his debts and provide for his family.

Indianapolis Diversion

In the midst of all the economic issues, Studebaker went racing at the Indianapolis 500 in 1932 and 1933. For both years, five special factory race cars were built up using the engine and chassis from Studebaker's President model. At this time, the President's 337 in^3 engine produced 122 hp. The output of the 3.5" bore and 4.375" stroke straight, eight-cylinder engine was increased to 200 hp for use in the Indy racers. In 1932, the top Studebaker finished in third place, averaging 102.66 mph. In 1933, two private Studebakers joined the five factory entrants. The seven Studebaker cars finished 6th through 12th, and all were on the lead lap. It was an impressive performance for a chassis and engine based on a production model.

Studebaker's Resurrection

In the wake of Erskine and Fish's resignations, Vance and Hoffman were put in charge of Studebaker. Vance, with his production background, became chairman of the board, and Hoffman, with his sales background, became president. Vance and Hoffman immediately worked to restructure the company, restart production (which had stopped on 18 March 1933), and reassure customers. Automobile production resumed in April, and a small profit was made.

Rockne production was moved from Detroit to South Bend and folded into Studebaker as the new 1934 Dictator. Cole became Studebaker's vice president of engineering. Studebaker sold off Pierce-Arrow in August 1933, and Studebaker autos were restyled for the 1934 model year. Vance and Hoffman worked closely with the bankruptcy court, and a new Studebaker Corporation was incorporated on 26 January 1935. Still struggling with stagnated sales in the low 40,000s, the company redesigned its vehicles for the 1936 model year.

In 1936, Studebaker began to claw its way back, with 91,999 units sold. However, the upward trend did not continue, with only 91,475 vehicles sold in 1937. Studebaker had retained designer Raymond Loewy and his team, including Virgil Exner, and they updated the 1938 product line. Loewy, the French-born designer, is known now as the *Father of Industrial Design*. Over his career, he would work on everything from razors to locomotives and from cookware to space stations. Loewy's association with Studebaker would span many years, as would Exner's.

However, an economic downturn in 1938 sent all auto sales plummeting, and Studebaker only sold 52,605 vehicles. Studebaker's sales for 1938 were only 58% of the 1937 sales volume. Studebaker did comparatively better than its competitors, which averaged only 45% of the previous year's sales. Studebaker's fortunes rebounded in 1939 with the introduction of the low-cost Champion that helped boost sales to 114,196 units. Sales for 1940 remained much the same, with 119,509 vehicles sold. Sales increased to 133,855 units for 1941.

World War II

Studebaker was just getting back on its feet as a solid automobile manufacturer when the impending war intervened. The government placed various restrictions on all automotive production, as materials were needed for manufacturing war equipment. As all resources were redirected for the war effort, the last Studebaker came off the assembly line on 31 January 1942. As it had done many times in the past, Studebaker would dedicate its vast production capabilities toward building whatever the government requested.

Under the Defense Plant Corporation, the U.S. government funded a plant at 701 West Chippewa Avenue in South Bend. Studebaker was to produce Curtiss-Wright R-1820 aircraft engines for the Boeing B-17 Flying Fortress bomber from the government-funded plant. During World War II, Studebaker produced 63,789 R-1820 engines and earned its Aviation Division an Army-Navy "E" Award for excellence in production.

Studebaker also worked to design and build the largest piston aircraft engine in the United States—the 5,000 hp XH-9350. The engine was designed for maximum fuel efficiency and installation in long-range bombers. Four single-cylinder and two twin-cylinder test engines were built. However, the war ended, and the project was cancelled before a complete XH-9350 engine was built.

In addition to aircraft engines, Studebaker also produced a variety of military vehicles during World War II, earning its Automobile Division an additional Army-Navy "E" Award. Actually, Studebaker's first World War II order was for 2,000 trucks placed by France in November 1939. As events played out, many of these trucks ended up in the hands of Germans after the fall of France. Through its auto production plants, Studebaker built over 197,678 US6 (M16A) trucks. Under the Lend-Lease program, many of these trucks were sent to the Soviet Union, where they became rather ubiquitous. Their use in the Soviet Union was so widespread that the word "Studebaker" became synonymous with "truck." Many of these trucks were still in service into the late 1950s, much to the chagrin of communist leaders.

Studebaker also designed and tested the T15/M28 and T24/M29 Weasel all-terrain tracked vehicles, ultimately producing over 15,124 of them. In their Vernon, California plant, Studebaker built engine assemblies for the Lockheed PV-1 Ventura patrol bomber. At the Vernon plant, Studebaker workers fitted the Pratt & Whitney R-2800 engines with mounts, cowlings, fuel and oil lines, and other components. The complete nacelle power package was then shipped to the Lockheed (Vega) plant in Burbank, California for installation on the Ventura aircraft.

Studebaker completed around $1.2 billion in contracts from the US government during World War II, but its net profit for the period was only around $26.9 million—2.24% of the contracted value. Studebaker's profit-to-sales ratio was no higher than what the company had achieved before the war, and its war profits did not account for the high cost of converting Studebaker operations back to vehicle production. Studebaker did not use World War II as an opportunity to profiteer.

As can been seen in the ads throughout this book, Studebaker took great pride in its contribution to the Allied war effort. Most of the artwork in the ads featuring machinery was created by Frederic Tellander (1878–1977), and most of the artwork featuring people was created by Robert Skemp (1910–1984). Some of the ads even highlighted Studebaker employees whose sons were fighting in the war. About 95% of Studebaker employees bought war bonds, and 5,600 served in the armed forces—111 were killed in action.

Post WWII to the Korean War

Government restrictions on automobile production were lifted on 15 August 1945, and the first Studebaker rolled off the assembly line on 1 October 1945. Various worker strikes plagued auto manufacturers throughout 1946, but Studebaker produced 120,763 vehicles. For 1947, Studebaker introduced entirely redesigned models and was the first auto manufacturer to do so. Shortages of various materials, including steel and iron, occurred as the United States transitioned away from war-time production. Studebaker bought a steel company to ensure its own uninterrupted supply.

The steel company purchase paid off handsomely; Studebaker production in 1948 hit a new record of 233,457 cars and trucks. Studebaker purchased the aircraft engine plant on Chippewa Avenue on 10 November 1948 and converted it for the manufacture of civilian and military trucks. Also in 1948, Hoffman left Studebaker to become director of the Economic

Cooperation Administration, overseeing the Marshall Plan that aided the rebuilding of Europe following World War II. In addition to serving as chairman of the board, Vance also became the president of Studebaker.

The war years had caused much pent-up demand for automobiles, and that demand was finally being met. Production continued to rise to 304,994 in 1949 and 334,554 in 1950. But the Korean War broke out in June 1950, and a cloud of uncertainty was again cast over the auto industry. The government again looked to Studebaker to build engines for bombers; this time it contracted Studebaker to build the General Electric J47 turbojet for the Boeing B-47 Stratojet. Engines were built and tested at the Chippewa Avenue plant, and 3,129 J-47 engines were made. Studebaker also continued to manufacture trucks for the military.

Studebaker made 285,888 cars and trucks in 1951 and 231,837 in 1952. Studebaker was now celebrating its 100th anniversary. On the surface, Studebaker looked like a solid company doing good business in the auto market and holding profitable government contracts. Under the surface, however, Studebaker had not been responding to the out-of-control labor costs that were severely eating into its profits. Studebaker's labor costs were the highest in the industry—about twice the average. While sales were good, the high labor costs meant that any issue with sales could knock Studebaker down.

In Search of Deep Pockets

The new 1953 Studebaker models turned out to be a production nightmare—some parts would not fit, while other parts were in short supply and held up production. The overall fit and finish of the vehicles was not good. To make matters worse, sedans were not very appealing to the end consumer, and production ran short on the desirable coupes. This situation left Studebaker with slow sales on some cars and missed sales on others. During the turmoil, Paul Hoffman came back and became chairman of the board. Vance continued as the president and chief executive officer. As soon as the production issues were solved, a strike occurred at Borg-Warner, Studebaker's supplier for manual transmissions, and resulted in further delays and shortages. Only 186,000 cars were produced in 1953.

The hope that Studebaker would regain ground in 1954 was shattered when Ford drastically increased production and dumped its cars on Ford dealers, forcing them to drastically cut prices. This was an attempt by Ford to regain the sales lead from Chevrolet. However, Chevrolet would have none of it and did the same as Ford. With heavily discounted Fords and Chevrolets, sales were very difficult for all other manufacturers, including Chrysler, whose sales and market share dropped by 40%.

In this time period, Vance passed twice on the opportunity to be the US distributor for Volkswagen. Volkswagen Beetle sales soon took off, and the Volkswagen sales could have provided much needed revenue to Studebaker had Vance moved forward with the agreement. Instead, Studebaker was negotiating a merger with the Packard Motor Car Company. On paper, the merger was a good fit, with Studebaker covering the lower end of the auto market while Packard covered the high end. Studebaker and Packard officially became the Studebaker-Packard Corporation on 1 October 1954, but there was more to this plan.

James J. Nance (1900–1984), president of Packard, had been discussing a four-way merger with George W. Mason, chairman and chief executive officer of the Nash-Kelvinator Corporation. The concept was Mason's idea. Mason felt there was only one way for the independent auto manufacturers to compete with the *Big Three*: Ford, General Motors, and Chrysler. They needed to merge and form a "big fourth." Under Mason's plan, Nash and Hudson Motor Car Company would merge, and Nance's Packard would merge with Studebaker. Later on, Nash-Hudson and Studebaker-Packard would merge to create another auto giant to compete with the Ford Motor Company, General Motors, and the Chrysler Corporation.

Nash and Hudson merged on 1 May 1954 to form the American Motors Company (AMC). And after Packard and Studebaker merged, Mason's plan for a "big fourth" seemed to be coming together. But it all fell apart just as quickly. Mason died on 8 October 1954, a week after the Studebaker-Packard merger. George Romney took charge of AMC and had no desire to merge AMC with Studebaker-Packard. The situation left Nance overseeing two, now combined, ailing companies. To make matters worse, Studebaker's health had been overstated; the company was in much worse shape than it had let on. Nance worked to cut costs and combine efforts, but sales collapsed, and consumer confidence evaporated. In 1955, Studebaker only built 138,472 cars and trucks.

There were 2,178 Studebaker-Packard dealers in 1954, but only 1,523 remained by 1956. A potential savior came in the form of Curtiss-Wright.

The Curtiss-Wright Corporation was created on 9 August 1929 with the merger of the Wright Aeronautical Corporation and the Curtiss Aeroplane and Motor Company. Wright Aeronautical's roots trace back to the Wright brothers, but the company mainly focused on aircraft engines from World War I on. Glenn Curtiss, a rival to the Wright brothers, initially produced engines, but his company increasingly focused on designing and building aircraft. After the two companies merged, the Wright Aeronautical Division (Wright) of Curtiss-Wright focused on aircraft engines, and the Curtiss division of Curtiss-Wright developed and produced aircraft.

At the close of World War II, Curtiss-Wright was one of the largest corporations in the world. However, the company failed to get its footing in the post-war economy. By the 1950s, Curtiss-Wright had failed to design a modern aircraft that appealed to the US military and subsequently stopped producing aircraft. Wright's piston engine business was strong, but the division had not designed a successful jet engine.

Curtiss-Wright was looking to diversify and entered into a three-year agreement to manage Studebaker-Packard in 1956. This arrangement allowed the tax burden of Curtiss-Wright's profits to be offset by Studebaker-Packard's losses. Backed by the Eisenhower Administration, the Curtiss-Wright deal went through, and Hoffman, Vance, and Nance all left the company. Long-time Studebaker worker Harold E. Churchill (1903–1980) was put in charge of Studebaker. Only 82,000 Studebakers were sold in 1956.

Packard production was moved from Detroit to South Bend. The Packards began to look much like Studebakers, earning them the unflattering moniker of "Packebakers." But a new scheme to help Studebaker emerged. Roy T. Hurley was the president of Curtiss-Wright, and he had been negotiating with Mercedes-Benz for United States distribution rights. The plan moved forward, and Studebaker dealerships began selling Mercedes-Benz automobiles imported from Germany.

However, selling Mercedes-Benz automobiles from Studebaker dealerships proved to be a poor match. The Studebaker dealerships were used to selling cars at the low end of the auto market and did not have the location or clientele needed to sell high end automobiles. In addition, the Mercedes-Benz vehicles were beyond the service abilities of most Studebaker dealerships. Studebaker built 74,738 cars in 1957 and sold 3,150 Mercedes-Benz autos.

Neither Studebaker-Packard nor Mercedes-Benz had gotten along well with Hurley at Curtiss-Wright. The Curtiss-Wright management agreement ended in 1958; Studebaker-Packard took over distribution rights for Mercedes-Benz, and Mercedes-Benz issued Studebaker-Packard some short-term loans. Sales for 1958 picked up, with Mercedes-Benz selling 7,704 vehicles and Studebaker selling 79,301 cars and trucks. The Packard line was killed off after only 2,000 cars were built, but the company was still called Studebaker-Packard.

With little money, Churchill and Studebaker worked on a new car for 1959 that they hoped would revitalize the brand and earn back market share. The compact Lark was born, and Studebaker sales went up to 182,323 units. The compact Lark was a popular car, so popular that the *Big Three* brought out their own compacts for the 1960 model year, and Studebaker's sales declined to 133,984. To make matters worse, dealers continued to abandon the Studebaker franchise and switch to other auto makers.

Studebaker-Packard had begun a campaign to diversify itself in the hope of finding profit outside the car business, as no end to the current hemorrhage of cash was in sight. Churchill retained the presidency of Studebaker. But through a contentious vote by the board of directors, Sherwood H. Egbert (1920–1969) became the new chief executive officer of Studebaker-Packard in February 1961.

112 Years in South Bend

Egbert had been a hardworking man since he was 12 years old, and he liked a challenge. It would certainly be a challenge to return Studebaker-Packard to profitability, especially when its own board of directors was showing less and less interest in the automotive manufacturing business. While further diversification continued, Egbert worked to shore up the Studebaker brand and get everything with the company in order, from its factories to its dealerships.

Although Studebaker sales continued to decline, Studebaker-Packard's financial situation improved as a result of diversification. Egbert realized that new Studebaker designs would be needed to revitalize the

9

marque, but a redesign of the Studebaker product line would be costly, and it was money the company did not have. Even before he took over the company, Egbert had imagined a new, revolutionary car that would set Studebaker sales on fire. The new car would be a stop-gap measure to give the company some financial breathing room, allowing Studebaker to redesign its other vehicle lines and put itself back in the car business. After cobbling together his basic ideas, Egbert called in Raymond Loewy in March 1961.

Loewy and his team had been let go in 1955 to cut costs. If Loewy had any apprehensions about working for Studebaker again, they quickly faded when he looked over the vehicle concept Egbert envisioned. Loewy quickly worked on the design, and the following month, a full-size clay model of the proposed Avanti was complete. Loewy bragged that the Avanti possessed no straight lines, an attribute that necessitated its molded fiberglass body. When shown to the board of directors in April 1961, they enthusiastically applauded the Avanti and approved its production.

Following disappointing sales of 92,434 cars and trucks in 1961, the Avanti made its debut on 26 April 1962, intended for the 1963 model year. Around this same time, the "Packard" name was dropped, and the company was once again simply "Studebaker." The Avanti car received a lot of attention. Andy Granatelli and his brothers, Vince and Joe, used a nearly stock example to set 29 records at the Bonneville Salt Flats in Utah where the car recorded a two-way top speed in the flying mile at 168.15 mph. The Granatelli brothers were closely associated with STP, and Studebaker-Packard had purchased the company in its efforts to diversify.

In the Avanti, Studebaker had a potential winner. But there were many problems associated with producing the new car and its fiberglass body. To further complicate matters, a series of strikes delayed everything at Studebaker. The production troubles, strikes, and delays did nothing to improve Studebaker's image. The delays with the Avanti used up precious cash resources, and with sales coming in low, there was no new money to put into the 1964 models.

Studebaker's product line was freshened up as much as the lack of funds would allow, and the Granatelli brothers again went to Bonneville—this time with one of everything Studebaker had to offer. Some 72

records were set, including a specially prepared, twin-supercharged Avanti reaching 196.62 mph. But it was sales, not speed records, that Studebaker needed. With an 86 day supply of unsold cars, Studebaker production at South Bend was nearly stopped. Only 67,918 cars were produced for 1963. Egbert resigned, and in December 1963, the board of directors decided to transfer remaining Studebaker production to the more modern plant in Hamilton, Ontario, Canada. The last Studebaker made in South Bend came off the assembly line in late December 1963, a month and a half shy of 112 years since Henry and Clement Studebaker opened a little business called H & C Studebaker.

Fade Into History

The Canadian government had placed severe restrictions on imports. Studebaker circumvented these restrictions by having an auto plant in Canada that manufactured and assembled vehicles for the Canadian market. The Hamilton, Ontario plant was purchased in 1947; it enabled Studebaker to sell cars in Canada and export them to other British Commonwealth nations.

Not all Studebaker products made the move to Hamilton, Ontario; the Avanti, for one, was abandoned. Gordon E. Grundy (1912–1975) was now in charge of the Studebaker automotive division, and he was determined to do what he could to continue the brand. However, diversification had gone well, and there was little interest in continuing automotive production. This meant that there would be no money to redesign existing vehicles or to design new ones.

Studebaker Canada made 17,614 cars in 1964. That same year, the Mercedes-Benz agreement ended amicably, leaving Mercedes-Benz to create its own dealer network. In 1965, 19,435 Studebakers were built. Gordon went to the board seeking funds to redesign the model line for 1967, but he was told there would be no 1967 models. The last Studebaker was built on 17 March 1966, one of only 2,045 cars the company produced that year.

What used to be the Studebaker Corporation was now a diversified conglomerate. Over the next decade, the company bought others, merged with others, and was purchased by others, until nothing named "Studebaker" remained. But memories of Studebaker did remain, along with the hopes, aspirations, and respect of a few.

Nathan D. Altman (1911–1976) was one of the leading Studebaker dealers, and he was truly taken by the Avanti. He arranged to restart production in 1965 on a small scale. Production slowly and steadily continued until 1985. After that, the rights to the Avanti changed hands several times, and a number of redesigns occurred. In 1987, production was moved from South Bend to Youngstown, Ohio. The last Avanti was built in 2006.

The Motor Machining and Assembly Plant (Building 72) on Sample Street, where the XH-9350 engine was designed and developed, remained in continuous use until Studebaker went out of business in 1963. The South Bend Lathe company then bought the building and occupied it until May 2002. It was later demolished with several other Studebaker buildings in the summer of 2008 to make way for a high-tech business park known as Ignition Park. Ignition Park is intended to help revitalize South Bend and place the city on the cutting edge of information technology.

Current Day

The Chippewa Ave plant that saw production of the R-1820 and J47 engines exists (in 2019) as the Studebaker Business Center. It houses a number of businesses, including Studebaker International Inc., the largest supplier of vintage Studebaker parts.

The Studebaker's storied history and unique styling are kept alive by thousands of enthusiasts and historians who meticulously restore and maintain Studebaker cars and trucks and preserve Studebaker history. Their passion ensures that Studebakers will still be on the road for years to come.

"Betcha Dad worked on those engines!"

They're talking about a Flying Fortress powered by Studebaker-built Wright Cyclone engines

JUST a little while back, expert machinist John H. Williams and his two sons, Evard and John, were working together at Studebaker.

Today, they're still working together in spirit—but many miles apart.

The father is building Wright Cyclone engines for the mighty Boeing Flying Fortress in the Studebaker factory. The boys have hung up their working clothes to put on the fighting uniforms of Uncle Sam.

Two on the firing line—one on the production line—each still giving "more than he promised"—each doing everything he can do to make victory sure.

There are many families such as the Williams family whose names shine brightly these war days on the Studebaker roster—families that are steadfastly maintaining the great Studebaker father-and-son tradition at home or far away.

And when the fighting job is done, that tradition will be carried forward, you may be sure, in finer Studebaker motor cars and motor trucks than ever for civilian use. The solid principles upon which Studebaker craftsmanship has been founded will remain unchanged.

BUY U. S. WAR BONDS

STUDEBAKER

Builder of Wright Cyclone engines
for the Boeing Flying Fortress, big multiple-
drive military trucks and other
vital war matériel

Craftsman father of craftsmen sons

John H. Williams, father of soldiers Evard and John, has been with Studebaker 21 years. He is one of many Studebaker veterans whose aptitude for fine work influenced and inspired their sons to become Studebaker craftsmen, too. Every Studebaker employee is proud of his organization's assignments in the arming of our Nation and its Allies.

2. Waldo Waterman and the Arrowbile

Inspiration

The automobile and the aeroplane both became relevant in the early 20th century. Many early auto pioneers and companies experimented in aviation by manufacturing either aircraft or aircraft engines—and some companies produced both. Bugatti, Daimler-Benz (as Benz, Daimler, and Mercedes), Duesenberg, FIAT, Ford, and Rolls-Royce were just a few of the innovative automobile companies aspiring to be involved in aviation. It was only a matter of time before someone endeavored to create a "flying car" or a "roadable airplane." Interestingly, powering such a machine was Studebaker's first foray into aviation.

Glenn Curtiss' Autoplane was one of the first attempted flying car machines. Officially unveiled at the Pan American Aeronautic Exposition on 8 February 1917, the Curtiss Autoplane was an enclosed, car-like cabin constructed of aluminum and supported by four wheels. Its tail, foreplane, and 40' 6" span triplane wings were removed for road travel. One aspect of the Autoplane that would make any pedestrian nervous was the 8' 8", four-blade, pusher propeller that provided the thrust not only for air travel but for road travel as well. Power from the 100 hp Curtiss OXX V-8 engine in the front of the machine was delivered to the propeller at the vehicle's rear via a shaft and belts. The Autoplane reportedly achieved 45 mph on the road and even made a few hops into the air, but it never actually flew.

Waldo Waterman's Arrowbile is considered the first successful flying car. It was Curtiss who directly inspired Waterman to design and build a flying car. Waterman was present when Curtiss successfully tested the first amphibian aircraft, the Curtiss Model E Triad, on 26 February 1911. After watching the Triad take off from water and then touch down on land, Curtiss remarked, "Now if we could just take off the wings and drive this thing down the road, we'd really have something." Waterman would never forget those words.

Top—The Curtiss Autocar displayed at the Pan American Aeronautic Exposition in February 1917. (AC) Bottom—The body of the Autocar without wings. (AC)

Glenn Curtiss taxing the Triad onto the beach from San Diego Bay. (AC)

Waterman

Waldo Dean Waterman was born in San Diego, California on 16 June 1894. Waterman was fascinated by mechanics and aviation from the start. Before he was eight years old, he was spending time in machine

The Curtiss Aviation School in San Diego. Waterman appears to be fifth from the right with arms crossed. (AC)

shops learning the techniques of the trade. By the age of 14, Waterman regularly serviced a neighbor's Ford Model K and other autos out of a garage he built behind his parents' house. His early work as a neighborhood mechanic provided Waterman with the funds for his next endeavor: a glider.

Waterman, already an avid kite maker, found instructions on how to build a Chanute-type glider in the April 1909 issue of *Popular Mechanics* magazine. He set to work constructing the craft in his garage and made various parts for his project at a local machine shop. By late June, the glider was ready. His first flight attempts were unsuccessful. The need for a steeper hill from which to jump quickly became apparent. On 1 July 1909, at age 15, Waterman jumped off a steep canyon and glided some distance before gently landing in the brush below. He spent the rest of the day making flight after flight. But getting to the top of the canyon was hard work. By August, Waterman had made an arrangement that allowed him more gliding time with less hard work—a friend would use his car to tow Waterman and his glider around the neighborhood. This arrangement (and the towed flights) ended when the glider hit a palm tree at a local park. Agitated neighbors called Waterman's mother, who quickly put an end to his early gliding days.

His gliding career cut short, Waterman focused his attention on building a powered aircraft for the first

American International Aviation Meet in Los Angeles. Waterman enlisted the help of his friend Kenneth Kendall, and together they rushed to build a biplane in time for the Aviation Meet in January 1910. They were able to borrow an engine for the plane. Unfortunately, the borrowed engine was damaged during a test run. Waterman had already received his credentials for the show, but with no funds to repair the engine, he went without a plane. It was there that Waterman first met Glenn Curtiss and did some volunteer work for him at the show.

When Waterman returned to San Diego after the aviation meet, he repaired the borrowed engine and installed it in the biplane for its first flight in February 1910. The engine was so underpowered that Waterman decided to have a car tow the biplane into the air and release it, hoping the engine could sustain the aircraft in flight. After a few successful flights using this method of takeoff, the tow release malfunctioned, leaving Waterman and his aircraft attached to the car. When the car turned, the biplane stalled and came crashing down. Waterman escaped the crash with eight broken bones: a broken ankle and several broken bones in his left foot.

By January 1911, Waterman had healed from his injuries and had reconnected with Curtiss, who was now in San Diego setting up the Curtiss Aviation School and Experimental Grounds on North Island.

(Because of Curtiss' work with the Navy, North Island, which was eventually connected to the Coronado Island peninsula, is known as the birthplace of naval aviation and is still a Naval Air Station.) Waterman became an aid to Curtiss at the facility. During this period, Curtiss worked on his amphibian, the Triad, and made mention of a roadable aircraft. Waterman had also built another airplane, but it was destroyed in a storm before it ever had the chance to fly. By the end of June, Waterman had taught himself how to fly at the Curtiss school.

Waterman attended the University of California at Berkley in 1912 to study mechanical engineering. This decision was influenced by Curtiss, who told Waterman that there were enough barnstormers but not enough people designing quality airplanes. While in college, Waterman designed and partially built a flying boat, but lack of funding left the project unfinished. With the United States entering World War I in 1917, Waterman tried to enlist as an aviation cadet in the Army. However, the injuries he had suffered to his ankle and left foot made him unfit for combat. Instead, he became the head of the Department of Theory of Flight in the Aviation School at Berkley, which was part of the U.S. Army Signal Corps. He taught some 500–600 cadets, including Jimmy Doolittle. In 1918, he left teaching and became involved with the United States Aircraft Corporation—a company set up to manufacture Curtiss JN-4 Jennys for the war effort. When the war ended on 11 November 1918, the corporation was left with a lot of equipment but no product, so it quickly folded.

Waterman purchased much of the corporation's equipment and founded the Waterman Aircraft Manufacturing Company in Venice, California in late 1919. Over the years, the new Waterman Company built a number of original aircraft (from a racer to a cabin monoplane) and modified others. However, none of the designs entered production. During this period, Waterman also continued to work in other areas of aviation: he helped start the predecessor to the Ontario Airport; started a small, short-lived airline out of Ontario, CA; helped build the Los Angeles Metropolitan Airport (now known as the Van Nuys Airport) and also worked as the airport's manager; did some movie flying; and bid for an airmail route.

Waterman also worked for the Bach Aircraft Company at Clover Field in Santa Monica, California. In 1927, he became the company's chief test pilot and experimental engineer. Waterman set an altitude

record with a 1,000 kg (2,200 lb) payload on 26 July 1929 at 20,820' in a Bach 3-CT Air Yacht trimotor. At the Cleveland National Air Races in Ohio, Waterman flew a Bach 3-CT to victory, averaging 136.41 mph in the muti-engine transport race (Event No. 20) on 25 August. The Bach Aircraft Company fell on hard times during the stock market crash of 1929. Also, a fire damaged the company's factory, and one of its aircraft crashed during a demonstration flight. These separate events forced the company to fold in 1931.

The Waterman W-1 Flex-Wing of 1930. Shock-absorbing struts varied the incidence and dihedral of the wings. While the design reduced structural loads by 25%, it had the unintended consequence of making a rough ride in the passenger cabin. (AC)

Whatsit

For over 20 years, the comments Curtiss had made about a roadable aircraft / flying car had intrigued Waterman. In April 1932, he set out to create just such an aircraft. To appeal to the masses and succeed, Waterman knew the aircraft needed to be stable, safe, easy to fly, and easy to land. He wanted to build an aircraft that was non-stalling and non-spinning, had a low landing speed, and was almost impossible to nose-over on landing.

Waterman decided that such an aircraft would need to have detachable wings and a tailless fuselage. With the wings left behind and no tail to begin with, the flying car's fuselage would take the shape of a streamlined coupe. Maximum pilot visibility was achieved by placing the engine in the rear of the craft. A tricycle undercarriage with a steerable nose wheel simplified the aircraft's ground handling and the vehicle's road handling. Early on, Waterman decided this project would be a proof-of-concept aircraft; it would not incorporate detachable wings or be used for road travel. As the odd aircraft took shape, many people asked Waterman, "What's it that you're building?" This constant question inspired the aircraft's name: Whatsit.

The Whatsit (registered as NX12272) had a short, two-place fuselage with side-by-side seating. The fuselage was placed on top of large wings swept back at 15°. With no tail, the Whatsit was one of the first flying wings. The wings used elevon control surfaces, which combined the functions of elevator and aileron. Each wing had a rudder positioned on its upper surface, near the tips. Power was provided by an air-cooled, five-cylinder, 100 hp Kinner K-5 radial engine that drove a two-blade propeller and was installed at the rear of the fuselage.

On the Whatsit's first takeoff attempt, the nose wheel encountered a gopher hole on the grass strip at the Los Angeles Metropolitan Airport (Van Nuys), and the Whatsit flipped over. During the rebuild, the sweep of the wings was increased to 25°, and a canard was placed on a boom that extended in front of the fuselage.

Waterman poses next to the Whatsit shortly after it was rebuilt following the flip-over on its first takeoff attempt. (AC)

The next flight attempt displayed the unusual aerodynamic characteristics of the machine, as it pitched up immediately after takeoff. Waterman cut the engine, and the Whatsit landed nose-high and hard, damaging the aircraft again.

The Whatsit was rebuilt a second time, and a slower, more careful course to flight was pursued. Waterman took short hops just above the runway to get a feel for the aircraft. Another pilot talked Waterman into letting him have a turn. The Whatsit quickly got away from its new handler and smashed back to earth, severely damaging the aircraft once again.

Waterman was ready to throw in the towel and give up. His faithful workers who had assisted him with the project asked if they could pick up the pieces and rebuild the Whatsit in their spare time. Waterman

The Whatsit demonstrating the relatively steep pitch-up during takeoff experienced by the flying wing aircraft. (SDASM)

agreed. With no money, no tangible projects, and with the country in the midst of the Great Depression, Waterman became an airline pilot for Trans-continental and Western Air (TWA).

Arrowplane

In November 1933, Eugene L. Vidal, the Director of the Bureau of Air Commerce, Aeronautics Branch, advocated the broader use of personal aircraft and issued a questionnaire to various aeronautical firms. Vidal hoped that a safe and easy-to-fly "everyman's aircraft" could be developed that would cost around $700 (about $12,000 in 2013 USD). Many believed that a $700 aircraft would create new jobs and opportunities and help revitalize the US economy. Twenty-two thousand copies of this questionnaire were sent out to just about every manufacturer involved in aviation, but a $700 airplane that was both easy to fly and desirable to the masses was deemed unrealistic by manufacturers.

Even so, Waterman was intrigued by this request and felt that the "everyman's aircraft" concept was in line with his own aspirations that had started with the Whatsit. Waterman took a leave from TWA to start again on the Whatsit. In January 1934, the repaired but disassembled Whatsit was taken out to Rosamond Dry Lake, north of Los Angeles (now part of Edwards Air Force Base). Here, the Whatsit was reassembled, and taxi tests were begun. Various minor changes and adjustments were made before the first flight. Toward the end of February, testing was complete, and the aircraft was flown to Waterman's home field in Santa Monica. Hoping that his aircraft fit the bill, Waterman

Waterman and the completed W-4 Arrowplane in late July 1935. The dark-colored panels on the wingtips were spoilers that only turned out. Note the airfoil balancers attached to the elevons to enhance their control. (AC)

began marketing the Whatsit as a possible answer to the Aeronautics Branch's request for an "everyman's aircraft."

This "everyman's aircraft" that the Aeronautics Branch was looking for had to meet specific requirements. It had to be non-spinning, non-stalling, and provide very good forward visibility. The aircraft needed to have a top speed of at least 110 mph, a 35 mph stall speed, and be powered by an engine of around 100 hp. Takeoff over a 35' obstacle was to be achieved with an 800' run, and landing after clearing a 35' obstacle was to be within 400'. In addition, the aircraft could not be prone to nosing over if the brakes were applied immediately upon touchdown. All of this was a tall order for the original price of $700, which explains why no serious prospects emerged.

To stimulate the quest for an "everyman's aircraft," Vidal appropriated $1,000,000 for a competition to find an aircraft that met the Aeronautics Branch's specifications and the subsequent production of 30 examples. This aircraft was dubbed the "Safety Airplane," and while a $700 aircraft was no longer the goal, the contest was still to meet the rest of the Branch's specifications for as little cost as possible.

Aircraft designs and bids to manufacture 30 examples were submitted to the Aeronautics Branch, and a winner was to be chosen in August 1934.

On 1 July 1934, the Aeronautics Branch was renamed the Bureau of Air Commerce. Waterman submitted his Whatsit-inspired design with an estimated $2,500 per unit cost. This new aircraft retained the basic layout of the Whatsit, but the wings were moved to the top of the fuselage. The change to a high wing was made because of unsatisfactory flight characteristics caused by the high thrust line and the low wing on the Whatsit. The front canard was omitted, and power was to be provided by a 100 hp, air-cooled, inverted, inline-four Wright-Gipsy L-320 (licensed-built de Havilland Gipsy) engine.

Despite being one of the lowest of the 16 bidders, Waterman did not win the contest. Although his bid was over $500 more than Waterman's, Dean Hammond won the competition with his Hammond Model Y design. As a sort of consolation prize, the Bureau of Air Commerce asked Waterman to build a 5' wingspan model of his proposal so that it could undergo wind-tunnel evaluation. Waterman would be awarded a $12,500 contract to build a prototype if his

Waterman sits in the cockpit of his Arrowplane before its flight to Washington D.C. The Arrowplane's designed provided a rather spacious cockpit for its two occupants. (AC)

model's wind tunnel evaluation indicated that the full-size aircraft could meet the desired specifications. A few other entries were also selected for prototype construction, including a design for the AC-35 roadable autogyro by Autogiro Company of America (Pitcairn Autogiro Company).

Waterman immediately set to work on the scale model of his design, and it was tested in the National Advisory Committee for Aeronautics' (NACA) wind tunnel at Langley, Virginia. The tests indicated that Waterman's performance claims for the full-size aircraft were valid and that the aircraft would meet the Bureau of Air Commerce's specifications. Waterman was awarded a contract for a prototype "Safety Plane."

Back in Santa Monica, construction of the aircraft progressed rapidly; Waterman wanted his to be the first of the Bureau of Air Commerce's aircraft to fly. The new aircraft was named the Waterman W-4 Arrowplane because its wings formed an arrow shape

and as a play on the word "aeroplane." The Arrowplane's wings were made out of wood and were covered with fabric. The wings incorporated elevons for pitch and roll control. A triangular vertical stabilizer fin with what appeared to be a rudder attached to its trailing edge was placed at each wingtip. The "rudders" were really spoilers that only turned outward to increase drag. The spoilers could be operated independently of each other for yaw control, or both could turn outward at the same time to act as an air brake. The engine was changed to a 95 hp Menasco B-4 Pirate because Waterman was able to obtain one for less money than the Wright-Gipsy. The Pirate had the same configuration as the Wright-Gipsy. The Arrowplane had a wingspan of 40', a length of 18.5', and a height of 8'. The Arrowplane weighed 1,310 lb empty and 1,900 lb loaded. Its top speed was 110 mph; cruise speed was 95 mph, and stall speed was 35 mph. The aircraft had a 26-gallon fuel tank and a 350 mile range. Although it was strictly an aircraft, Waterman had designed the Arrowplane for possible conversion to a flying automobile.

In early 1935, the Arrowplane was completed, and registration number X13 was applied to its wingtips. The aircraft was taken to Rosamond Dry Lake for flight tests, where it became the first of the "Safety Airplanes" to fly. After a series of successful flights, Waterman flew the Arrowplane to Santa Monica, where it underwent a few modifications and a registration change to NS13. After another round of flight testing in July, the Department of Commerce deemed the craft airworthy. By early August 1935, the Arrowplane was ready for a flight to Washington D.C., three months ahead of the delivery deadline. John Geisse, a Bureau of Air Commerce representative, flew the aircraft to Washington D.C. It is interesting to note that Geisse was a new flyer with only 35 hours. A few technical difficulties did crop up, but the Arrowplane arrived at Bolling Field, Washington D.C. on 12 August. On 15 August, Amelia Earhart took the Arrowplane up for a flight. Eventually, the Arrowplane met all the specifications except having an 800' takeoff run and clearing a 35' obstacle; it was close, but it could not meet the specifications in still air. With a small penalty deducted, Waterman received payment for the Arrowplane and returned to California. Later in 1935, Charles Lindberg also flew the Arrowplane.

After it was delivered to the Department of Commerce, the Arrowplane was test-flown at various locations. Above, the aircraft is at Roosevelt Field on Long Island, New York. (SDASM)

Vidal was enthusiastic about the Arrowplane and felt it achieved what he had envisioned. Although the Arrowplane met almost all of the Bureau of Air Commerce's criteria, nothing more came of the project. The Arrowplane was essentially destroyed in a flood at Bolling Field in March 1936. Ultimately, the Hammond Model Y did not fare much better. The

Bureau of Air Commerce's order was reduced from 30 aircraft to 12, and only around 15 were built. Also, the Model Y's price jumped to $7,000. The aircraft was certainly not a success.

Arrowbile

In 1935, Harris "Pop" Hanshue, former President of TWA and Fokker, and General Manager of Easter Air Lines, was looking for a new aircraft project. He had spoken with Vidal, who sold him on the idea and merit of the Arrowplane. Hanshue and Waterman were already acquainted through their mutual involvement in aviation over the years. Back in Santa Monica, Hanshue approached Waterman to discuss business opportunities originating from the Arrowplane. Waterman discussed his thoughts on a flying car version and found that Hanshue was very interested. The men decided to proceed with the flying car project, and the Waterman Arrowplane Corporation was incorporated in late 1935, with Waterman as the president and Hanshue as vice president.

The Waterman W-5 flying car project was christened the Arrowbile. The similar name was chosen to capitalize on media exposure from the Arrowplane. It was decided that as many automotive components as possible would be incorporated into the Arrowbile. In addition, the craft was to be powered by a regular automotive engine. Using automotive components would reduce the cost of the machine and increase the ease of maintenance; an auto engine would allow the Arrowbile to be fueled and serviced at any normal station, just like a standard car. In late 1935, Hanshue left for the eastern states to raise capital. Waterman followed shortly after to help raise funds and also to acquire a suitable engine for the Arrowbile.

The Arrowbile's engine needed to be fairly light, pressure lubricated, and produce around 100 hp at 3,500 rpm. This was a challenge in 1935; many engines used splash lubrication and only produced around 70 hp. Over a five-week period, Waterman stayed in Detroit, Michigan and met with the engineering departments of General Motors, Ford, Chrysler, and Hudson in an attempt to find a suitable engine. Unfortunately, all the reviewed engines were either too heavy or underpowered; some were too heavy *and* underpowered.

There was one big auto manufacturer that Waterman and Hanshue had not spoken with, and that was Studebaker in South Bend, Indiana. Hanshue called up his old friend and current Studebaker President Paul

The first completed W-5 Arrowbile in March 1937. Although the layout was similar to the Arrowplane, the Arrowbile was an entirely new aircraft and fulfilled the "flying car" role. (PM)

G. Hoffman. Hanshue and Hoffman first became acquainted when they were competing car salesmen in Los Angeles. In early 1936, Hanshue and Waterman visited Hoffman at his house and went over their Arrowbile proposal, which included film of the Arrowplane. After the presentation, Hoffman insisted that Waterman and Hanshue visit the Studebaker plant to discuss the Arrowbile and the ideal engine with Studebaker's engineering department.

The next day, Hoffman introduced Waterman and Hanshue to Stanwood W. Sparrow, designer of Studebaker's recent engines, and William S. James, Chief Engineer at Studebaker. Before joining Studebaker, Sparrow and James had worked together at the National Bureau of Standards where they wrote a number of reports dealing with the mechanics of internal combustion engines. The men cross-referenced the desired engine traits with what was available from Studebaker and found a potential engine.

Both James and Sparrow believed that good engineering could make a power plant lighter and more efficient. Where possible, their new engine designs incorporated stressed steel rather than heavy iron castings. James and Sparrow also experimented with Studebaker's 218 in^3, straight, six-cylinder, flathead engine. This engine was derived from the 190 in^3 engine first used in the 1932 Rockne cars. It originally had a 3.125" bore and a 4.125" stroke. When the engine was used in the 1934 Studebaker Dictator, the bore was enlarged to 3.25", which increased displacement to 205 in^3. The stroke was then increased to 4.375", resulting in a displacement of 218 in^3 for the 1936 and 1937 Dictator. (Due to events in Europe, the name Dictator was dropped for the 1938 model year and was replaced by Commander.) The engine's displacement was increased again in 1939 to 226 in^3, followed by a final increase in 1949 to 245 in^3. The engine was in production until 1960—28 years after its introduction.

The experimental 218 in^3 engine that James and Sparrow were working on had an aluminum cylinder head and used multiple carburetors. In this configuration, the engine produced 105 hp, an increase from the normal 90 hp. The 218 in^3 engine was exactly what Waterman was looking for, and Studebaker was interested in the Arrowbile.

Waterman, with his signature pipe, about to drive off in the Arrowbile car. For road use, the propeller locked into place and did not rotate. Note the three intake ports in the cowling. A group of six belts drove the propeller from the engine's crankshaft. (AC)

Dorothy Hoffman, Paul Hoffman's wife, and Studebaker each invested $5,000 into the Arrowbile. Part of the agreement with Studebaker allowed Waterman to purchase 50 engines at $100 apiece. These engines were to be supplied without carburetors or manifolds but would include starters and generators. This was exactly the arrangement Waterman had wanted. Plans were discussed to produce 1,000 Arrowbiles a year to be sold in Studebaker dealerships across the country for $3,000 plus accessories. Waterman returned to California to start construction while Hanshue continued to raise additional funds until he passed away unexpectedly on 8 January 1937.

Constructed during 1936, the Arrowbile was a direct descendent of the Arrowplane, having a very similar shape and layout but with a more refined appearance. Two people sat side-by-side in a streamlined fuselage with the propeller at the rear. Attached to the top of the fuselage were large wings swept back 25°. As with the Arrowplane, the wings used elevon control surfaces and had a vertical stabilizer fin at each tip. Attached to the trailing edge of the vertical fin was a rudder that only turned outward to increase drag. The wings had wooden spars, but the rest of their internal

structure was aluminum. The leading edge of the wings were covered with aluminum back to the first spar. The rest of the wings were fabric-covered. A V-strut extended down from the underside of each wing and attached near the bottom of the Arrowbile's fuselage. For road travel, each wing would detach separately from the fuselage and be left behind at the airport. The fuselage had a tube steel frame and was covered with aluminum-alloy sheets. The light-weight fuselage allowed the road-going part of the Arrowbile to be classified as a motorcycle. This classification allowed the use of a tricycle undercarriage rather than a four-wheel arrangement.

To detach the wings from the fuselage, pins were removed from the struts where they attached to the fuselage. The struts were then separated and swung away from the fuselage so that they were perpendicular to the ground. Levers in the cabin then released each wing from its attachments above the fuselage. This allowed the wing to pivot up and away from the fuselage until the bottom of the vertical stabilizer fin rested on the ground. The fuselage could then be driven away from under the wings. The entire process of detaching the wings took only three minutes.

The Arrowbile's Studebaker 218 in³ engine was a water-cooled inline-six with a 3.25" bore and a 4.375" stroke. The engine's actual displacement was 217.7", but it is sometimes noted as having a 217 in³ displacement. As installed in the Arrowbile, the engine was officially known as the Studebaker-Waterman S-1 and was awarded Type Certificate No. 178 on 15 July 1937. The S-1 engine had a sea level power rating of 90 hp at 3,500 rpm. The engine had a 7:1 compression ratio and was stock with the exception of the intake manifold and the three Stromberg AK-3 carburetors. A standard Auto-Lite distributor was used for the single ignition system. The Arrowbile's S-1 engine was connected to the 7' 4" wooden propeller via belt-driven drive shafts at a .52 ratio so that the propeller turned a little more than half engine speed. The engine had a dry weight of 579 lb.

Example of a Studebaker Dictator and Commander flathead, straight-six engine. The specific engine pictured was installed in a car and not in an Arrowbile. (AC)

The six drive belts attached to the propeller shaft in the Aerobile, which had a similar drive system as the Arrowbile. Using a larger pulley, the propeller shaft turned at .52 times engine speed. (SDASM)

The Studebaker engine was to be installed as low as possible for the best center of gravity. Ultimately, the engine was positioned right above the rear axle. The propeller shaft was positioned above the engine so that the propeller had 9" of ground clearance. Six V-belts rode in aluminum-alloy sheaves on both the engine output shaft and the propeller shaft. The belts were controlled by a clutch pulley that made it easy to transition power from the propeller to the drive wheels. Remotely, the pilot raised or lowered the front end of the propeller shaft to alter the tension on the belts. When the belts were under tension, the engine was connected to the propeller. When the belts were totally slack, the propeller was disconnected, and power went to the drive wheels. For road travel, the propeller was locked in place so that it did not spin. The engine and propeller drive passed a 150 hour endurance test operating at 90–100% throttle.

Originally, the Arrowbile had one forward and one reverse speed. Power to the drive wheels was provided by floating axles with universal joints splined into a custom-made differential. The differential had a Duralumin case and weighed 20 lb. Waterman constantly worked to improve the Arrowbile's powertrain. A three forward and one reverse speed transmission with an automotive-type clutch was under development, but it appears that it was never installed.

In addition to the Studebaker engine, the Arrowbile incorporated a Studebaker radiator and battery. Other automotive parts were used from Ford, Willys-Overland, and American Austin. Eight of the 11 instruments were automotive in nature. The remaining three instruments were a compass, an altimeter, and an airspeed indicator.

The Arrowbile had a 38' wingspan, was 19' 4" in length, and was 8' 8" high. The aircraft weighed 1,941 lb empty and 2,500 lb loaded. The Arrowbile's maximum speed was 120 mph, cruising speed was 102 mph, and stalling speed was 45 mph. Fuel capacity was 26 gallons, and range was 400 miles. On the road, the Arrowbile had a top speed of 70 mph (sources vary between 50 and 75 mph).

As the Arrowbile was coming together in mid-1936, Amelia Earhart visited Waterman and was given a ride in the road-going fuselage frame before any exterior sheet aluminum was installed. Being a flying car, the Arrowbile faced some monumental technical problems that took time to sort out. In February 1937, the first Arrowbile was complete and ready for its first

1. Out of Waldo D. Waterman's garage, his Arrowbile is wheeled. It is more convenient and less expensive to keep the plane in the family garage than in a hangar. Daughter Jane is at the wheel.

2. Down to the airport goes Arrowbile, a wingless, three-wheeled auto, engine driving wheels instead of propeller.

3. At the hangar, the wings are lowered and attached firmly to the body. Waterman has seven Arrowbiles under construction, five of them ordered by Studebaker whose engines power this plane.

4. The Arrowbile races down the airport runway. Its engine is now linked to propeller which, the plane being a "pusher," is in rear.

5. The Arrowbile takes off. A curious-looking machine, it is made mostly of automobile parts. It has a Studebaker engine and generator, Willys-Overland brakes and differential, Ford steering assembly, battery and radiator.

6. In flight along the coast (*above*), the Arrowbile has a top speed of 120 m.p.h., can carry two passengers 350 miles. Its price is $3,000.

An aviation article excerpt featuring the Arrowbile from the 16 August 1937 issue of LIFE Magazine. (LIFE)

flight. Rather than tow the craft to the airport, Waterman drove the fuselage to the Long Beach airport while others followed in a truck carrying the wings. The Long Beach airport provided more room for flight testing than Clover Field in Santa Monica (Waterman's home field), and it was a lot closer than Rosamond Dry Lake.

On 27 February 1937, the Arrowbile took to the sky for the first time. The flight was a disappointment, because the aircraft's handling and performance were poor. The flight issues were caused by tape along the wing, where the aluminum and fabric met; the tape had peeled back and disturbed the airflow around the wing. The tape was quickly removed, and Waterman took the Arrowbile up again. This time, everything was perfect. The next few test flights proved that the Arrowbile was very stable and easy to fly. The aircraft was nearly impossible to spin or stall. Its general maneuverability and ground handling were good. The

Arrowbile was flown to Clover Field to prepare it for its introduction to the press.

Controlling the Arrowbile was fairly straightforward. While on the road, the vehicle had conventional controls: a steering wheel and gas and brake pedals. Since the transmission had one forward and one reverse speed, it did not require a clutch to change gears like a normal manual transmission. However, Waterman did envision a better, three-speed transmission that would have a proper clutch and be geared to the Studebaker engine. While in the air, pushing or pulling the steering wheel controlled the aircraft's pitch via the elevons on the wings. Rotating the steering wheel rolled the aircraft via the elevons and rudders. Unlike a conventional aircraft, there were no rudder pedals.

In March, Arrowbile No. 1 (registered as NX262Y) was shown to the press. The concept of an affordable

The second (pictured, NR18932) and subsequent Arrowbiles were finished in Studebaker colors and trim. Note the revised grille and headlight arrangement. (PM)

flying car garnered much interest. In mid-March, the Arrowbile was present at the 1937 National Pacific Aircraft and Boat Show in Los Angeles. At the show, Morrow Crumb, Studebaker's head of publicity, ordered five Arrowbiles for Studebaker. Studebaker's intent was to have them all displayed at the National Air Races in Cleveland, Ohio in early September. The Arrowbiles would then tour the country, stopping in at many Studebaker dealerships. Additional orders were also received, all based on a $3,000 sale price.

Now the challenge was how to complete Studebaker's five Arrowbiles in six months. To emphasize the Arrowbile-Studebaker connection, the new Arrowbiles were to be finished with a 1938 Studebaker-style grill, painted in Studebaker colors, and include some Studebaker interior trim. Although construction began on Studebaker's five Arrowbiles, it quickly became apparent that they would not all be ready in time. Two new Arrowbiles were completed, and the first Arrowbile was modified with the new Studebaker grill, paint, and trim. Arrowbiles 2 (registered as NR18932) and 3 (registered as NR18933) were finished in August. Arrowbile 3 was christened *Miss South Bend* by Dorothy Hoffman, Paul Hoffman's wife. It is not clear if Arrowbile 2 was

christened with a name, but there is some indication that it may have been called *Miss Indiana*.

In late August, Arrowbiles 2 and 3 left for Cleveland, respectively flown by Latham A. "Slim" Perrett and Jerry Phillips. A few days later, after being updated with the Studebaker scheme, Arrowbile 1 left for Cleveland flown by Chuck Sisto. However, Arrowbile 1 had mechanical issues, and Sisto crash landed near Gila Bend, Arizona. Inspection of Arrowbile 1 revealed that a fitting in the sheave adjustment had failed, resulting in the belts going slack and not transferring engine power to the propeller. The pilot took responsibility for this failure because he was experimenting with the tension of the belts while in flight. The crash landing damaged the gear, and Arrowbile 1 was trucked back to Santa Monica for repairs.

Arrowbiles 2 and 3 were demonstrated daily at the Air Races in Cleveland by Perrett and Phillips. The demonstration consisted of one Arrowbile landing and shedding its wings. It would then drive around while the other Arrowbile took flight and performed a demonstration for the crowd. To further its presence at the event, Studebaker had arranged to provide its vehicles as the official cars of the 1938 National Air

Waterman, with his pipe, sits in Arrowbile 2. This view illustrates the revised cowling. A simple scoop provided induction air to the engine. Note the exhaust stack protruding from the engine access panel. (PM)

Races. The demonstrations were considered a success, and the Arrowbile continued to tour the country after the air races.

In October, Arrowbile 3 made a promotional stop in South Bend. An article reported that it had flown 2,200 miles averaging 18 miles per gallon and consumed two quarts of oil. The reported numbers were respectable for those days, but the information released to the paper may have had some bias. The undeniable truth was that a flying car existed and was in use. The future of the Arrowbile seemed so bright that Studebaker considered taking over production and moving it to South Bend.

However, by late 1937, the Waterman Arrowplane Corporation was in trouble. Hanshue's passing and the pressure to complete the Arrowbiles for Studebaker meant that no additional efforts to raise capital had occurred. In addition, the Arrowbile's initial price of $3,000 was too low, forcing the company to refund deposits that had been placed. The Arrowbile needed

to sell for around $6,000 to be profitable. During this time period, the country had experienced another economic downturn as it struggled to free itself from the effects of the Great Depression. This downturn had a major economic impact on Studebaker, which saw its vehicle sales for 1938 plummet. Studebaker now had to watch its money and investments, and that meant there were no funds for flying cars. However, Studebaker, through Hoffman, continued to fund the rebuild of Arrowbile 1, and Hoffman authorized the completion of an Arrowbile 4 (registered as NR2621) strictly as an airplane. Anytime an Arrowbile was altered for pure aircraft use and lost its ability for road travel, Waterman considered it to be an Arrowplane conversion. This activity kept a very small crew working at the Waterman Arrowplane Corporation.

Arrowbile 3 made a number of demonstration flights in the Northeast to promote the plane and also the 1938 Studebaker automobile line. It then returned to Studebaker's headquarters in South Bend, Indian and was placed in storage.

Arrowbile 4 was converted to a pure aircraft, which Waterman referred to as an "Arrowplane." (SDASM)

Arrowbile 2 made a number of demonstration flights in the Midwest but was abandoned in Detroit by Perrett when he was let go by Studebaker. In Detroit, Waterman demonstrated the aircraft before the Society of Automotive Engineers during its annual meeting. Waterman then flew Arrowbile 2 to Chicago, where it was displayed at the Air Industry Show in January 1938. After the show, Waterman flew on to South Bend, where Arrowbile 2 joined Arrowbile 3 in storage. While in South Bend, Waterman met with Hoffman to discuss the future of Studebaker's involvement with the Arrowbile. Simply put, there was no future.

The six aircraft that comprised the entire Arrowbile production run are seen under construction at the Waterman Arrowplane Corporation. Note the propeller shaft with attached pulley on the workbench in the foreground. (SDASM)

Once Arrowbile 1 was repaired following its crash landing, it was used in a 1938 movie called *Tail Spin.* In June 1938, the use of Arrowbile 1 was authorized to proceed with the aircraft's type certification as the Waterman W-5A Arrowbile. However, the certification was never completed, as Waterman's appendix burst in late 1938. His treatment included 13 blood transfusions and a year-long hospitalization in those pre-penicillin days. Waterman's absence effectively ended fundraising efforts to continue the Arrowbile project.

The conversion of Arrowbile 4 into an Arrowplane was completed in 1939. In this example, the propeller was geared directly to the Studebaker engine, making the V-belts used in the previous versions unnecessary. Test flights were done by Jerry Phillips, as Waterman was still recovering from his illness. Overall, Waterman found the aircraft's performance disappointing but had no funds to continue experimentation, so Arrowbile 4 was put in storage.

Arrowbile 5 (registered as NR18934) joined Arrowbiles 2 and 3 in South Bend. It is unlikely that Arrowbile 5 was ever completed. All were supposedly kept for a short time at Studebaker's proving grounds west of South Bend and later scrapped during the early part of World War II.

In late 1940, Waterman worked with Hoffman to take possession of Arrowbile 1, which was technically owned by Studebaker. Waterman then replaced the Studebaker engine with a 120 hp, air-cooled, horizontally opposed, six-cylinder Franklin engine. The engine used a planetary gear reduction and was mounted in line with the propeller. New main gear was installed that had a wider track but lacked a drive system for road travel. The changes meant Arrowbile 1 could no longer be converted for road use.

In 1943, William B. Stout was working on a variety of projects when Convair bought out his engineering company in Dearborn, Michigan. Convair wanted to continue his projects, and Stout felt Waterman would be an asset to his team. Stout negotiated with Waterman to join Convair and also to purchase the Waterman Arrowplane Corporation's assets, including whatever could be obtained from Studebaker. An agreement was made, and Arrowbile 1 was sent to Dearborn. Later, flaps were added to the aircraft to evaluate their effect on the flying wing and its elevon controls. Apparently, Arrowbile 1 was later cannibalized for other projects.

Arrowbile 4 was eventually shipped off to Dearborn, where it joined Arrowbile 1. It was converted back to a flying car, and Waterman referred to it as Arrowbile 6. Convair had an interest in the flying car and eventually made two versions of its own design. In Dearborn, the Arrowbile was used to test the possibility of folding wings that could be towed behind the vehicle when it was operated on the road. Mockups of the wings were towed behind the Arrowbile, but the results were not satisfactory. A non-detachable cantilever wing was installed, and the aircraft was shipped to Convair's facility (formerly owned by Stinson) in Nashville, Tennessee in 1944. It is possible that the aircraft flew with the new wing, but there is no additional information regarding its history.

While working with Stout, Waterman was mostly interested in a helicopter project and not really interested in working on anything related to a flying car. Management changes were forced upon Stout's Dearborn location by Convair's home office in San Diego and caused much friction. When his year-long contract with Convair was up, Waterman returned to San Diego and essentially retired.

Aerobile

In 1946, The Whatsit was flown to Washington D.C. and donated to the Smithsonian Institution. The fuselage is currently in storage. The wings may be lost, but much of the aircraft does exist.

Starting in 1947, Waterman modified the last Arrowbile (the original number 6) into what became the Aerobile 7 or just Aerobile (registered as N54P). It was powered by a Franklin (Aircooled Motors) O-335 opposed, six-cylinder engine that had been converted to water-cooling by the Tucker Corporation for use in the 1948 Tucker sedan. This engine produced 166 hp. The extra power compared to the Studebaker engine allowed the Aerobile to be built as a three-place aircraft. The fuselage was elongated, and the pilot was moved forward. Also, the wings detached as a single unit, as Waterman had originally envisioned.

After 10 years of working on the Aerobile in his spare time, Waterman was at the controls when it first took to the air on August 1957 at Gillespie Field in San Diego, California. In the spring of 1959, Waterman donated the aircraft to the Smithsonian Institution. It is currently on display in the Boeing Aviation Hangar at the Steven F. Udvar-Hazy Center in Chantilly, Virginia.

Postscript

Waldo Waterman continued to be involved in aviation for the remainder of his life, building a number of replica and reproduction aircraft, including copies of his original glider. He also became very involved in sailing and participated in many yacht races. Waterman passed away on 8 December 1976 at the age of 82.

The Franklin-powered Aerobile after it was completed in 1957. (SDASM)

There has always been some confusion regarding the Arrowplane, Arrowbile, and Aerobile. Given their similar names and how Waterman referred to converted Arrowbiles as Arrowplanes, their history is anything but clear. Simply put, there was only one true Arrowplane; it was built for the Safety Plane competition. There were six Arrowbiles. Five of them were completed as such, even if some of them were modified with different wings and engines and lacked the ability to travel by road. What started out as the last Arrowbile was heavily modified and completed as the only Aerobile. The grand total of production was seven aircraft: one Arrowplane, five Arrowbiles, and one Aerobile.

Many have pursued the idea of a flying car over the years. In 1940, Henry Ford said, "Mark my words: A combination airplane and motorcar is coming. You may smile, but it will come." However, none of the flying car concepts have met with much success. The fact is a good flying car will never be a good car or a good airplane. It is a compromise, by its very nature, and typically an expensive one that exceeds the combined price of a good car and good airplane.

Author's note: The Arrowbiles' history is often recorded either incorrectly or incompletely. While researching the Arrowbiles, I found many conflicting reports, and I realized that just about no two sources agree completely on the history of these machines. What I have written about the Arrowbiles, I mainly extrapolated from Waterman's autobiography. Even though my information was taken from Waterman's own account, there are contradictions in that text and questions left unanswered. I have exercised great care to present the Arrowbiles' history accurately, but I cannot be certain that my research is without error. I hope that my efforts will help to preserve the complicated and often confusing history of the Arrowbiles.

"*Automobile that flies*" is powered by Studebaker engine

"STUDEBAKER WORKMEN ARE THE WORLD'S GREATEST ENGINE CRAFTSMEN"

says Waldo Waterman, designer of amazing new line of Arrowbiles

ARTHUR FINCH DRILLS OIL HOLES IN DICTATOR SIX CRANKSHAFTS... It's his kind of expert attention to minute detail that enables Studebaker Dictator engines to live up to the boast of Studebaker's unique 7000 veteran workmen—"the finest 6-cylinder engines in any American car at any price."

Wings are attached at the hangar and the Arrowbile takes the air!

THE NEWEST IN AVIATION—"THE FLYING AUTOMOBILE." Even the traffic cops can't figure it out, it's so different. When Waldo Waterman selected an engine for his line of Arrowbiles he carefully tested ten different makes. And as usual, Studebaker led in reliability, flexibility, power and economy. Flying, or on the road, the Studebaker engine does not require premium high test gasoline. And its economy equals and often betters that of even the lowest priced cars.

THEY got a kick out of it, of course, on the Studebaker engine assembly line, when they heard that a motor they built for a Studebaker passenger car was chosen to power the world's first practical automobile-airplane.

And yet, unusual and unintended uses for Studebaker engines have long since ceased to startle these famous craftsmen whom Waldo Waterman calls the greatest in their field in the world.

For two years in a row, 5-car Studebaker teams not only finished, but finished well up among the leaders in the Indianapolis 500-mile Memorial Day classic—and last year a Studebaker powered car finished ninth with a speed of 101.331 miles and an average of 14.08 miles to the gallon of gasoline.

It is this stamina and this almost flawless performance that you can count on getting from every Studebaker engine. Men who have been working together longer than any similar group in any other automobile factory see to it that you do. The Studebaker Corporation, South Bend, Indiana.

GEZU ORBAN IS A 16-YEAR STUDEBAKER VETERAN... He's 48 years old and they call the job he's pictured doing on a President Eight crankshaft "finish grinding". The average age of Studebaker's 7000 craftsmen is almost 40 years. They have the greatest guild spirit you'll find in any automobile factory. And here in South Bend, where every workman is a neighbor, you'll see the finest type of craftsmen—devoted to their task of producing the world's most expertly built cars...jealously safeguarding Studebaker's reputation for engine excellence.

STUDEBAKER CRAFTSMAN JOSEPH MASSEY INSPECTS AND TUNES AN ENGINE... And when he says OK you can depend upon it that this 6-cylinder Dictator engine will be OK. Every man on the Studebaker engine assembly line is a great mechanic as well as a skilled inspector.

28

3. Studebaker-Built Wright R-1820 Cyclone

When Germany invaded Poland on 1 September 1939, the United States Air Corps had 26,000 officers and airmen and a heavy bomber force of only 23 Boeing B-17 Flying Fortresses. The aerial assets of the United States amounted to only a few thousand frontline aircraft, most of which were outdated and outclassed by the *Luftwaffe*.

At this time, the aviation industry in the United States had already begun a large expansion to accommodate the influx of French and British orders. The French and British, both declaring war against Germany on 3 September 1939, had seen the trouble ahead and purchased as many warplanes from the United States as they could, even though some types were obsolete. This expansion had nearly doubled the aviation industry's production capacity from 6,000 planes a year to 12,000. However, more than foreign funded expansion was needed to rearm and modernize the air forces of the United States.

The political situation in Europe continued to deteriorate when German forces invaded Denmark and Norway on 9 April 1940. Even the most optimistic could see that there would be no return to peace once Germany invaded Belgium, Luxembourg, the Netherlands, and France on 10 May 1940. A full-fledge war was now raging in Europe, and there was no end in sight.

The United States needed to continue the expansion of its aviation industry and inventory of warplanes. Addressing a joint session of Congress on 16 May 1940, President Franklin D. Roosevelt made the following statement:

> I should like to see this nation geared up to the ability to turn out at least 50,000 planes a year. Furthermore, I believe that this nation should plan at this time a program that would provide us with 50,000 military and naval planes.

President Roosevelt requested the immediate appropriation of $896 million ($16.2 billion in 2018 USD) to meet this goal.

Roosevelt's plan was laughed at in hushed tones, because there was no foreseeable way the aviation industry could produce the quantity of aircraft he requested. However, President Roosevelt was serious about this goal. To mobilize the industry, he set up the National Defense Advisory Commission (NDAC) and appointed William S. Knudsen (the president of General Motors) as its chairman. The NDAC brought together many heads of industry to organize all of the nation's rearmament efforts. George Mead was one of the founders of Pratt & Whitney Aircraft but had recently left that organization; he was quickly recruited and tasked with planning the 50,000-aircraft program. A short time later, Congress provided funds in excess of what President Roosevelt had requested, to ensure the development of both strategic and tactical air forces. (The NDAC was replaced by the Office of Production Management in January 1941, and that entity was subsequently replaced by the War Production Board in January 1942.)

As massive expansions of the aircraft industry were planned, it quickly became apparent that the industry was already near its production and management limit with the French and British orders. The only other group with the requisite mechanical experience and managerial ability to swing into aircraft and aircraft engine production was the automobile industry. The change from producing automobiles to aircraft would not be simple, but the two industries shared the same foundational skills. With minimal development, the automobile industry could produce aircraft and their engines.

At the time, the rather small aircraft industry was hesitant to transfer its knowledge and designs to the large and powerful automotive industry; the aircraft industry felt it had everything to lose and nothing to gain. However, what the auto industry had that the aircraft industry did not was the ability to employ mass production techniques using completely interchangeable parts. As the expansion plan moved forward, production assignments were handed out to the automobile industry.

The Wright R-1820 Cyclone was one of the most reliable radial engines ever built. The nine-cylinder engine was in production from 1930 to the mid-1960s, and over 120,000 R-1820s were produced. (AEHS)

The Boeing B-17 Flying Fortress is perhaps the most famous bomber of World War II and most were powered by Studebaker-built R-1820 engines. (USAF)

There were only three main producers of military aircraft engines in the United States: Allison, Pratt & Whitney Aircraft, and Wright Aeronautical. Allison

continued to be the sole supplier of its engines, and Packard was brought in to produce the Rolls-Royce Merlin. Pratt & Whitney felt that it did not have the managerial manpower to oversee the expanded production and were more than willing to license its engines. Buick and Chevrolet produced the Pratt & Whitney R-1830. Chevrolet also produced the Pratt & Whitney R-2800, as did Ford. Nash-Kelvinator was brought in later than the other firms, also to produce the Pratt & Whitney R-2800. Unlike Pratt & Whitney, Wright was resistant to licensing and wanted to complete all final engine assembly itself. Ultimately, licenses for production were issued to Studebaker for the Wright R-1820 and to Dodge (brought in later) to produce the Wright R-3350. By February 1942, all automobile production in the United Sates came to a halt and was supplanted with the production of war machines.

Studebaker was brought into the production program in November 1940. Under the Defense Plant Corporation, the U.S. government funded a plant in which Studebaker could manufacture aircraft engines at 701 West Chippewa Avenue in South Bend, Indiana. Ground breaking for the 1,560,000 ft^2 (over 35 acres) plant occurred in January 1941, and the plant became known as the Studebaker Aviation Division Aircraft Engine Plant. Studebaker was contracted to manufacture 6,500 14-cylinder Wright R-2600 radial engines. Wright objected to this assignment, because it wanted to avoid making the same engine in two plants. Wright proposed an expansion of its Lockland, Ohio plant (which was under construction and intended for R-2600 production) to meet the future demand for the R-2600 engine.

While deliberations continued over which Wright engine would be produced, equipment was installed in the new Studebaker plant so that engine production could begin as soon possible. In June 1941, the government changed Studebaker's production assignment from the R-2600 to the Wright R-1820 engine. The government asked Studebaker to make the change because it felt Studebaker was more adaptable than Wright. The main reason for this change was that Wright R-1820 engines were urgently needed for the Boeing B-17 Flying Fortress heavy bomber.

The Boeing B-17 originated as the Boeing Model 299, first flown in 1935, from an AAC request for a multi-engine, long-range bomber. Boeing built the Model 299 at company expense, and many changes were made between the prototype aircraft and the B-17s that entered service during World War II. First utilized by the Royal Air Force, the B-17, along with the Consolidated B-24 Liberator, formed the backbone of the American bombardment campaign against Germany. The aircraft was also used extensively in the Pacific theater. Most B-17s that served in World War II were the F and G models. On a regular mission, hundreds of B-17s carrying between 4,000 lb and 5,000 lb of bombs each would take off from bases in Britain, bound for targets within the European continent. With the exception of the Model 299 prototype and a few other experiments, four Wright R-1820 engines powered each of the 12,731 B-17s built.

The Wright R-1820 (or Cyclone 9) engine was a rather dated design at the start of World War II. The engine was a direct descendant of the Wright R-1750 Cyclone designed by Edward T. Jones and Sam D. Heron when they first joined Wright Aeronautical in 1926. The R-1750 was a nine-cylinder, air-cooled radial engine with a 6.0" bore and a 6.875" stroke. The engine initially produced 525 hp at 1,900 rpm and weighed around 760 lb.

In 1930, the R-1750's bore was enlarged by 0.125" to 6.125". This increased the nine-cylinder engine's displacement to 1,823 in^3, and the Wright R-1820 Cyclone 9 was born. The first of the R-1820s was the E-series, with A- through D- being applied to various versions of the R-1750. The R-1820 E-series used a barrel-type, aluminum crankcase. The cylinders were made of cast aluminum with integral rocker arm housings and machined cooling fins. The two valves per cylinder operated in a hemispherical combustion chamber, and the exhaust valve was sodium-cooled—a design pioneered by Heron. A one-piece master connecting rod was used on a two-piece crankshaft that joined at the crankpin. The engine was available with and without a planetary gear reduction for the propeller. A General Electric supercharger was used; its purpose was to mix the fuel and air rather than to provide boost. Initially, the R-1820 E-series produced 575 hp at 1,950 rpm. The engine weighed 850 lb for the direct drive version and 920 lb for the geared version.

Development of the R-1820 continued, resulting in the F-series of 1932. The F-series used a forged aluminum crankcase split on the cylinders' centerline. The speed of the supercharger's impeller was increased to provide additional boost and true supercharging of the incoming mixture. The cylinder design was improved, and the cooling fin area was increased. Special dynamic counterweights were developed to eliminate crankshaft vibrations encountered with increased

engine power and adjustable pitch propellers. The R-1820 F-series engine produced up to 900 hp at 2,300 rpm and weighed around 1,000 lb.

A cutaway R-1820 G engine showing the master connecting rod in the upper cylinder. Just visible is the planetary gear reduction for the propeller. (AEHS)

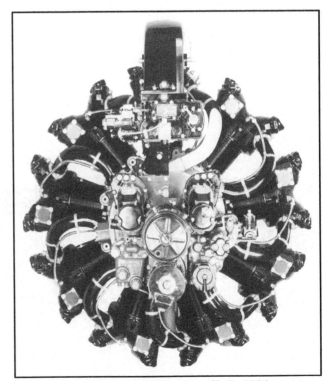

Rear view of an R-1820 G. All R-1820 engines incorporated an engine-driven supercharger in the accessory section. Engines in the B-17 also used a turbosupercharger. (AEHS)

Major Applications of the Wright R-1820 Cyclone Engine			
Boeing	B-17 Flying Fortress bomber	**Grumman (cont)**	FF / SF fighter
	Model 307 airliner		F3F fighter
Brewster	F2A Buffalo fighter		F4F Wildcat fighter (various versions)
Curtiss	CW-21 fighter		HU-16 Albatross amphibian
	P-36 Hawk fighter (various versions)		J2F Duck utility amphibian
	SBC Helldiver dive bomber		S-2 Tracker anti-submarine warfare aircraft
	SC Seahawk scout seaplane	**Lockheed**	Model 14 Super Electra airliner
	T-34 Condor II		Model 18 Loadstar transport
Douglas	A-33 attacker		A-28 Hudson recon bomber
	B-18 Bolo bomber	**Martin**	B-10 bomber
	SBD Dauntless dive bomber	**North American**	O-47 observation aircraft
	DC-2 airliner		P-64 fighter
	DC-3 airliner (early versions)		T-28 Trojan trainer
	DC-5 transport	**Northrop**	YC-125 Raider transport
FMA	AeMB.2 light bomber	**Piasecki**	H-21 Shawnee cargo helicopter
Grumman	C-1 Trader transport	**Ryan**	FR-1 Fireball mixed-power fighter
	E-1 Tracer carrier warning aircraft	**Sikorsky**	H-34 Seabat/Seahorse/Choctaw helicopter

Introduced in 1935, the G-series continued to improve the R-1820 engine. The G-100 engines of 1937 featured cylinders that were further refined, incorporating over 2,800 in^2 of cooling fin area per cylinder. The aluminum pistons had cooling fins machined into their inner walls to take full advantage of internal oil cooling. The General Electric supercharger was replaced with a 25% more efficient Wright-designed unit. The aluminum crankcase was discarded in favor of a specially designed, thin-wall, steel forging. The R-1820 G-100 series engines produced 1,100 hp at 2,300 rpm for takeoff and had a maximum continuous power rating of 900 hp at 2,300 rpm.

The B-17 Memphis Belle *is perhaps the most famous of all the Flying Fortresses. The aircraft was one of the first U.S. bombers to complete 25 combat missions in Europe. The* Memphis Belle *has been preserved and is on display at the National Museum of the United States Air Force in Dayton, Ohio. (USAF)*

The G-200 series was introduced in 1939 and was a further refinement of the R-1820. The cylinders had 3,500 in^2 of cooling fin area, which included around 1,100 in^2 of fins that were machined into the steel cylinder barrel. Direct-drive versions of the engine were available, but most used gear reduction. The G-200 engine had a takeoff rating of 1,200 hp at 2,500 rpm and a normal rating of 1,000 hp at 2,300 rpm. The R-1820 G had a diameter of approximately 55 inches and weighed approximately 1,310 pounds.

The last version of the R-1820 was the H-series, which entered production in 1942. Some of the later H-series engines produced up to 1,525 hp at 2,800 rpm.

The Wright R-1820 Cyclone 9 engine was used in over 30 different types of production aircraft—perhaps more than any other large piston engine made in the United States. The R-1820 was in production until the mid-1960s, and over 120,000 were produced.

Under Contract W-535-ac-17399, the Studebaker Corporation focused on manufacturing Wright R-1820 G-200 engines for Boeing B-17 bombers. The engines Studebaker produced carried the military designations R-1820-65 and R-1820-97. The -97 engines differed from the -65 engines in that they had an external oil scavenge and external oil lines for the propeller governor control. Complete engines were built at the Aviation Division Aircraft Engine Plant in South Bend. Studebaker's Fort Wayne, Indiana and Chicago, Illinois plants (both leased from the government) supplied gears, connecting rods, and other engine components. Each R-1820 engine required some 45,000 machine operations. All of the Studebaker-built components shared the same part numbers as the Wright-built components and were completely interchangeable. Between the three plants, over 9,400 Studebaker employees were involved in R-1820 production.

In his State of the Union address delivered on 6 January 1942, president Roosevelt made the following statement regarding aircraft production:

> [T]o increase our production rate of airplanes so rapidly that in this year, 1942, we shall produce 60,000 planes, 10,000 more than the goal that we set a year and a half ago. This includes 45,000 combat planes—bombers, dive bombers, pursuit planes. The rate of increase will be maintained and continued so that next year, 1943, we shall produce

125,000 airplanes, including 100,000 combat planes.

With the Engine Plant nearly finished, Studebaker was now in a position to help meet those goals.

The first R-1820-65 engines came off the assembly line in January 1942, six months after the order was placed. Only four were made that month, with another seven following in February. For July, the production output had risen to 600 engines, and over 1,000 were built in September. Production shifted to the R-1820-97 in October and continued at around 1,000 engines per month. Total production for 1942 was 6,091 engines, 2,587 of which were R-1820-97s.

An R-1820 supercharger and accessory section being lowered into position at the Studebaker plant. (AC)

The first Studebaker engines did have some problems; it has been noted that they ran rough, and that some bomber crews preferred Wright-built R-1820s. The auto industry's initial deficiencies are not surprising, considering it began mass production of an unfamiliar product requiring increased precision. But early

A line of Studebaker-built R-1820 engines at the Chippewa Avenue plant await cleaning before being packed in crates and shipped out for installation on Boeing B-17s. The engines have completed their initial and final test runs. As a whole, the automotive industry performed a miracle with its rapid, precision production of complex engines during World War II. (National Automotive History Collection, Detroit Public Library)

production issues were quickly overcome, and the Studebaker-built R-1820 engine served reliably throughout the war.

May 1943 saw Studebaker build 2,000 R-1820-97 engines, and total production for 1943 was 23,066 engines. From 1944 on, Studebaker was the sole supplier of R-1820 engines for the B-17. Peak production occurred in March 1944 when 2,479 engines were built. The total production for 1944 was 27,920 engines, an average of over 2,326 engines produced each month. From the high output of 1944, Studebaker's production wound down in 1945. Studebaker's R-1820 contract was terminated in May, and production came to a halt by 1 July 1945, shortly before the war ended. Only 6,712 engines were built in 1945.

From January 1942 to July 1945, Studebaker built 3,504 R-1820-65 engines and 60,285 R-1820-97 engines. The grand total of 63,789 engines produced by Studebaker was about 2/3 of the war-time R-1820 production. Including spare parts, Studebaker's R-1820 production accounted for some 92,549,203 hp. For its efforts during World War II, the Studebaker

Aviation Division earned an Army-Navy "E" Award for excellence in production.

Studebaker Wright R-1820 Production	
Year	Quantity
1942*	6,091
1943	23,066
1944	27,920
1945**	6,712
Total	**63,789**

*3,504 -65 and 2,587 -97 engines were produced in 1942. Remaining production was solely -97 engines.
**Production had stopped by 1 July 1945

There are still a fair number of R-1820 engines flying. These engines have been rebuilt many times over the years, and since Studebaker and Wright used the same part numbers, it is impossible to say exactly which manufacturer built each part in every engine. Most

Having passed all inspections and tests, eight of the 63,789 R-1820 engines built by Studebaker are crated and prepared for shipping. (AC)

likely, a large number of Studebaker-built parts are still in service. Modern engine overhaulers state there is no discernible difference between the Wright-built R-1820 components and the Studebaker-built components. In their experience, all parts share the same high level of quality and are interchangeable. The same cannot be said for some of the other license-built engines.

The engine's data plate proudly carries the builder's name, and a number of R-1820 engines in World War II aircraft still carry the Studebaker data plate. It is a lasting tribute to all the men and women involved in the World War II expansion programs. Incidentally, the R-1820 engine on display in the Smithsonian National Air and Space Museum in Washington, DC is a Studebaker-built R-1820-97.

Right—R-1820 engines being installed on left and right B-17 inner wing sections. The sections were then mated with aircraft fuselages. (LoC)

A273

Contract No. _____ ROUTINE ENGINE INSPECTION TEST LOG INSTRUCTIONS: Made in duplicate by testers. Original to Air C...

THE STUDEBAK... / AVIATIO... / SOUTH BE...

St'r. Model	WAC 1820 G 666	St'r. Test Spec.	WACET 1001	St'r. Fuel Spec.	
St'r. No.	SW 099,999	U.S. Test Spec.	AN 9503 a	U.S. Fuel Spec.	ANF 28-1
U.S. Model	R 1820-97	Comp. Ratio	6.7:1	Oct. No.	100
U.S. No.		Blower Ratios	7.0:1	St'r. Oil Spec.	
Rated H.P. at L	1000	Red. Gear Ratio	0.5625	U.S. Oil Spec.	AN-VV-O-446a
Rated R.P.M.	2300	Tach. Dr. Ratio	½:1	Viscosity S.A.E.	120 @ 210°F

Test Stand No.	2	Carb. Mfr.	STROMBERG	Mag. Mfr.	AMER. BOSCH
Test Stand Type	PROD. RIGID	Carb. Model	PD 12 H 2	Mag. Model	SF 9 LC 3
Dyn. Constant		Carb. Set. No.	68973 N-12F	R.H. Mag. No.	CC 57795
Counter Weight Sta.		Carb. Ser. No.		L.H. Mag. No.	DD 58461
Test Club No.	26179	Press. Reqd.	15-19 LB.	Advance L.H. 20° R.H. 20°	
Test Club Dia.	91"	Gravity Feed	FUEL PUMP	Spark Plugs	ACLS 55

Time A.M. P.M.	Start or Stop	Time At Spec. Cond.	% Rated Speed	Mix. Cont. Pos.	Abs. Man. Press. In. Hg.	Man. Press. In. Hg.	R.P.M. By Counter	Torque Load At Rad.	Corr. H.P. Std.	Obs. H.P. Test	Lbs. Fuel Per Obs. H.P. Hr.	Lbs. Oil On Scale	Lbs. Oil Per Hour	Lbs. Oil Per Obs. H.P. Hr.	Engine Oil Press. P.S.I.	Hydro. Oil Press. P.S.I.	Clutch Low P.S.I.	Clutch High P.S.I.	Oil Temp In °F.	Oil Temp Out °F.	Oil Temp Rise °F.	Oil Flow Lbs./Min.	Heat Reject To Oil B.T.U.
1	2	3	4	5	6	7	8	9	10	11	12	13	14	15	16	17	18	19	20	21	22	23	24
A 6:07	Start			PT	AR	16.26	-12.4	1060							86	75			122	108	-14		
6:10	Stop																						
6:55	Start			PT	AR	16.36	-12.3	1070							86	73			112	118	6		
7:15		10	58	AR	21.96	-6.7	1590				115.0				80	64			186	192	6		
7:25		10	67	AR	23.96	-4.7	1700				113.0				79	62			185	210	25		
7:35		10	74	AR	25.96	-2.7	1800		456	449	.550	107.0				80	61			185	214	29		
7:45		10	84	AR	29.86	1.2	2010		644	636	.569	104.0				80	60			186	218	32		
7:55		20	84	AR	29.86	1.2	2010		644	636	.569	103.0				80	60			185	221	36		
B 8:05		30	84	AR	29.86	1.2	2010		644	636	.569	100.5				80	60			185	221	36		
8:10	Stop																						
8:45	Start			PT	AR	16.48	-12.1	1040							76	64			137	137	0		
8:55		5	95	AR	35.88	7.3	2230		866	854	.653	97.0				74	53			185	226	41		
9:00		5	95	AR	Magneto Check [TACH]										74								
9:10		10	79	AL	27.98	-0.6	1910		555	550	.450	93.0				74	56			185	218	33		
9:20		0	95	AR	35.88	7.3	2230		866	854	.653	116.5				73	52			186	229	41		
9:30		10	95	AR	35.88	7.3	2230		866	854	.653	116.0				73	52			185	230	45		
9:35		Change to 100 Octane Fuel								Valves O.K.				Tester John Danks							Observer Han...		
9:40		20	95	AR	35.88	7.3	2230		866	854	.653	115.0				73	52			185	230	45		
9:50		30	95	AR	35.88	7.3	2230		866	854	.653	114.0	5.0	.0058		73	52			185	230	45		
9:55		0	100	AR	39.80	11.2	2340		1018	1004	.678	115.0				73	49			187	233	46		
10:05		10	100	AR	39.80	11.2	2340		1018	1004	.678	114.5				73	49			185	234	49	70.5	1725
10:15		20	100	AR	39.80	11.2	2340		1018	1004	.678	113.5				73	49			185	234	49		
10:25		30	100	AR	39.80	11.2	2340		1018	1004	.678	112.5	5.0	.0050		73	49			185	234	49		
10:26			100	AR	39.80	11.2	2340		1018	1004	.678	112.5				73	49			185	234	49	70.5	1725
10:31			85	AR	Magneto Check [Counter]																		
10:36			IDLE	AR	16.20	-12.4	1150								68	57			185	210	25		
10:41			TO	AR	46.80	18.2	2500	1230	1215	.761	110.0				73	48			185	236	51		
C 10:46	Stop																						
11:30	Start	0	PT	AR	16.30	-12.3	1040								48	40			150				
11:40		10	PT	AR	16.30	-12.3	1040								37	30			220				
11:50		20	PT	AR	16.30	-12.3	1040								33	26			230				
11:55	Stop																		236				

Test Complete

NOTES: Fuel, Oil and Water Leaks. Etc.

A - Initial check for leaks - Replaced broken bolt on barrel ring
B - Scheduled check - Adjusted oil pressure 3/8 turn out
C - Final Inspection - Prepare for Clear Fuel run

Magnetic Plug - O.K.

CARBURETOR PERFORMANCE
Accel. Slow OK Rapid OK
Idling 520 OK Flood OK
Oper. Below 1000 R.P.M. OK
Fuel Cut Off Secs. 4.8 @ 700
Idling Oil Press. 28 @ 186°

MAGNETO PERFORMANCE
Both Mags. 1960
R.H. Only 1930
L.H. Only 1910
Shut Off OK
Spark Plugs OK

Above and on the following page is a Final Acceptance Test chart example for a Studebaker-built R-1820. After an engine was completed, it was run in one of around 200 test cells at the Aircraft Engine Plant. After the test, the engine was disassembled and inspected. The engine was then reassembled and run again for its final inspection. The chart indicates that the test for this engine was conducted from 6:07 PM to 11:53 PM on 19 September 1944. The engine was run for a total of three hours and eight minutes, which included 30 minutes at 100% throttle (1,018 hp) and five minutes at takeoff power (1,230 hp). (A)

Opposite page, bottom—The data plates on Studebaker-built R-1820s were stamped with the Studebaker wagon wheel logo. Similar data plates can be found proudly attached to many engines on airworthy B-17s. (AC)

ER CORPORATION
ON DIVISION
END, INDIANA
Corps Inspector, duplicate filed. Blue Print to Statistical Department.

Sheet No. ONE OF ONE   Date SEPT. 19, 1944

ACCESSORIES		TYPE	SER. NO.	ENGINE TIMING	WEATHER
Starter	ECLIPSE			Cyl. No. ONE	TIME 9:55 PM
Generator				Inl. Open 18° Close 42°	Obs. True Barom. FAIR 6:07 29.16 6:55 29.14 8:45 29.14 9:55 29.13
Control				Exh. Open 74° Close 27°	Dry Bulb °F. 86 83 86 85
Fuel Pump	PESCO	R 600 CEB	21788-155	Clearance .010" COLD	Wet Bulb °F. 68 67 70 69
Vacuum Pump				M. Rod Cyls. ONE	Vapor Press. .50 .48 .56 .53
					Dry Air Press. 28.66 28.66 28.58 28.60

Fuel Press. P.S.I.	Fuel Temp. °F.	Lbs. Fuel Rota Temp.	Time Min. Rota Reading	Lbs. Fuel Per Hour	CARBURETOR AIR			W.O.T. H.P. Corr. Factor	Dyn. Blower Press. In.H2O	Dyn. Blower Temp. °F.	Cowl Air Temp. °F.	Engine Gear Case Temp. °F.	SPARK PLUG THERMOCOUPLES						CORR. OIL FLOW	CORR. HEAT REJECT TO OIL				REAR SECT. PRESS.	BACK PRESS. MAIN FILTER
					Temp. °F.	Press. In. H2O	Press. In. Hg.						#1	#5	#6	#7	#8								
25	26	27	28	29	30	31	32	33	34	35	36	37	38	39	40	41	42	43	44	45	46	47	48	49	
17.0																									
16.9																									
17.4	70	79	6.5	166		0.0						79	150	260	270	275	270	270						1.2	7.0
17.5	68	79	8.5	206		0.0						78	160	280	290	290	285	285						1.6	7.0
17.6	69	79	10.5	247	77	0.0						78	165	290	300	300	300	300						1.8	7.5
17.6	68	78	16.1	362	73	0.0						78	170	300	315	310	310	305						2.4	7.5
17.6	69	76	16.1	362	73	0.0						78	170	300	320	315	310	310						2.4	7.5
17.6	69	75	16.1	362	73	0.0						78	170	300	320	315	310	310						2.4	7.5
16.9																									
17.6	67	76	25.0	558	75	0.0						78	170	300	320	325	320	310						3.2	8.0
17.6	69	74	10.5	247	71	0.0						76	170	305	320	315	315	310						3.0	8.0
17.6	67	74	25.0	558	75	0.0						78	175	300	325	330	320	320						3.2	8.0
17.6	68	72	25.0	558	75	0.0						78	180	300	325	325	320	315						3.2	8.0
ry-boc 17.6	68	72	25.0	558	75	0.0						78	175	300	325	325	320	315						3.2	8.0
17.6	68	72	25.0	558	75	0.0						78	175	300	325	325	320	315						3.2	8.0
17.7	67	72	30.2	680	75	0.0						78	180	310	320	330	320	320						3.6	8.0
17.7	67	72	30.2	680	75	0.0						78	185	310	320	330	320	320	69.0	1560				3.6	8.0
17.7	67	72	30.2	680	75	0.0						78	185	310	320	330	320	320						3.6	8.0
17.7	68	72	30.2	680	75	0.0						76	185	310	320	330	320	320						3.6	8.0
17.7	68	72	30.2	680	75	0.0						78	185	310	320	330	320	320	69.0	1560				3.6	8.0
17.1																									
17.5	68	72	40.5	925	73	2.0						78	185	310	325	355	350	350						4.4	8.5
17.2													70	165	185	195	200	200	200						13.0
17.2													70	195	205	220	220	220	220						10.0
17.2													69	195	210	225	220	220	220						8.0

ACCESSORY PERFORMANCE			TEST EQUIPMENT		
Starter	OK			Tester John Drake	PERFORMANCE SATISFACTORY
Generator				St'r. Inspector a. Plane	Rated J. Smith
Gen. Control				U.S. Inspector J. Smith	Take-off J. Smith
Fuel Pump	OK				Accepted J. Smith U.S.A.
Vacuum Pump				Type of Test FINAL ACCEPTANCE TEST U.S.A.	Inspector

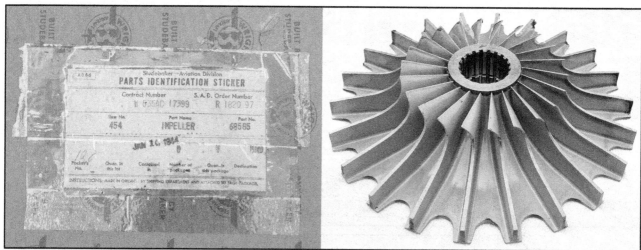

In addition to complete engines, Studebaker made many spare parts for the R-1820 engine. At top is a piston packed on 4 January 1944, and at bottom is a supercharger impeller packed on 14 January 1944. Note the Wright Aeronautical logo with "Built by Studebaker" printed on the boxes. These parts can still be found today covered with cosmoline and in their original boxes. The fit and finish of the parts is remarkable considering they were mass-produced during wartime. These 75-year-old, "New Old Stock" parts are routinely used in rebuilding R-1820 engines. (A)

The proudest assignment in our 90-year history

Studebaker BUILDS WRIGHT CYCLONE ENGINES FOR THE *Flying Fortress*

At flying fields throughout the world, airmen speak with unqualified admiration of the Flying Fortress, designed by Boeing and powered with mighty Cyclone engines. Studebaker, America's oldest manufacturer of highway transportation, welcomes the opportunity to work for victory with Wright, America's oldest builder of airplane engines. The same skill, the same Studebaker plus, that have gone into every Studebaker passenger car and truck, are today going into every implement of war being produced by Studebaker. We're proud of our assignments in the arming of our United States.

★ STUDEBAKER'S 90TH ANNIVERSARY 1852-1942 ★

© 1944 The Studebaker Corporation

Tom Hinkle's boys do him proud in the Army
just as they did on their Studebaker jobs

IT'S a long way from the Fiji Islands to the Studebaker factories where Wright Cyclone engines for the Boeing Flying Fortress are built.

It's still farther to the American air bases in India from which vital war cargo is flown into China across the towering Himalayan "hump."

But there's a link that spans those distant spots where Tom Hinkle's boys are now stationed and their father in South Bend. That link is a comradeship in craftsmanship which had its beginning when all three were working close together in the Studebaker plants.

Like large numbers of other Studebaker automobile craftsmen, Tom Hinkle is now building aircraft engines while his sons serve their country in combat areas overseas. Instead of manufacturing Studebaker

Champion, Commander and President cars as a family team, they're working together for victory although many miles apart.

For over 92 years, the tradition of fine craftsmanship has been fostered in many families like the Hinkle family in Studebaker's home community. The painstaking efforts of many such father-and-son teams have been considerably responsible for the surviving soundness that puts so much solid wartime value into Studebaker motor cars and trucks.

STUDEBAKER
Builder of Wright Cyclone engines for the Boeing Flying Fortress — big multiple-drive military trucks — and other vital war matériel

Lieutenant, corporal and craftsman—the Hinkles still "work together"—Tom Hinkle now builds Flying Fortress engines at Studebaker where his record as a motor car craftsman goes back nearly 23 years. At last reports, one son, George, is an Army Air Forces lieutenant in India, Bill Hinkle, Tom's other son, is a Coast Artillery corporal in the Fiji Islands.

BUY MORE AND _MORE_ WAR BONDS

© 1944 The Studebaker Corporation

617 combat hours for Studebaker-built engine 43-58319

As great armadas of Flying Fortresses swarm across invaded Europe, it's interesting to read what the squadron engineering officer of an Army Air Forces base in England has to say about one remarkable Studebaker-built Wright Cyclone engine.

It's engine four in the Fortress "Miss Carry," in service 617 combat flying hours.

"This engine's performance," said the officer, "exemplifies war-winning co-operation at its best. The workers in the factories back home produce the world's finest equipment. Our ground crews work day and night to keep that equipment in operational trim. Our combat crews do an outstanding job in blasting enemy targets and knocking out the Luftwaffe."

Studebaker is proud, of course, of its record of building more than 45,000 of the Wright Cyclone engines that power the famous Boeing Flying Fortress.

But this war is being won, not by production statistics, but by men in combat all over the world—on the ground, on the seas and in the air.

It's of those valiant Americans that the workers in the five great Studebaker factories are thinking as they build aircraft engines, multiple-drive military trucks and other units of vital war matériel.

Awarded Studebaker Aviation Division

Awarded Studebaker Automotive Division

Proud to be of service to her country

And all America, in turn, is proud of every member of the Women's Army Corps. General Marshall says the need is critical for many more women from 20 to 49 inclusive. What can you do? Encourage WAC recruiting in your community.

JOIN THE WOMEN'S ARMY CORPS

★ BUY MORE AND MORE U. S. WAR BONDS ★

Studebaker BUILDS WRIGHT CYCLONE ENGINES FOR THE BOEING FLYING FORTRESS

©1944 The Studebaker Corporation

"Thanks a million for those fine engines!"

A FLYING Fortress pilot, on the last leg of his training before leaving for overseas, wrote this note to Studebaker:

"Thanks a million for those fine, high-speed Wright Cyclone engines. You keep building them. We'll keep them flying. Wish us good luck."

Today, all over the world, the good luck that bomber pilot asked for is smiling more and more on America's armed forces —thanks to their own resourcefulness and valor plus the unremitting thoroughness of the preparations of our Army and Navy general staffs.

With our government's wholehearted co-operation, the Studebaker organiza-tion, for example, has thus far built more than 45,000 Wright Cyclone engines for the mighty Boeing Flying Fortress—more than 135,000 big, multiple-drive Studebaker military trucks—and great quantities of other vital war matériel.

But no one at Studebaker forgets for a moment that it's on the battle fronts, not the production fronts, that the war's outcome is decided. And so Studebaker gratefully salutes the valiant men and women in our country's uniform as the Americans to whom the cause of freedom owes its biggest debt.

Awarded To All  *Studebaker Plants*

Studebaker BUILDS WRIGHT CYCLONE ENGINES FOR THE BOEING FLYING FORTRESS

4. XH-9350 in Context

Background

In the early 1930s, the United States Army Air Corps' Power Plant Branch at Wright Field, Ohio began studying engine cylinder designs to develop an engine of increased power. Led by Sam Heron, these tests involved highly-supercharged air forced into a single-cylinder test engine operating at high rpm. The cylinder featured a hemispherical combustion chamber, sodium-cooled valves, and high-pressure liquid cooling maintained at 300° F. The resulting cylinder was termed a "High Performance" or "Hyper" cylinder and produced more than 1 hp/in^3. At the time, the Hyper cylinder produced more power for its displacement than any engine then in production or under development. The ultimate goal was to use Hyper cylinders to create an engine that produced more than 1 hp/in^3 and weighed less than 1 lb/hp.

In 1932, the Continental Motors Company began working with the Power Plant Branch to build an engine that incorporated Hyper cylinders. Lycoming Engines followed in 1933; eventually, Allison Engine Company, Pratt & Whitney Aircraft Company, and Wright Aeronautical were involved. The light, compact, and powerful high-performance engines being designed by these companies would be ideal for fighter aircraft, but there was little funding available, and development was slow.

By July 1933, as the high-performance engine development continued, the Air Corps became interested in a separate project focused on a long-range bombardment aircraft. The goal for the bomber was to cruise at 200 mph and carry 2,000 lb of bombs over 5,000 miles, an incredible distance for the time. The aircraft would have a maximum bomb load of 20,000 lb. The Air Corps referred to this program as Project A and issued a proposal for an experimental long-range bomber in April 1934. The Boeing Airplane Company's Model 294 design won the competition, and Boeing was contracted to build an example, which was designated XBLR-1 (eXperimental Bomber Long Range-1).

The Engineering Section at Wright Field foresaw that a high-performance engine would not be a suitable power plant for a long-range bomber. As early as 1935, it began studies to create two different aircraft engine classes. The engines for each class would be designed to meet specific aircraft roles rather than being all-purpose aircraft engines.

The first class of engines were high-output and low weight and would be used in fighters, light bombers, attack aircraft, and other applications in which aircraft range was not a primary concern. The second class of engines were specifically designed for long-range aircraft in which low fuel consumption was the primary concern. Other concerns were for the engine to be durable under cruise conditions and have sufficient maximum power for takeoff without requiring an excessive ground run. It was understood that these long-range "bomber" engines would be larger, heavier, and have a higher compression ratio than the "fighter" engines.

Also in 1935, the Air Corps began Project D, which would push the long-range bomber concept even further than Project A. The objective of Project D was to build a bomber that would achieve the greatest range possible using existing technology. In 1936, the Douglas Aircraft Company was contracted to build the XBLR-2 to fulfill Project D's goal.

The Boeing XBLR-1, now designated XB-15, made its first flight on 15 October 1937. The aircraft had a span of 149' and a length of 87.6'. Originally, it was to be powered by four 1,000 hp Allison V-1710 engines; however, Allison was experiencing developmental issues with the V-1710. As a result, the XB-15 was powered by four 850 hp Pratt & Whitney R-1830 engines—the most powerful engines available at the time. This change left the XB-15 underpowered and

The Boeing (XBLR-1) XB-15 in flight with a Boeing P-29 Peashooter fighter. Each of the four 14-cylinder Pratt & Whitney R-1830 engines produced 850 hp but were not powerful enough for the large aircraft. (USAF)

unable to achieve its design goal of carrying 2,000 lb of bombs 5,000 miles. Although the XB-15 had a maximum bombload of 12,000 lb, with range factored in, the best the aircraft could do was carry 2,500 lb of bombs for 3,400 miles at a cruise speed of 152 mph. Even though its performance fell short of Project A's goals, the aircraft was a success from an engineering standpoint, and much was learned regarding the construction and operation of large aircraft.

In 1938, the US Army conceived the Hemisphere Defense policy to protect the United States and the rest of the Western Hemisphere against military attack by an enemy located on another continent. Deteriorating political relationships within Europe indicated that war was imminent. However, Army and Navy planning officers concluded that the continental United States could not be threatened seriously by either air or surface attack unless a hostile power first secured a foothold somewhere within the Western Hemisphere.

Under the Hemisphere Defense policy, the United States would work to defend the Western Hemisphere

from attack. This was a shift in policy from protecting the country's shores to protecting all countries in the Western Hemisphere. The US also needed the capability to strike the aggressor nation whether they were in Europe or elsewhere. This was another policy switch, from mainly focusing on defense, to having a formidable offensive capability.

On 14 November 1938, President Franklin Roosevelt called for the Air Corps to have an inventory of 10,000 planes, a production capacity of 10,000 planes a year, and for the US to protect both North and South America. The Hemisphere Defense policy and events in Europe, which centered on the activities of German leader Adolf Hitler, also encouraged the development of long-range bombers.

Due to budget issues, construction on the Douglas XBLR-2, now designated XB-19, did not begin until 1938. This aircraft had a 212' wingspan and was 132.2' long, making it the world's largest aircraft at the time. The XB-19 was to be powered by four 1,600 hp Allison X-3420 engines; however, Allison was pre-occupied with developmental issues on the V-1710,

The Douglas (XBLR-2) XB-19 was powered by Wright R-3350 engines. However, the four 18-cylinder, 2,000 hp engines were not enough, and the aircraft underperformed. The XB-19 is seen here during World War II with an olive drab paint scheme. Note that the left inboard engine is stopped. (USAF)

and the X-3420 never proceeded beyond the design phase. A switch to four 2,000 hp Wright R-3350 18-cylinder engines was made, and the aircraft first flew on 27 June 1941. The XB-19 had a maximum bombload of 37,000 lb and could carry 6,000 lb of bombs 7,300 miles at a cruise speed of only 135 mph. At 135 mph, it would take over 54 hours to cover 7,300 miles. The Wright R-3350 engines experienced constant cooling issues and were replaced by 2,600 hp Allison V-3420s in 1943, resulting in the aircraft being re-designated XB-19A. With the V-3420 engines, speed increased but range and payload decreased.

Request for Data R40-A was issued on 11 September 1939. This request sought new liquid-cooled engines that could produce 1,800–2,400 hp for fighters, attackers, and medium bombers. A committee was convened at Wright Field, Ohio on 18 October 1939 to discuss the engine proposals from Allison, Continental, Pratt & Whitney, and Wright. The Pratt & Whitney X-1800 and the Wright Tornado (R-2160) were judged the winners. However, a supplement to the committee report noted the following regarding engines for the next generation of heavy bombers:

In connection with the recommendation included in the Committee Report to the affect that a Request for Data covering engines of the 4000–5000 horsepower category be issued to the industry, it appears that there will be a definite requirement for engines of this power rating for installation in Long Range Heavy Bombardment type airplanes by the time such an engine can be developed.

The statements to the Committee by representatives of the engine manufacturers indicated that very little study and no work is being devoted to the project. In addition, there is a positive lack of interest in this development because it is essentially a military type with limited commercial application.

During the XB-19's development, Request for Data R40-B was issued on 29 January 1940 and called for a "Hemisphere Defensive Weapon." This was to be a very heavy bomber with a 16,000 lb maximum bombload and the ability to deliver 2,000 lb of bombs to the midpoint of a 5,333 mile unrefueled flight. The bomber would have a top speed of 400 mph; this speed was later reduced to 300 mph with a 450 mph top speed listed as desirable. The payload and range were a step back from what was expected from the XB-19, but the maximum speed was significantly higher. In a sense, the performance requirements outlined for R40-B's "Hemisphere Defensive Weapon" acknowledged the technological limitations that hindered the XB-15 and XB-19 programs but continued to advance aircraft design by using the lessons learned in those earlier programs.

Boeing's Model 341 was deemed the best R40-B proposal, and the design was built as the B-29 Superfortress. Consolidated's Model 33 was judged as the runner up. It was ordered as insurance against issues with the B-29 program and was designated the B-32 Dominator. Both the B-29 and B-32 would use the Wright R-3350 engine (the same engine first used on the XB-19), which was not the ideal long-range engine envisioned by the Air Corps. While neither the XB-15 nor the XB-19 were considered successful aircraft, their development paved the way for designing, constructing, operating, and maintaining very large aircraft, and the engineering experience gained made subsequent large aircraft, like the B-29 and B-32, possible.

The Wright R-3350 engine powered the Air Corps' long-range bombers developed from R40-B. The engine's development was rushed, which resulted in several shortcomings. The urgencies of war prevented some of the issues from being fully resolved. (AEHS)

On 20 February 1940, Request for Data R40-C was issued for a new fighter aircraft with a top speed of 450 mph, with 525 mph listed as desirable. In addition, R40-C promoted and funded the continued development of high-performance engines for these new fighters. Engines that were part of this program included the Allison V-3420; Continental IV-1430; Lycoming H-2470 (funded by the Navy); Pratt & Whitney X-1800 (H-2600), H-3130, and H-3730 (all Navy funded); and Wright R-2160 Tornado.

However, as the Air Corps had already predicted, high-performance engines would not be suitable for long-range aircraft. With the fighter class engine development underway, resources could now be turned to a long-range bomber engine. The XB-15 and XB-19 illustrated the need for fuel efficient engines of a high-power output for long-range aircraft. An engine for long-range aircraft needed a low fuel consumption to maximize range, but its power output needed to be high to get the large aircraft into the air and maximize cruise speed. The problem was how to fulfill the paradoxical requirement of a fuel efficient, high-powered engine. To that end, request for Data R40-D was issued to initiate development of special engines ideal for long-range aircraft.

Request for Data R40-D

On 6 March 1940, Request for Data R40-D was issued for the design of a 4,000 to 5,500 hp aircraft engine. R40-D also requested a table of the proposed engine's guaranteed specific fuel consumption (SFC) at 40%, 50%, 60%, and 70% takeoff power. Ultimately, the R40-D engine was to complete a 275-hour approval test for long-range operation. The following quote from the request describes the engine's purpose:

> [F]or test and experimental installation in airplanes to explore the effect of durable, low fuel consumption engines on the performance of long range aircraft. Whereas the performance requirements represent a substantial increase over the performance of existing models now under construction, it is hoped that the industry will be able to produce articles required without resort to radical departures from accepted practices or principles of aeronautical engine design.

The R40-D request was sent to Wright, Pratt & Whitney, Allison, Continental, and Lycoming.

Initially, the engine designs needed to be submitted by 6 May 1940, but this date was pushed back to 7 June 1940. However, because of the tight time frame and current production commitments (orders from Europe), the designs that were submitted consisted of existing engines geared together. Allison offered the DV-6840—basically two separate V-3420s driving a common remote gearbox for contra-rotating propellers. Lycoming offered the XH-4940—a doubled H-2470. The Air Corps was looking for an entirely new engine design and felt that none of the submitted designs met the requirements outlined in R40-D. As a result, on 25 July 1940, it was recommended that the Request for Data R40-D be cancelled.

Long-Range Necessities

Late in 1940, Hitler's war machine was controlling much of Europe, and the Battle of Britain had just ended. "The Few" had managed to keep Britain free and hold off the Germans, but many wondered if the next battle would have a different outcome. Britain stood alone against the Axis Powers; Winston Churchill referred to this period as the *Darkest Hour.*

In the United States, involvement in the war seemed inevitable. There were serious concerns regarding the possible fall of Britain. The Air Corps saw an urgent need to develop a bomber capable of attacking German targets in Europe from North America. Engineers at the Consolidated Aircraft Corporation quietly began design studies for an intercontinental bomber. On 11 April 1941, the Air Corps issued official requirements for a very long-range bomber with a 275 mph cruise speed, 45,000' service ceiling, and 12,000 mile range. The aircraft was to carry 10,000 lb of bombs 10,000 miles or 72,000 lb of bombs 4,700 miles.

This intercontinental bomber aircraft's capabilities would far exceed those of the Boeing B-17 Flying Fortresses and Consolidated B-24 Liberators just then entering service. Even the Boeing B-29 and Consolidated B-32, both under development, paled in comparison. Boeing and Consolidated seriously pursued the design of this new bomber and submitted proposals to the Air Corps. Douglas and Northrup also entered the competition, but their proposals fell short of the requirements.

On 15 November 1941, Consolidated was issued a contract for the intercontinental bomber designated XB-36. From the start, the B-36 Peacemaker was a massive aircraft with a wingspan of 230' and a length of 163'. Power for the B-36 came from six 3,000 hp Pratt & Whitney R-4360 engines. The R-4360 was first run on 28 April 1941 and was the largest, most

The Consolidated (later Convair) B-36 Peacemaker pushed the long-range bomber to its technological limits. The planned six 3,000 hp Pratt & Whitney R-4360 engines powering the aircraft were barely adequate, and the Air Corps realized that engine technology must be advanced in order to develop aircraft beyond the B-36. The B-36 missed the war, with its first flight taking place on 8 August 1946. (USAF)

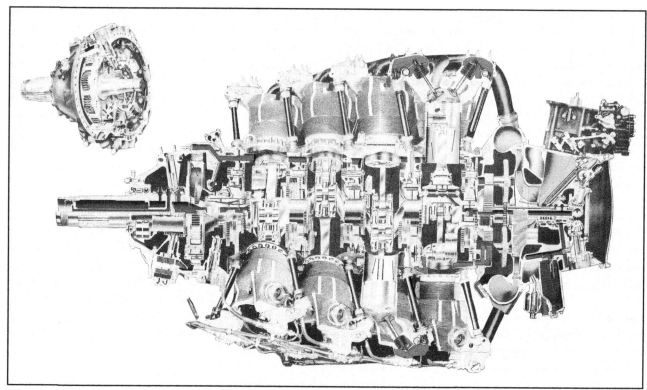

The Pratt & Whitney R-4360 was the most powerful aircraft engine running when the B-36 contract was awarded. The 28-cylinder engine was very complex and never a favorite with maintenance crews. The R-4360 had a 5.75" bore and 6.0" stroke. The engine weighed in excess of 3,500 lb. (AC)

powerful engine under development during the B-36's design phase. The B-36 was built upon lessons learned from the Boeing XB-15 and the Douglas XB-19, and it took the "World's Largest Aircraft" title from the XB-19.

Long-Range Engine

With the B-36 intercontinental bomber moving forward and even more ambitious projects on the drawing board, the need for a long-range engine was even more apparent. On 4 December 1941, the Army Air Force (AAF, renamed from the Army Air Corps in June 1941) prepared a report for an aircraft engine designed specifically for low fuel consumption and for installation in long-range bomber aircraft. The power goal of around 5,000 hp from Request for Data R40-D remained. Generally, as engine displacement increases so does the power output. One way to increase the displacement of an engine is to increase the number of cylinders. However, numerous cylinders add weight and complexity. The decision was made to enlarge the long-range engine's bore and stroke beyond anything that was in current use or being developed. A larger bore and stroke would increase the engine's displacement while maintaining a manageable number of cylinders. Larger cylinders,

rather than more cylinders, would produce the required power, achieve the most efficient operation possible, and simplify the engine overall. The AAF thought that success would be achieved via a high compression cylinder with a bore of 6–8" and a similarly long stroke. To reach the 5,000 hp goal, an engine displacing 6,500–8,000 in^3 was needed.

It was believed that the development of such an engine would take at least four years and be very expensive. Because of the war situation in Europe and the development time involved, the AAF recommended that engine development be started as soon as possible. Beyond the military applications, the engine was seen as a very valuable power-unit for the emerging market of commercial intercontinental air transport.

Lt. Col. Franklin O. Carroll was the Chief of the Experimental Engineering Section at Wright Field and a proponent of the long-range engine. Lt. Col. Carroll was at the center of every major experimental and engineering project that originated from Wright Field during World War II. In a memorandum dated 23 December 1941 to the AAF Materiel Division in Washington, DC regarding the long-range engine, Lt. Col. Carroll noted the following:

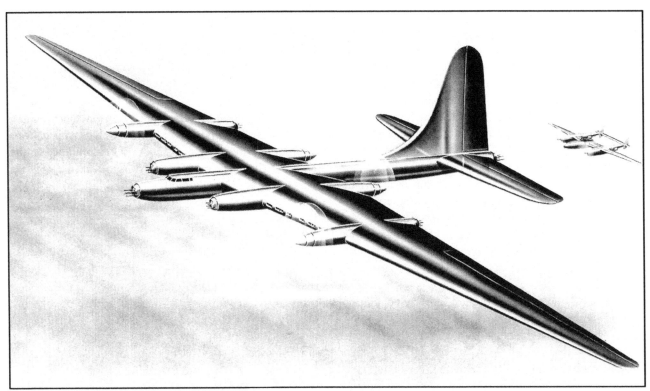

With a wingspan of 280', the Materiel Command Design (MCD) 392 was a possible answer to the question of what would come after the B-36. Other ambitious designs were on the drawing boards of just about every aircraft manufacturer. However, aircraft were developed much faster than aircraft engines, so the Air Corps wanted to start development of the next generation of large and powerful aircraft engines as soon as possible. (AC)

To develop such an engine will require considerable time, of the order of four years, a large amount of money, and sound engineering talent. Because of the magnitude of the project, it is recommended that the development be started now because the experimental funds could be allocated in the amounts required and the present emergency [war in Europe] will undoubtedly indicate the need for engines of this type. ... It is becoming more evident that technically a universal aircraft engine will not be suitable for all types of applications. It is recommended, therefore, that development be started on an engine specifically for long range bombardment having a take-off output of approximately 4500 h.p., a cruising specific fuel consumption of not to exceed .38 pound per horsepower and having the durability characteristics required. It is urgently recommended that this project be undertaken before the actual need arises and while adequate experimental funds are available.

A survey of companies involved with aircraft engine production was conducted to see if one of them could take on the project. This survey included not only aircraft engine manufacturers, like Wright and Pratt & Whitney, but also automobile manufacturers that were beginning to produce aircraft engines on license, such as the Packard Motor Car Company, Ford Motor Company, and Chrysler Corporation. Aircraft engine manufacturers were all overwhelmed with existing production and the development of new engines of up to 3,000 hp. Automobile manufacturers were equally overwhelmed with aircraft engine production and the construction of other war equipment. There was one exception: the Studebaker Corporation.

In addition to available plant space, Studebaker had an extensive automobile test laboratory that could accommodate single- and two-cylinder test engines. It had an engineering department with around 250 engineers, draftsmen, experimental machinists, and dynamometer operators. Studebaker also had two men on its engineering staff who had experience with aircraft engines: William S. James (Chief Engineer) and Stanwood W. Sparrow. Lt. Col. Carroll praised Sparrow as an "outstanding research engineer on aircraft engines during and following the last war

[World War I]." Before joining Studebaker, the men worked together at the National Bureau of Standards and authored a number of reports dealing with the mechanics of internal combustion engines. They also investigated the relation between improved fuels and engine performance in high compression test engines. James and Sparrow most likely joined Studebaker's engineering department in the mid to late 1920s.

What the AAF felt Studebaker lacked was a designer thoroughly familiar with modern aircraft engine design. With wartime production ramping up, there was an extreme shortage of designers that met the AAF's requirements. However, there was one qualified aircraft engine designer who the AAF felt could be made available: Mr. N. N. Tilley.

Interestingly, the success of the long-range engine seemed somewhat assured, with Lt. Col. Carroll stating the following:

> If this company [Studebaker] were interested in such a development, and with an adequate experimental contract from the Air Corps would employ Mr. Tilley and give him technical supervision of the design, a satisfactory engine for long range bombardment aircraft should result. ... If the National Emergency terminates prior to the completion of this development, then Studebaker Corporation should have available an ideal transoceanic commercial engine which should make the project attractive to this company [Studebaker].

N. N. Tilley

Norman Nevil Tilley was born on 29 January 1892. In June 1915, he graduated from Cornell University in Ithaca, New York with a degree in Mechanical Engineering. He stayed on at Cornell as an Experimental Engineering Instructor in the Sibley College of Mechanical Engineering and Mechanic Arts while he worked on a graduate degree. In 1918, in the midst of World War I, he was commissioned as a 2nd Lieutenant in the newly formed United States Army Air Service.

By 1920, Tilley was discharged from the service and worked as a civilian engineer for the Air Service at the Power Plant Section at McCook Field in Dayton, Ohio. Later, Tilley served in the same capacity when the Power Plant Section was moved to Wright Field (also in Dayton) and renamed the Power Plant Branch.

While with the Power Plant Branch, he worked alongside the likes of Sam Heron, Glenn Angle, Edward T. Jones, and many others. Some of the projects he was associated with were investigations on cylinder and exhaust valve cooling and the Engineering Division W-1 and Allison X-4520 24-cylinder engines. Ultimately, Tilley became the Chief of the Engine Development and Specifications Unit before he left the Power Plant Branch for the Kinner Airplane and Motor Corporation in 1929. He was the Chief Engineer at Kinner but left around 1933 for Continental, where he was the Chief Engineer of the Detroit, Michigan plant.

While at Continental, he worked on the GSV-750A— a 500 hp, 754 in^3, air-cooled, inverted, V-12 engine that was never built. More importantly, Tilley found himself again working with Heron, now developing the Hyper No. 2 cylinder. The Hyper No. 2 project developed into the 1,000 hp, 12-cylinder, horizontally-opposed Continental O-1430 engine. During the O-1430 project, Tilley took out two US patents: 2,016,693 for mounting a large, 12-cylinder, horizontally-opposed engine and 2,053,354 for a reversible starter and generator drive. The O-1430 was run in 1938 and passed its 50-hour development test in 1939. However, the concept of a horizontally-opposed engine had fallen out of favor, and the engine was redesigned as the inverted Vee XI-1430.

In late 1939, Tilley was a Project Engineer at Lycoming and involved with the development of the company's high-performance engines: the O-1230 and H-2470. Lycoming's O-1230 was a horizontally-opposed, 12-cylinder engine very similar to the Continental O-1430. Lycoming had decided that the O-1230 would not produce enough power for the next generation of aircraft. The company's solution was basically to put two O-1230 engines on their sides and gear them together. The resulting engine was the XH-2470, a 24-cylinder vertical "H" engine.

Perhaps the most intriguing project Tilley worked on while at Lycoming involved the Bell FM-1 Airacuda. In mid-1940, Bell Aircraft Corporation initiated a design study of powering the Airacuda with two XH-2470 engines. Tilley worked with Robert J. Woods (Bell's chief engineer) on the aircraft, which Bell designated Model 17. Within each wing, a XH-2470 engine was to be positioned on its side and turned 90° so that the rear of the engine was near the fuselage and the propeller shaft was pointed toward the wing tip. A right-angle gearbox would take the engine power and deliver it to a propeller shaft that extended behind the Airacuda's wings. It was estimated that the engine change would have made the heavy fighter capable of 400 mph and able to cruise at 300 mph for eight hours. A desired delivery date was set for June 1941, but the Bell Model 17 never proceeded beyond the design stage. Another project that Tilley worked on, which foreshadowed things to come, was a remote, two-speed gearbox to drive contra-rotating propellers for the XH-2470.

Tilley was also involved with Lycoming's submission to the Air Corps' Request for Data R40-D: the twin XH-2470. Exactly how far this project proceeded or the exact configuration of the engine has not been found, but Tilley's notes indicate that the XH-4940 would have had slightly less than twice the frontal area of the XH-2470, indicating some sort of side-by-side arrangement. This 48-cylinder engine had the same 5.25" bore and 4.75" stroke individual cylinders as the XH-2470 and was to displace 4,935.6 in^3. Tilley's notes indicate an expected 4,800 hp at 3,100 rpm up to 8,500' with the aid of a single-speed, single-stage supercharger. The engine had a projected 3,400 rpm maximum and would weigh 6,200 lb. Engine power would be transferred to contra-rotating propellers via a two-speed gear reduction, and a minimum SFC of .38 lb/hp/hr was given.

While still serving as a consultant for Lycoming, Tilley had moved on to the Lawrence Engineering & Research Group in 1941 and was involved in developing a three-cylinder auxiliary engine. By late 1942, with Lawrence's engine entering production and the Lycoming XH-2470 design completed, Tilley was free to join a new project. The AAF wanted Tilley to head up the long-range engine project, which it had made a priority.

Development Begins

Early in 1942, the AAF approached Studebaker and Tilley regarding the possibility of designing a large, durable, high-compression aircraft engine of around 4,500 hp with a low SFC not to exceed .38 lb/hp/hr for maximum range. Opie Chenoweth, Chief Civilian Engineer of the Power Plant Laboratory (formerly the Power Plant Branch until 1939), met with Tilley around 19 January 1942 to discuss what was referred to as the *Special Engine Project*. The engine's configuration, bore, stroke, and other parameters would be determined after developmental analysis and testing of single-cylinder engines with a variety of bores and strokes. With automotive production stopped because of the war, and with its engineering

Norman N. Tilley circa 1940. (LoC)

department free, Studebaker had already considered the possibility of becoming involved with aircraft engines beyond the license manufacture of the Wright R-1820. Studebaker and Tilley had numerous discussions regarding the *Special Engine Project*, and they decided to accept the AAF's request.

On 3 March 1942, Roy E. Cole, Vice President of Studebaker, sent a proposal outlining Studebaker's development of the long-range engine to Col. Edwin R. Page, Chief of the Power Plant Laboratory at Wright Field, Ohio. This proposal outlined the use of four different cylinder bores to be tested on four different single-cylinder test engines. The bores were 6.5", 7.0", 7.5", and 8.0". The cylinder that exhibited the best SFC would be used on two twin-cylinder test engines. These test engines would serve as the basis for the construction of six full-size test engines.

The engine would be liquid-cooled, fuel injected, turbosupercharged and would have a two-speed drive to the contra-rotating propellers. Studebaker chose to use two separate and remote gearboxes: one for the two-speed drive and the other for the contra-rotating gear reduction. Studebaker believed the remote gearboxes would allow for a number of different engine installation options and enable more aircraft to use the engine. The combination of engine, two-speed gear drive, propeller gear reduction, and associated shafting could be configured based on the specific needs of different aircraft.

On 18 March 1942, Authority for Purchase No. 224892 was submitted for the long-range engine. Per Col. Page's request, the engine project was given a "Confidential" status on 23 March 1942, and Project Number (Materiel, Experimental) MX-232 was assigned under the title "Studebaker XH Engine." However, the engine's configuration had yet to be determined.

Authority for Purchase No. 224892 was rewritten by Col. Carroll (who had been promoted from Lt. Col.) and resubmitted on 10 April 1942. This request was to cover the first phases of development for the engine, and it is not known how much it differed from the earlier request. In the updated document, Col. Carroll wrote, "An engine has never been built wherein the first consideration in its design has been fuel consumption." According to Col. Carroll, the engine's estimated displacement was 6,500–8,000 in^3, and development would be costly and require several years to accomplish. Col. Carroll made the following statement:

> There is no known means of saving time by bypassing the many preliminary tests which should be undertaken prior to the building of the full scale engine. It is therefore urgently recommended that the early phases of this project be undertaken while the money and the Studebaker engineering organization are available and interested in undertaking a development which will have outstanding military applications.

On 24 April 1942, Cole sent a letter notifying Tilley that Studebaker was awarded the contract for the long-range engine. In another letter, dated 30 April 1942, Cole's eagerness to start the project was apparent when he asked Tilley to come to South Bend, Indiana on 4 May 1942 to "sit down and sort of map out a tentative program as to how [they] will start" the engine's development. Tilley was placed in charge as the Chief Engineer of the Studebaker Special Engine Project.

It was not until 10 July 1942 that Contract W-535-ac-28386 covering the development of a long-range engine was approved, but the contract did not cover the construction of any complete engines. Studebaker was to proceed with the design and development of the single- and twin-cylinder test

engines and also the design (but not construction) of the full-scale engine.

The largest cylinder bore used in a then-in-production aircraft engine was 6.125" (used in various Wright engines). The 6.5" bore cylinder for the MX-232 program represented a slight stretch from the current state-of-the-art and was included in the testing mainly to serve as a baseline by which the larger cylinder bores would be judged. All other aspects of the engine, such as stroke, compression ratio (CR), and configuration, were to be determined based on the testing of each cylinder. The engine's height needed to be kept to a minimum to enable its installation buried in an aircraft's wing, and "H" or "X" configurations were considered.

The MX-232 program was run out of the Studebaker Motor Machining and Assembly Plant (Building 72) on Sample Street in South Bend, Indiana. This location was about three miles from the government-built Aviation Division Aircraft Engine Plant on Chippewa Avenue where Studebaker was building Wright R-1820 engines. Studebaker moved quickly to design the 6.5", 7.0", 7.5", and 8.0" cylinders. The 8.0" cylinder and test engine (AF-1) were given priority, followed by the 6.5" cylinder (AF-2), the 7.5" cylinder (AF-3), and the 7.0" cylinder (AF-4). The "AF" in the engines' names stood for "Air Force."

Original Cylinder Design

The cylinder was made of a hardened (Rockwell C 34–38) forged alloy steel barrel shrunk into a cast cylinder head of heat-treated Alcoa 355 aluminum alloy. The cylinder barrel coolant jacket was an aluminum casting of the same alloy as the head, shrunk to the barrel at the crankshaft end and retained against a shoulder on the barrel with a large nut. The jacket was fastened to the head with studs. The cylinder assembly was held to the crankcase with four long, heat-treated, hold-down through bolts and eight (two per side) smaller fasteners. The four hold-down through bolts were tightened to bear a load in considerable excess of any combustion loads. While there may have been some size variation between the different cylinder sizes, the hold-down bolts for the 7.5" cylinder had a diameter of .75" and were 18.0" long.

The cylinder was designed for high temperature coolants, such as ethylene glycol or water, under pressure up to 30–40 psi. Coolant entered the jacket at a flanged connection near the crankshaft end of the cylinder. It passed around the barrel and into the cylinder head jacket through large, cored passages in the head casting. The wetted surfaces of the head included the dome, the ports, around all spark plug bosses, and completely around the valve guide bosses. Two coolant outlets were located fore and aft of the uppermost part of the head casting.

All cylinder bores had a hemispherical combustion chamber. The head of the 8.0" cylinder had a radius of 5 5/32" blended to the 8.584" outer diameter of the cylinder sleeve with a radius of .75". The 6.5" cylinder head had a radius of 4.375" blended to the cylinder bore with a radius of .512". The head of the 7.5" cylinder had a radius of 5.0" blended to the 7.5" inside diameter of the cylinder sleeve with a radius of 1.25". The 7.0" cylinder head had a radius of 4 11/16" blended to the 7.0" inside diameter of the cylinder sleeve with a radius of 1.0".

The cylinder head had one intake port and one exhaust port. Both ports were in a plane perpendicular to the axis of the crankshaft. The exhaust was expelled from the cylinder head via a side outlet, and the intake port entrance was on the cylinder centerline. On the 8.0" cylinder, the intake valve seat had an inside diameter of 4.0", and the exhaust valve seat was 3 11/16". On the 6.5" cylinder, both the intake and exhaust seats had a 3 5/32" inside diameter. On the 7.5" cylinder, the intake seat had an inside diameter of 3.75", and the exhaust seat was 3 11/16". On the 7.0" cylinder, both the intake and exhaust seats had an inside diameter of 3.5".

The valve seat inserts were of the shoulder type and made from steel (Silchrome No. 1 or Cichrome X-Be) shrunk into the head at the smaller outside diameter of the insert. The valve seat angle was 45° for both intake and exhaust inserts for all test cylinders except the first series of preliminary runs with a 6.8:1 CR (6.16:1 CR for 6.5" cylinder) and 7.25" stroke for the 8.0" and 6.5" cylinders, and a 6.75" stroke for the 7.5" and 7.0" cylinders. For those runs, the valve seat angle was 30°.

The intake and exhaust valves were directly above the cylinder and fully enclosed. The valves had a hollow head and were cooled with a sodium-mercury mixture. The valves ran in SAE no 62 Bronze guides inclined 27° to the cylinder axis. The seating surface of the valves was Stellite faced.

The valves for the 8.0" and 6.5" cylinders were operated by individual cams on the center line of the valves, acting on cup-type tappets surrounding the outer end of the valve springs. Cam lobes for the 8.0" cylinder had a .900" lift, and the 6.5" cylinder had a .750" lift. The tappets were guided in a housing cast integral with the cylinder head. A wear-resistant coating of Colmonoy was applied to the cam lobe contact surface of the tappet. Running clearance adjustment was provided by shims of various thickness inserted between the end of the valve stem and tappet. Oil was supplied through jets to each side of the cam lobe at the rubbing surface.

The valves on the 7.5" cylinder were operated through lever followers by individual .865" lift cam lobes on the center line of the valves. The lever followers (which had a wear-resistant Colmonoy coating on the cam lobe contact surface) bore on the valves through a ball and socket member. Running clearance adjustment was provided by shims of various thicknesses inserted between the cam housing and the cylinder head and also by grinding the face of the socket, which was made thick enough to permit this.

Valve action for the 7.0" cylinder differed in that they were actuated by rocker arms and push rods through roller followers. The intake and exhaust cam lobes were on a single shaft and had a lift of .640". The rocker arm ratio was such that the valve lift was .779" with the specified clearance. Running clearance was set by an adjusting screw on the valve end of each rocker arm, the screw being held tight by a locknut. Pressure lubrication was applied through drilled passages in the cam lobe followers, push rods, and rocker arms.

Other cylinder designs included four-valve and three-valve heads. Different versions of the four-valve head were drawn with flat, pent roof, and hemispherical combustion chambers. The flat combustion chamber featured dual overhead camshafts. Two designs were made: one with intake port diameters of approximately 2.76" and exhaust port diameters of approximately 2.64", and a more compact design with port diameters around 2.85" for the intake ports and a 2.36" for the exhaust ports.

The pent roof design had a single overhead camshaft and was drawn with two different valve angles. The 15° valve angle design had 2.85" intake port diameters and 2.76" exhaust port diameters. The 25° valve angle design had 2.98" intake port diameters and 2.84" exhaust port diameters.

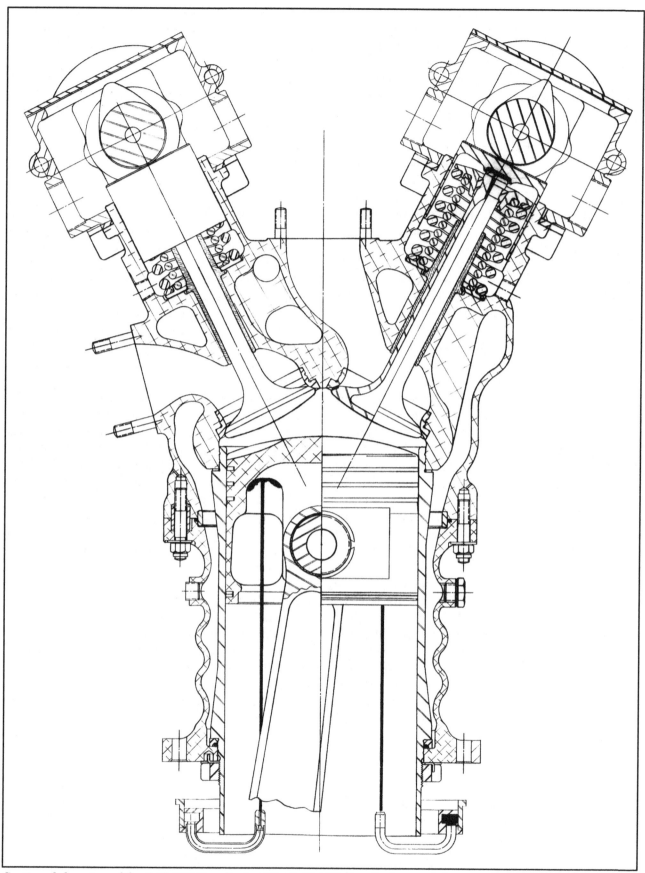

Sectional drawing of the 6.5" (AF-2) cylinder. The 8.0" (AF-1) cylinder used the same head design. Note the jets of oil that sprayed the underside of the piston for cooling. The intake valve is on the right. (NARA)

The 8.0" (AF-1) cylinder undergoing a deflection test while mounted on the test engine. The cam housings have been removed, and the very tip of the valve stem is visible. (AC)

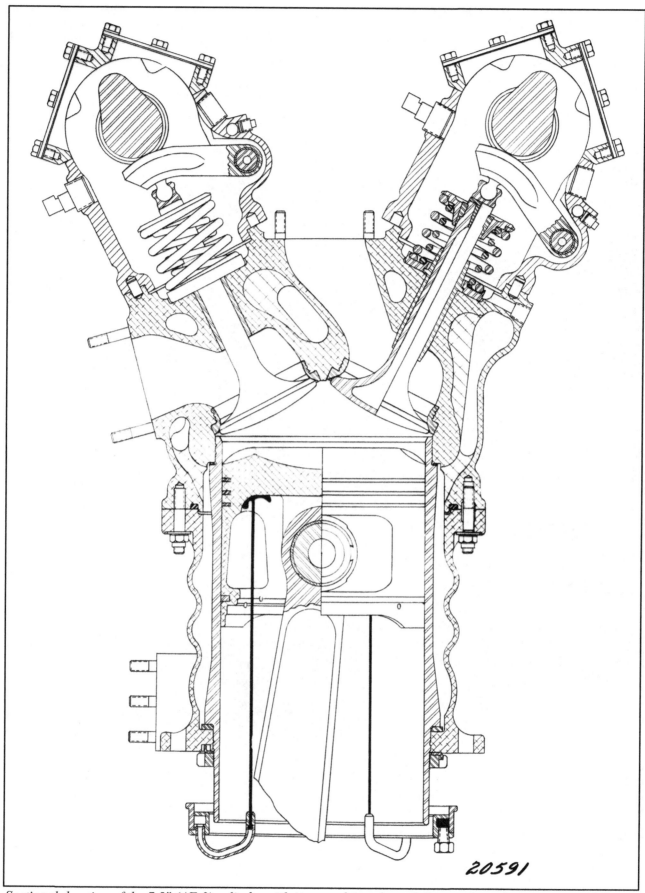

20591

Sectional drawing of the 7.5" (AF-3) cylinder with its cam-driven lever followers for valve actuation. (AC)

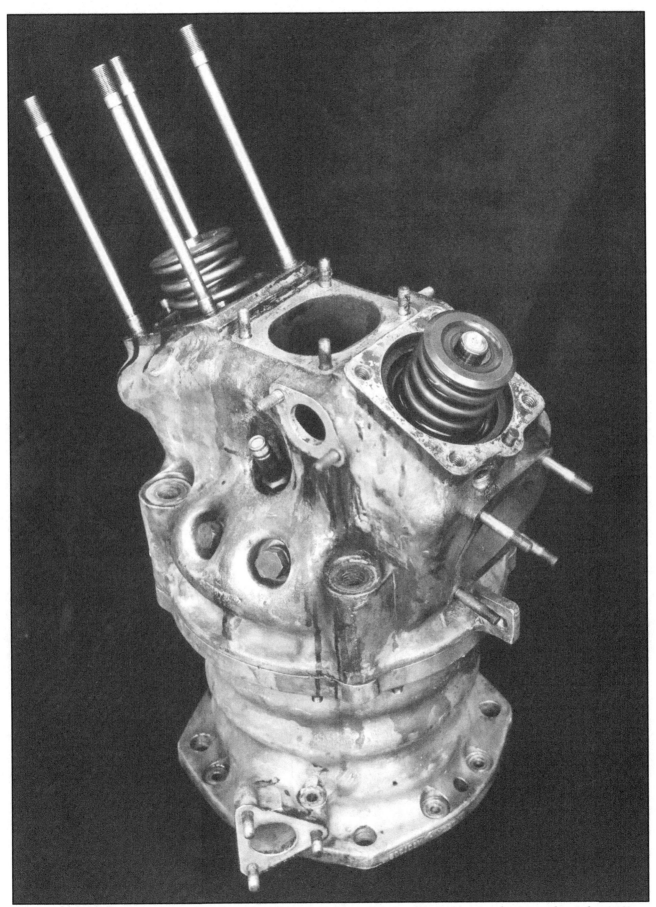

The 7.5" (AF-3) cylinder without its cam housings and through bolts. The exhaust valve is on the right. (AC)

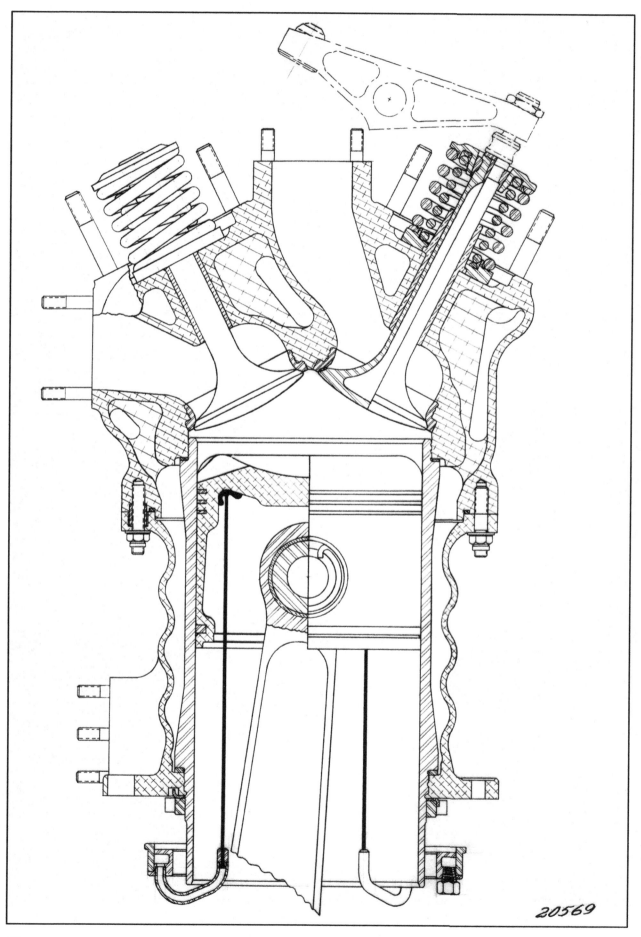

20569

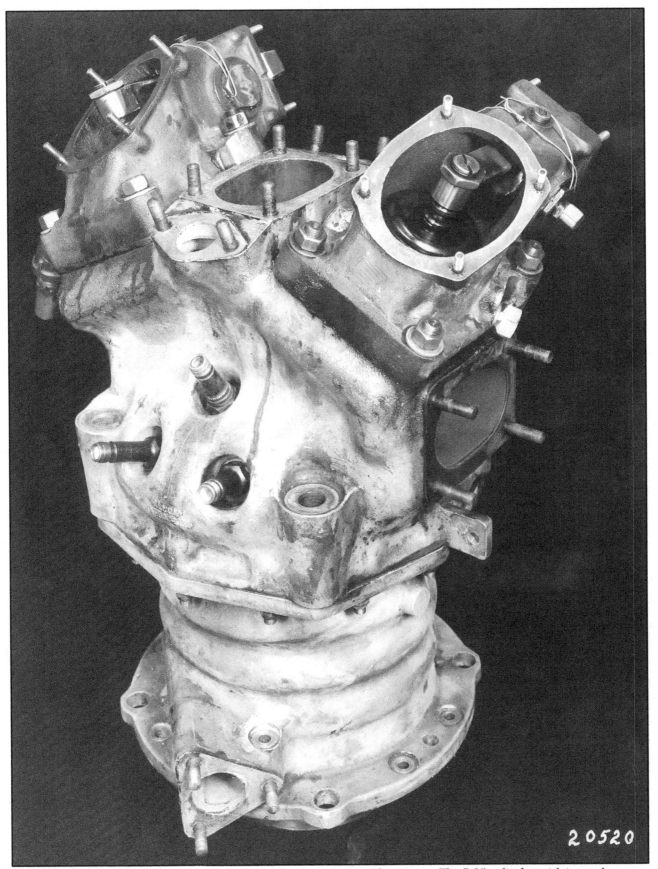

20520

Previous page—Drawing of the 7.0" (AF-4) cylinder. (NARA) This page—The 7.0" cylinder with its rocker arms visible above the valves. Note the three spark plugs on this side of the cylinder. The drawing and image are from a report dated 27 October 1944. (NARA)

The hemispherical four-valve combustion chamber featured a single overhead camshaft. The hemispherical four-valve head had a valve angle of 25°, and port diameters were approximately 3.23" for the intake ports and 2.73" for the exhaust ports.

The three-valve head design had a hemispherical combustion chamber, and the valves were actuated by a single overhead camshaft. The camshaft had three lobes for each cylinder—the two intake valves flanked the single exhaust valve. The angle of the two intake valves was 15°, and the exhaust valve angle was 20°. Port diameters for the three-valve head were approximately 3.175" for the intake ports and 3 33/64" for the exhaust port. Notes indicate that the three- and four-valve head designs would not leave enough material between the valves, spark plugs, and fuel injection boss to prevent cracks from developing.

The basic cylinder design was revised with lessons learned through testing. The first three cylinder designs were very similar. They differed in valve seat angle and port contours and included some additional changes to the head casting. A third-design cylinder that had a 1.3" shorter barrel was also used to test a 3.0" shorter connecting rod. Different heads were used that were either flush with the inside diameter of the cylinder barrel or flush with the outside diameter of the barrel. Six 18 mm holes were provided in the head dome for spark plugs and fuel injector nozzles. The thread inserts were Aero Thread helicoils.

The complete 8.0" cylinder was approximately 83 lb in weight and 26.6" tall.

Pistons

The pistons were forged of Lo-Ex alloy and were without ribs. Lo-Ex is a light aluminum alloy made up of approximately 82% aluminum, 14% silicon, 2% nickel, 1% copper, and 1% magnesium. Heat expansion for Lo-Ex is about 20% less than pure aluminum, and the alloy is heat and wear-resistant. Pistons with a thick domed (convex) crown were initially used for the 8.0" and 6.5" bore cylinders. Pistons with a cupped (concave) crown were originally used for the 7.5" and 7.0" bore cylinders.

The first piston design had three 3/32" compression rings above the pin and two 1/8" oil control rings in a single groove in the crankshaft end of the piston. These oil rings had scalloped lower faces. The second piston design differed only in that the oil rings were relocated above the piston pin. The second piston design was used on the 6.5" bore engine. As development progressed, domed, cupped, and flat top pistons were used in various engines, but they were all very similar with the exception of their crowns. The 2.75" diameter, case-hardened piston pin was a full-floating type retained by snap rings in a groove on each end of the piston pin boss. A complete 8.0" piston weighed 24.54 lb. Each piston was cooled by four oil jets located at the crankshaft end of the cylinder. The jets sprayed up the cylinder to the underside of the piston. The four jets combined to flow approximately 2.5 gpm of oil.

Cam Lobe

For the 8.0" and 6.5" cylinders, the intake lobe was designed for an open duration of 250° and the exhaust

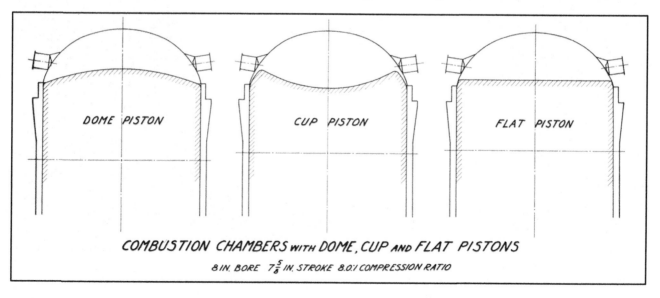

COMBUSTION CHAMBERS with DOME, CUP and FLAT PISTONS

8 IN. BORE 7⅝ IN. STROKE 8.0:1 COMPRESSION RATIO

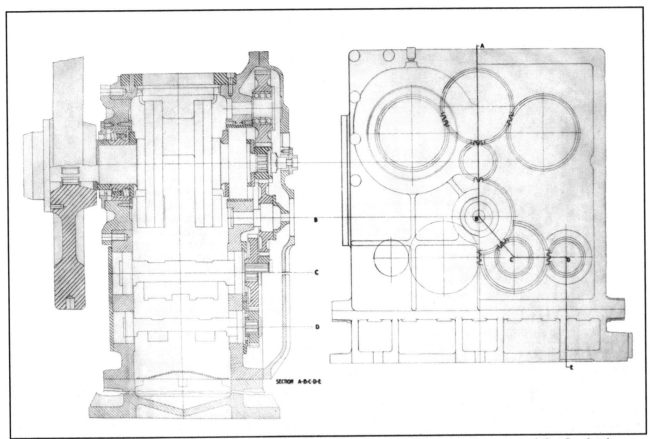

The single-cylinder test engine crankcase without a cylinder mounted on top. Opposite of the flywheel was a dynamometer that could be used to motor the engine or absorb its power when running. (NARA)

lobe for an open duration of 260°. The 7.5" cylinder's intake and exhaust lobes were both designed for an open duration of 258°. The 7.0" cylinder's intake lobe was designed for an open duration of 252° and the exhaust lobe for an open duration of 276°.

The 8.0" cylinder intake lobe had opening and closing ramps of .020". The first exhaust camshaft's lobe had a .020" opening ramp and a .030" closing ramp. This camshaft was replaced by a second camshaft with the same opening interval but with opening and closing ramps both equal to .020". The 6.5" cylinder camshaft lobes' opening and closing ramps were .030" except for an intake opening ramp of .020". The valves of the 7.5" cylinder on AF-3 originally had issues with excessive acceleration during the initial opening period and did not permit operation above 2,000 rpm. A new camshaft was made that had opening and closing ramps of .020". The 7.0" cylinder camshaft lobes' opening and closing ramps were .035".

On all of the test engines except for the 7.0" cylinder, the intake and exhaust cams were driven independently and could be set to give any desired time of opening. The intake and exhaust cams for the

7.0" cylinder were integral with the driving shaft and had a fixed overlap of 45° crankshaft rotation. Valve timing was adjusted to give the best overall maximum power performance for the speed range tested.

Single-Cylinder Test Engines

The test engines were constructed of plate steel that was welded together and then machined for the cylinder mount and crankshaft. The 8.0" bore cylinder and AF-1 test engine were planned to operate with 6.75–8.0" strokes up to 2,500 rpm. The 6.5" bore cylinder and AF-2 engine were planned to operate with 6.0–8.0" strokes up to 3,150 rpm. The 7.5" bore cylinder and AF-3 engine were planned to operate with 6.75–8.0" strokes up to 2,700 rpm. The 7.0" bore cylinder and AF-4 engine were planned to operate with 6.0–7.625" strokes up to 2,700 rpm. The operational speed for each engine was limited by its respective valve mechanisms. The cylinders and engines were designed to operate at CRs between 6.5:1 and 10:1 (6.0:1 to 10:1 for the 6.5" cylinder). Ultimately, 18 different bore, stroke, and CR combinations were tested.

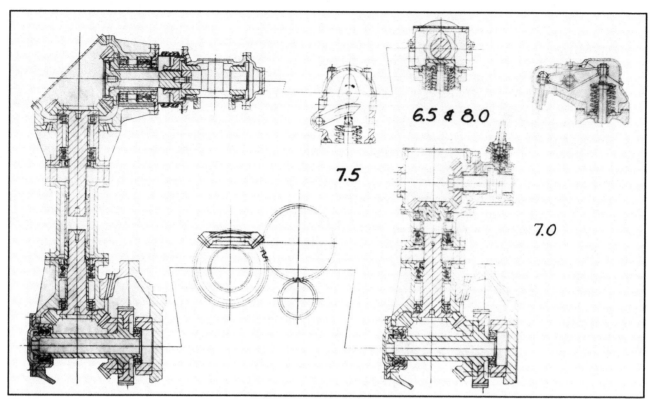

Even though each cylinder used a different valve operation, only two cam drives were used with the test engines. The 7.0" cylinders (AF-3) used a direct cam drive with a fixed valve overlap. The other cylinders used adjustable cam drives. (NARA)

The crankshaft was supported by two main bearings, most likely 4.75" in diameter. It originally had 4.0" diameter crankpins, but new crankshafts were made with 4.75" diameter crankpins after tests revealed the original design had excessive deflection.

Single-Cylinder Engine Tests			
Bore	Stroke	Disp.	Comp. Ratio
6.5	6.00	199.10	8.0
6.5	6.375	211.54	6.16/8.0
6.5	7.25	240.58	6.16/8.0
7.0	6.75	259.77	6.8
7.0	7.625	293.44	8.0
7.5	6.75	298.21	6.8/8.0
7.5	8.00	353.43	8.0
8.0	7.25	364.42	6.8/8.0
8.0	7.625	383.27	8.0
8.0	7.75	389.56	8.0
8.0	8.00	402.12	6.8/7.5/8.0/8.7

Single-Cylinder Testing

The 8.0" cylinder AF-1 engine ran for the first time in February 1943. The 6.5" cylinder AF-2 was the next to run, firing up for the first time in March 1943. The 7.0" cylinder AF-4 followed, with its first run in July or August 1943. In late October or early November 1943, the 7.5" cylinder AF-3 made its first run. Early issues were encountered with the engines' three-piece crankshaft deflecting. A one-piece crankshaft was substituted. There was also the issue of cracks forming in the cylinder water jackets. This issue was lessened by the various cylinder redesigns. Likewise, issues with valve float were encountered but were slowly resolved by the use of valve dampers, although a perfect damper was never found.

Extensive testing was conducted during the MX-232 program, using just about every conceivable variable. For example, an engine was tested with a single spark plug, and the test was run six times, trying the spark plug in each hole to determine which location resulted in the best performance. Eleven different bore and stroke combinations were tested. Engines were run with the three different piston types, many different combinations and locations of spark plugs, different locations and types of fuel injectors, different cylinder heads, and different CRs. Head air flow and crankshaft deflection was even compared to a captured German Junkers Jumo 211 engine.

The AF-2 (6.5") cylinder on the test engine. The dynamometer drive is on the back side. The crankshaft drove the two cam drives at the front of the engine. A vertical shaft linked the cam drive at the front of the engine to the actual cams above the cylinder. The vertical pipe above the cylinder brought in air. The pipe leading from the cylinder to the ground took away exhaust gases. The two horizontal lines on the left side of the image are the cooling water supply. (NARA)

Engine test conditions varied depending on the nature of the test, but the general specifics were as follows:

Intake air temp:	100° F
Coolant outlet:	250° F ethylene glycol or water or a mix at 15–17 gpm
Oil:	SAE 60
Oil inlet:	170–180° F at 4–13 gpm
Fuel:	Shell 100/130
Induction length:	40.5"
Exhaust length:	41.0"
Valve timing:	Intake opened at 25° BTC and closed at 45° ABC
	Exhaust opened at 60° BBC and closed at 20° ATC
	Intake tappet clearance .018"
	Exhaust tappet clearance .034"
Ignition:	two to six sparkplugs with Scintilla battery timer
Advance:	5–25° BTC
RPM:	1,000; 1,200; 1,600; 1,800; 2,000; 2,200; and 2,400
inHg MAP:	25, 30, 35, 40, and 45

AF-1 was always run with an 8.0" cylinder. The different strokes used were 7.25", 7.625" and 8.0" (634.42, 383.27, and 402.12 in^3 respectively). The different CRs tested were 6.8:1, 7.5:1, 8.0:1, and 8.7:1. This engine was run throughout the program and accumulated 1,734 hours, the most hours of the four test engines.

AF-2 was always run with a 6.5" cylinder. The different strokes used were 6.0", 6.375", and 7.25" (199.10, 211.54, and 240.58 in^3 respectively). The different CRs tested were 6.16:1 and 8.0:1. This engine was disassembled and put in storage at the end of March 1945. AF-2 was the third most run of the four test engines and accumulated 1,024.5 hours.

AF-3 was run with a 7.5" cylinder until November 1944. The different strokes used were 6.75" and 8.0" (298.21 and 353.43 in^3 respectively). The different CRs tested were 6.8:1 and 8.0:1. After it had accumulated 460 hours, it was then converted to an 8.0" cylinder with a 7.25" stroke (364.42 in^3) and run another 260 hours. This engine was also used to test the shorter connecting rod with a shorter 8.0" cylinder. The engine ran for a total of 750 hours. It was placed into storage in June 1945. AF-3 was the least run of the four single-cylinder test engines.

AF-4 was run with a 7.0" cylinder until October 1944. The different strokes used were 6.75" and 7.625" (259.77 and 293.44 in^3 respectively). The different CRs tested were 6.8:1 and 8.0:1. After accumulating 474 hours, AF-4 was converted to an 8.0" cylinder and run another 753 hours. While using the 8.0" cylinder, the engine was only run with a 7.625" stroke (383.27 in^3). AF-4 was the only single-cylinder engine to run the XH-cylinder. The XH-cylinder was fitted in June 1945, and the engine ran 211.5 hours with that style of cylinder. AF-4 was being equipped with a 7.75" stroke crankshaft (389.56 in^3) to simulate the XH-9350 engine, but the program was terminated, and the combination was never run. The AF-4 engine was run throughout the test program and had the second highest run time at 1,227 hours.

"H" Configuration

While the single-cylinder engines were under test, the design of the 5,000 hp engine continued to evolve. Originally, an "X" or "H" engine was considered, both with an 8.0" bore, 7.25" stroke, and a total displacement of 8,750 in^3. In December 1942, The "X" engine configuration featured one camshaft for each side of the engine. It was situated in the Vee made by the upper and lower rows of cylinders but moved away from the crankcase and toward the top of the cylinders. The camshaft was positioned between the valves of the upper and lower cylinders. The camshaft actuated the cylinders' valves through short pushrods and rockers.

Two connecting rod designs are known to have been considered for the "X" engine's single crankshaft. The 1942 design had side-by-side connecting rods of the master and articulated type. This design had two rows of cylinders staggered slightly behind the other two and would increase the engine's length. A later design had four articulated connecting rods attached to a master carrier mounted on the crankpin. A link connected to an eccentric boss on one of the articulated rods would prevent the master carrier from rotating but allow it to move in a circular motion.

However, the single crankshaft design was eliminated because it would create too much stress on the crankpins.

Studebaker's focus shifted to a horizontal "H" engine with an upper and lower crankshaft. Early designs (from December 1942) of this configuration also used a single overhead camshaft for each side of the engine. The camshaft was positioned above and between the two cylinder rows and acted directly on the inner valves (exhaust) of each cylinder row. The outer valves (intake) for each row were actuated by short pushrods and rockers. While this design would save weight, it added complexity. The camshaft arrangement for the complete XH-engine was redesigned so that each cylinder row had a single overhead camshaft actuating the valves from directly above.

Cylinder: Bore, Stroke, and Number

Single-cylinder tests indicated that 32 of the 6.5" or 7.0" bore cylinders would be needed to reach the desired 5,000 hp output. This essentially eliminated those cylinders from consideration and put the main focus on the 8.0" cylinder that had always outperformed the others.

8.0" Piston Comparison Tests						
	Max Power IMEP			Min SFC lb/hp/hr		
RPM	Dome	Cup	Flat	Dome	Cup	Flat
30 inHg						
1200	172	172	179	.313	.315	.313
1600	182	181	184	.303	.300	.308
2000	184	187	187	.300	.301	.304
35 inHg						
1200	202	206	206	.317	.316	.312
1600	217	217	218	.312	.311	.312
2000	219	220	221	.308	.300	.308
40 inHg						
1200	229	227	229	.326	.321	.325
1600	233	239	239	.327	.315	.309
2000	246	247	246	.311	.322	.313

With the cylinder size set on an 8.0" bore, the next task was to determine the desired stroke. AF-1 displaced 402.12 in³ with its 8.0" bore and 8.0" stroke. This combination yielded the best performance of all the cylinder bore and stroke combinations tested. The lowest SFC was recorded as .292 lb/hp/hr achieved at

2,400 rpm with 25 inHg MAP and an 8.0:1 CR. At these settings, AF-1 had an indicated mean effective pressure (IMEP) of 138, which corresponded to 168 hp indicated. Using a 6.8:1 CR because of detonation experienced at 8.0:1 CR, the engine produced a maximum of 277 IMEP at 2,400 rpm and 45 inHg MAP. That IMEP corresponded to 338 hp indicated. At this power, SFC was .413 lb/hp/hr.

A 24-cylinder engine with this bore and stroke combination would displace 9,651 in³. Power at the best SFC would be 4,035 hp (indicated) and 3,630 hp at a 90% mechanical efficiency. At maximum power, the engine would have an output of around 8,100 hp (indicated), and at 90% mechanical efficiency, the engine would produce around 7,290 hp. Of course, the numbers achieved with a single-cylinder engine cannot be directly extrapolated to a 24-cylinder engine, but they do give some insight as to the complete engine's performance.

The single-cylinder tests had shown that a longer stroke increased fuel economy. However, a long stroke would also increase the engine's height. Studebaker was told to keep the engine under 36" for installation buried in an aircraft's wing, but this was impossible with the 8.0" stroke. A compromise was reached in which the engine grew to 40" to enable a 7.75" stroke. The 7.75" stroke was not one of the crankshaft options available, and new parts had to be made. The AF-4 single-cylinder engine was later configured with an 8.0" cylinder and a 7.625" stroke to simulate the XH engine. The 7.625" stroke was used because it was the closest stroke available to the 7.75" of the XH engine. Again, a longer stroke would have been preferred, but the height restriction would not allow it.

Cylinder Test Comparison*				
Bore	6.5	7.0	7.5	8.0
Best Stroke	7.25	7.625	8.0	8.0
Displacement	240.58	293.44	353.43	402.12
IMEP at Max Pwr	228	255	243	277
Max IHP	175	227	260	338
Best ISFC	.310	.300	.310	.292
Cyl # Cmplt Eng	32	32	24	24
Cmplt Eng Disp	7,698	9,390	8,482	9,651
Cmplt Eng IHP	5,595	7,255	6,245	8,100
HP 90% Mech Eff	5,035	6,530	5,620	7,290
*Detonation issues limited some test results				

In September 1944, Studebaker's MX-232 project officially became an H engine with an 8.0" bore and 7.75" stroke, displacing 9,350 in³—the XH-9350 was born. All efforts were now focused on this combination. AF-3 and AF-4 were converted to run 8.0" cylinders. The twin-cylinder engines, AF-5 and AF-6, would be built up with an 8.0" bore and 7.75" stroke. In addition, a new "XH-cylinder" design would be used on the twin-cylinder engines.

XH-Cylinder Design

The cylinder intended for use on the XH-9350 differed from the previous experimental cylinders in the weight and arrangement of its parts, details of construction, and valve action. These changes permitted a more compact and lighter full-scale engine. The complete XH-cylinder was around 12.5 lb lighter than the original cylinder, resulting in a 300 lb weight savings for the complete engine. In addition, the reciprocating weight for each cylinder was reduced by almost 7.0 lb. The new cylinder did away with the four long hold-down bolts that passed through the head, and reverted to a conventional hold-down flange. This design would alleviate stress points in the cylinder barrel and cylinder head, thereby eliminating the frequent water jacket cracks of the original cylinder design. The XH-cylinder design was only made with an 8.0" bore and had a flatter combustion chamber than earlier cylinders. The intake and exhaust ports were situated tangential to the cylinder bore instead of in the plane perpendicular to the crankshaft. The exhaust port was 68% of the intake area, instead of 85% as was the case with the earlier 8.0" cylinder.

Like the original cylinder, the XH-type cylinder was made of a hardened (Rockwell C 34–38) forged alloy steel barrel. But, the cast cylinder head was made of heat-treated "Y" alloy (Alcoa 142) and was screwed and shrunk onto the cylinder. The cylinder coolant jacket was made from thin sheet steel that was silver soldered to shrink bands at each end. The shrink bands were made from thin, high-strength steel. The head end band was shrunk on a land of aluminum that was part of the cylinder head jacket. The crankshaft end band was adjacent to the cylinder hold-down flange. The cylinder was held to the crankcase (or adapter, for the single- or twin-cylinder test engines) by 24 short hold-down studs and nuts.

The XH-cylinder was designed for coolant pressure up to 50 psi or more. The coolant passed around the barrel, around the portion of the head shrunk over the barrel, through cored passages over the top of the head, around the exhaust port, and to an outlet at the inner end of the exhaust port. The wetted surfaces included the dome, exhaust port, valve seat insert portion of the inlet port, surfaces around all spark plug bosses, and completely around the exhaust valve guide boss.

When the exhaust port was directed downward (as in the upper banks of the 24-cylinder engine), a coolant outlet was provided at the then upper part of the sheet metal cylinder jacket near the cylinder head. In the event that the cylinder was used in a vertical position (as in the single-cylinder test engine), the top of the jacket adjacent to the port was vented separately to the coolant expansion tank.

In the head dome of the cylinder, adjacent to the outer shrink band of the water jacket, were four 18 mm holes for spark plugs and/or a fuel injector nozzle. The holes were inclined radially at 30° from vertical. The piston for the XH-cylinder had a flat crown with a broad rib between piston bosses. It had the same ring arrangement as the second piston design. As a result of a lighter piston and piston pin, the complete piston weighed 16.83 lb, which was 7.71 lb less than the piston assembly used for the earlier 8.0" cylinder.

As with the earlier cylinders, each piston was cooled by four oil jets that flowed approximately 2.5 gpm when combined. For the complete XH-9350 engine, the cooling oil flow to the underside of the piston would be automatic. Above 30 inHg MAP, oil would flow to the cooling jets, but there would be no oil flow under 30 inHg MAP.

The combustion chamber of the head was hemispherical with a radius of 9.0" inches blended to the cylinder bore with a radius inside diameter of 1.25". There were two ports using valves with a 3 15/16" seat inside diameter for the intake and 3.25" for the exhaust. The plane through the valve stem made an angle of 40° to the crankshaft axis. The valve guides were inclined to the cylinder centerline at 13° for the intake and 16° for the exhaust. The intake port entrance and exhaust port outlet were away from the cylinder centerline and the crankcase.

The complete XH-cylinder weighed 70.5 lb and was 21.75" tall.

Valve Actuation

The XH-cylinder used one camshaft to actuate both the intake and exhaust valves. Unlike the original cylinder design, in which the camshaft could act directly on the valve, each valve in the XH-cylinder was operated by its own rocker arm. The rocker arm had a roller to follow the cam lobe and an adjusting screw, both on the same side of the rocker pivot. The adjustment screw allowed for the proper clearance and had a ball-ended tappet. The ball-ended tappet had a large diameter foot that was spherically concave to match the slightly smaller diameter spherical end of the valve stem. The axis of the tappet was inclined between the plane of the rocker and the axis of the valve. This mechanism arrangement was required since the axis of the valve was inclined to the plane of the rocker. The fixed rocker shaft was between the camshaft and the cylinder head on the cylinder centerline. Oil was fed through this rocker shaft, into the rocker arm, through the silver-plated cam roller shaft, to the bearing of the rocker roller, and through the tappet to its two spherical seats. The XH-cylinder's intake cam lobe had a .900" lift and 250° open duration. The exhaust cam lobe had a .890" lift and a 260° open duration.

Connecting Rod

The engine was to use a conventional fork-and-blade connecting rod. The connecting rod was 14.75" long (center-to-center) and had a 4.5" diameter big end and a 2.5" diameter piston pin. Four bolts secured the big end of the fork rod, and two bolts secured the blade rod.

XH-9350-1 Order Placed

Encouraged by the results, the AAF sat down with Studebaker in December 1944 to discuss building a complete XH-9350 engine. Gen. Carroll was a major proponent of the engine and saw it as a power plant for both military and commercial use. Tilley and Cole felt that the XH-9350 engine and any aircraft in which it was installed would be too expensive for commercial use and that the engine would only be used by the military. Furthermore, Cole made it clear that Studebaker was primarily interested in manufacturing cars and trucks, and while it was not interested in making the engine on a production basis, Studebaker was happy to move forward with the construction of test engines as part of the company's current work.

Originally, back in 1942, six test engines had been proposed. The AAF inquired about purchasing three XH-9350-1 engines. Studebaker agreed, but it was not until 2 July 1945 that the order for the three engines was approved with a forecasted completion date of 1 March 1947.

XH-Cylinder Tests

The XH-cylinder was put into service in June 1945 by adapting the AF-4 single-cylinder engine. Also, the twin-cylinder engines had been built up and run. The two twin-cylinder engines were essentially the same, with the same welded sheet steel construction as the single-cylinder engines. They were made to run an 8.0" XH-cylinder with a 7.75" stroke crankshaft and with 8.0:1 CR. The twin-cylinder engines each displaced 779.12 in³.

AF-5 was first run in June 1945, and AF-6 followed in July 1945. Oil flow issues between the main bearings and crankshaft resulted in an overheated crankshaft and damage to AF-5's crankcase after 8.25 hours of operation. AF-5 was being repaired when the XH-9350 program came to an end. AF-6's CR was reduced from 8.0:1 to 7.5:1 because of detonation. The engine continued to run until the project was cancelled. It accumulated 104 hours.

Although the twin-cylinder engines never completed testing, preliminary results indicated a maximum IMEP of 234 at 2,200 rpm and 38 inHg MAP, with a SFC of .450 lb/hp/hr. This represented 506 hp indicated for the twin-cylinder engine or 6,077 hp indicated for the 24-cylinder engine. With a 90% mechanical efficiency, the output would be 5,469 hp for the XH-9350. The best SFC recorded was .300 lb/hp/hr at 1,350 rpm and 30 inHg with an IMEP of 140. This corresponded to 186 hp indicated or 2,230 hp for the complete engine. With a 90% mechanical efficiency, the output would be 2,000 hp.

When compared to the original cylinder, the XH-cylinder exhibited a maximum power IMEP reduction of less than 2% at 2,200 rpm. For maximum economy, the XH-cylinder showed less than 3% higher SFC at 1,200 rpm and less than 2% higher SFC at 2,200 rpm. Some issues were experienced with spark plug fouling, and a revised XH-cylinder head was being designed that would relocate the spark plugs to a more vertical position to improve the cylinder's performance. In addition, the new XH-cylinder would include a thicker head to prevent cracks, and a simplified intake port. The new cylinder head was expected by 1 December 1945.

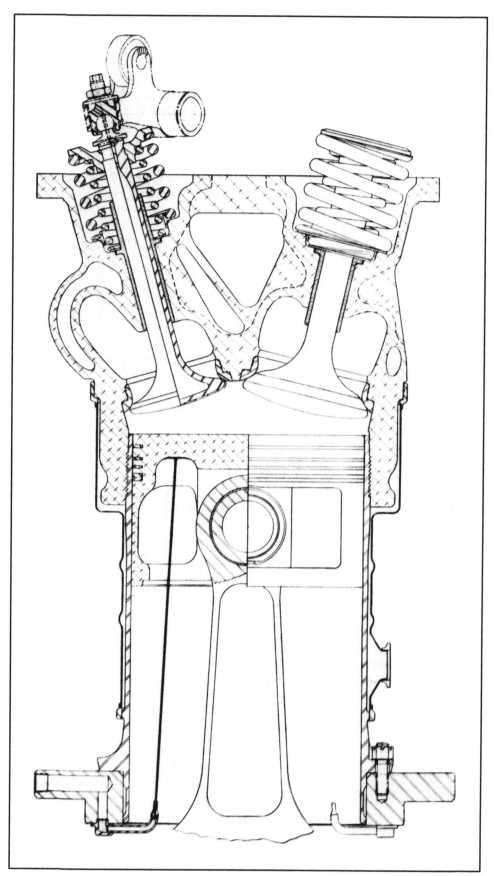

The final cylinder design was known as the XH-cylinder. It was an 8.0" cylinder that had been simplified and refined from lessons learned during all of the previous testing. The drawing is from 25 September 1945. (NARA)

The XH-cylinder had only four spark plug bosses, but the intent was to use two plugs and a fuel injector. The cylinder was flange-mounted to the crankcase and did not use any through bolts. Compared to the previous 8.0"-cylinder designs, the XH-cylinder was approximately 5" shorter and 12.5 lb lighter. With 24 cylinders, the weight savings was 300 lb per engine. The above image was taken on 22 August 1945. (NARA)

Twin-cylinder test conditions mirrored those of the single-cylinder engines except for the following specifications:

Coolant outlet: 250° F ethylene glycol at 14–16 gpm per cylinder
Oil inlet: 180–190° F
Oil pressure: 95–105 psi main bearings and 45–55 psi cams
Valve timing: Intake opened at 20° BTC
                      Exhaust opened at 55° BBC
                      Intake and exhaust tappet clearance .035"

Twin-cylinder AF-6 with two XH-cylinders on the test stand on 12 October 1945. See the photograph on page 136 for the engine's internal components. (BL)

Twin-Cylinder Engine Tests			
Bore	Stroke	Disp.	Comp. Ratio
8.0	7.75	779.12	7.1/8.0

A Change in Course

In August 1945, most military programs and orders were cancelled with the end of the war. Programs that were not cancelled suffered severe budgetary cutbacks. Accordingly, two of the XH-9350-1 engines were cancelled, but the AAF wanted Studebaker to proceed with one test engine. Both Cole and Paul M. Clark, General Counsel for Studebaker, made it clear that Studebaker was not interested in building any additional XH-9350 engines and planned to focus the company's resources on automotive work. However, if the AAF requested more engines, Studebaker would do what it could to accommodate the AAF's wishes.

In a letter dated 21 August 1945, Cole made Studebaker's position clear:

We are not interested in the commercial possibilities of such an engine [H-9350] and from the standpoint of our own interests the time and energy of our organization devoted to such work could be much more profitably employed in our own work. However, if this development work is necessary, we feel that we should, purely as a matter of accommodation to the Government, try to assist the Government in working out an arrangement for the performance thereof. With this in mind, we would be willing to undertake the construction of additional engines.

The XH-9350 as Designed

The XH-9350-1 was designed to operate up to an altitude of 40,000' with a low SFC over a wide power range, enabling long-range operations of over 30 hours non-stop. The engine would use two crankshafts, each with six 4.5" crankpins and supported by seven 5.0" main bearings. Viewed from the non-propeller end, The XH-9350's upper crankshaft rotated counter-clockwise while the lower crankshaft rotated clockwise. Because the crankshafts

rotated in opposite directions, they could be directly geared together via a combining gear set at the front of the engine. This gear set also drove the engine's two magnetos, four camshafts, and front oil scavenge pump.

As seen in a blueprint and clay models from October 1945, the camshafts were driven from a smaller gear that was incorporated into each crankshaft's large combining gear. This smaller gear drove an idler gear on each side of the engine. The idler gear drove a shaft that had beveled gears on both sides. The other side of the shaft drove the camshaft above each cylinder row at half crankshaft speed.

In addition to the camshafts, the lower combining gear also drove the magnetos. This was achieved through another gear in line with the combining gear but larger and in front of the camshaft drive gear. This larger gear drove a compound idler gear on each side of the crankshaft. At the center of this compound idler gear was a smaller gear that drove the magneto drive gear at half crankshaft speed. The magneto was mounted on the front combining gear and accessory housing so that its shaft would engage the center of the magneto drive gear.

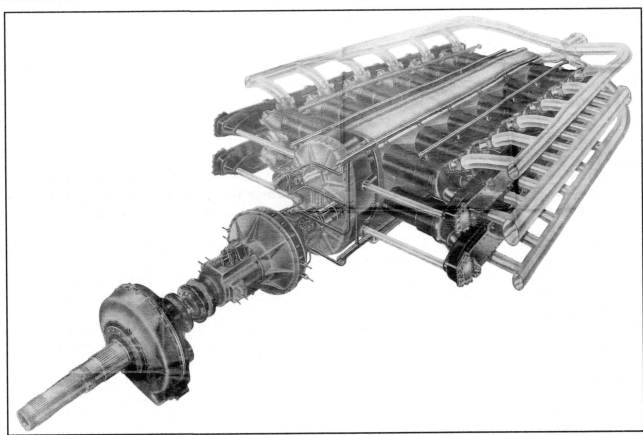

Drawing from 1944 depicting the complete XH-9350 engine with a remote, two-speed gear reduction unit and a remote, contra-rotating propeller gear reduction. (NARA)

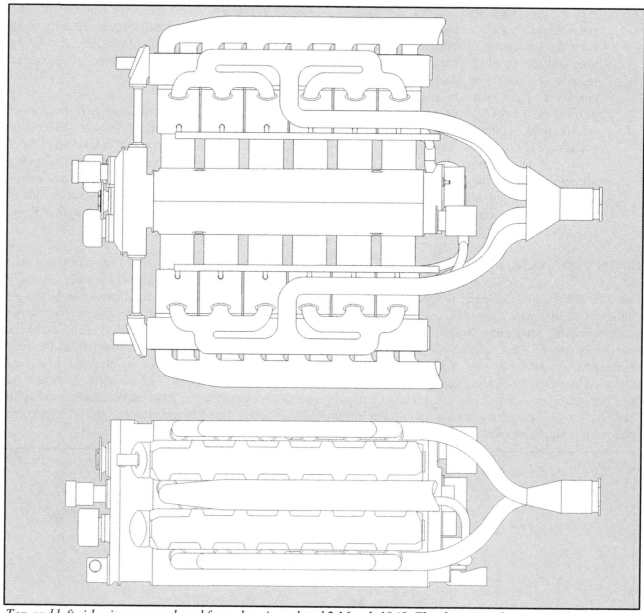

Top and left side views reproduced from drawings dated 2 March 1945. The drawings do not include the remote gear units. The exhaust manifolds on the sides of the engine led back to turbosuperchargers. The pressurized air from the turbosuperchargers would have been fed into the intake manifold at the rear of the engine. (A)

The front oil pumps were driven at the bottom of the lower combining gear. The engine's starter was also incorporated into the front combining gear and accessory housing. The starter was positioned so that it engaged the upper crankshaft's combining gear. The engine's output shaft was in line with and coupled to the upper crankshaft.

The rear engine accessory drive accommodated the engine's main and rear engine scavenge oil pumps. With the engine running at 2,200 rpm, oil flowed at a rate exceeding 85 gpm. Geared to the rear engine accessory drive were also the water pump and the fuel

injection pump. The rear housing also accommodated the Cuno oil filter and the speed density control unit for fuel injection. All other accessories were mounted on the rear of the contra-rotating gear reduction unit.

Originally the XH-9350's crankcase would have had evenly spaced cylinders. By October 1945, this design had changed. The cylinders were spaced 11" apart at their center, except for the middle cylinders, which were spaced 11.75" apart. The extra distance allowed a wider center main bearing for the crankshafts, which were 16.75" apart vertically. The crankcase was made of two pieces: a left and a right side. The sides were

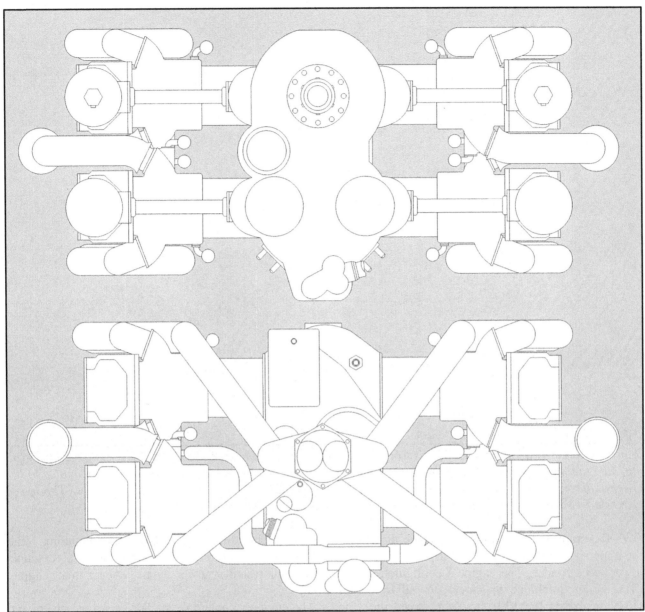

Front (at top) and rear (at bottom) reproduction drawings of the XH-9350 from 2 March 1945. Engine output was taken from a shaft in line with the top crankshaft. (A)

identical and attached together by 19 bolts at both the top and bottom of the crankcase. The seven main bearing supports for each crankshaft were machined into the crankcase halves. Twenty-eight through bolts supported the crankshaft main journals as well as the center of the crankcase. And finally, the front and rear accessory cases were bolted to the assembled crankcase. As designed, the crankcase was 69 9/64" long, 17 13/32" wide, and 39 61/64" tall.

For the intake, pressurized air from the turbosuperchargers passed through intercoolers and entered an air valve. The air valve branched into four 4.5" diameter induction pipes, each leading to a bank

of cylinders. The induction pipe then branched into two intake manifolds. Each manifold was 4.0" in diameter and supplied air to three cylinders.

Once the fresh air charge was in the cylinder, fuel was injected and the mixture ignited by two Champion RP-43-S (or equivalent) spark plugs. The spark plugs were fired by two high-frequency, low-tension magnetos positioned at the front of the engine. The XH-9350's preliminary firing order was as follows: Bottom 1 Left, Top 6 Right, B4R, T2L, B5L, T3R, B1R, T6L, B3L, T5R, B5R, T3L, B6L, T1R, B3R, T5L, B2L, T4R, B6R, T1L, B4L, T2R, B2R, and T4L. The No. 1 cylinders were at the rear of the engine.

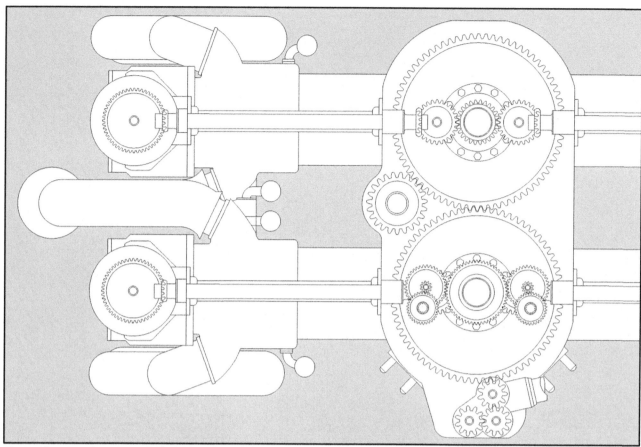

Reproduction drawing of the XH-9350's front gear system from 11 October 1945. The starter engaged the gear mounted to the upper crankshaft. With the crankshafts rotating in opposite directions, the gears mounted to the crankshafts meshed at the front of the engine. Each crankshaft also drove the camshaft drives. The lower crankshaft drove magnetos and an oil pump mounted to the front of the engine. (A)

With the crankshafts rotating in opposite directions, the upper right cylinder fired 30° degrees behind the lower left cylinder. The engine's configuration and firing order combined to cancel out all orders of vibration except the 12th. It was believed the 12th order of vibration would not be present in the engine's operating rpm range.

Exhaust for each cylinder was expelled through the 3.75" port and into a 4.5" diameter pipe. On each side of the engine, these pipes merged into a 6.5" diameter exhaust manifold that was positioned above and between the cylinders. The two exhaust manifolds traveled behind the engine where they met two General Electric CH-5 turbosuperchargers. Each CH-5 turbosupercharger had an 11" impeller and, spinning at 20,000 rpm, could supply 265 lb of air per minute (about 14,500 cfm) at 35,000' altitude. The CH-5 could be over-sped to 22,000 rpm for 15 minutes. Each CH-5 turbosupercharger weighed 260 lb. Notes mentioned using the turbosuperchargers for compound operation, but no descriptive information

has been found. In Turbo-compounding, the turbocharger turbine is geared to the engine's crankshaft so that power can be fed back to the engine.

The engine's coolant was a 70% ethylene glycol and 30% water mixture circulated by a centrifugal pump driven from the rear accessory gear case. The coolant pump had a flow capacity of over 700 gpm. Via a 4.5" diameter inlet, this pump brought in coolant from the radiator and distributed it to the engine. The pump had two outlets, one for each side of the engine. Each outlet pipe split into two 2.0" diameter manifolds to supply the upper and lower cylinder bank. Coolant entered at the bottom of each cylinder barrel and then flowed through the cylinder barrel water jacket and up into the head. The coolant exited each cylinder and flowed into a 2.0" diameter manifold to be taken to the radiator.

The complete XH-9350-1 engine was to have a length of 109", a width of 105" with manifolds (80" without), and a height of 40". The complete engine was to weigh

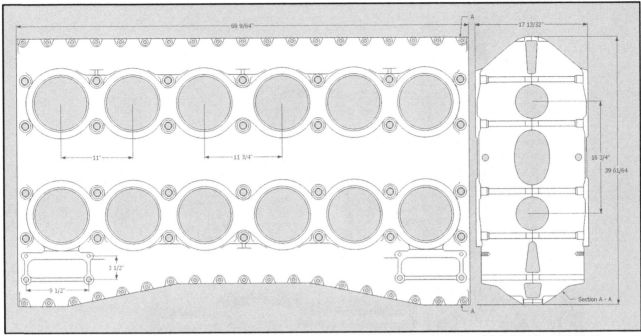

The XH-9350's crankcase design with dimensions reproduced from a drawing dated 11 October 1945. Fourteen through bolts secured each crankshaft in seven main journals. (A)

over 5,580 lb, not including the contra-rotating gear reduction, two-speed gear unit, propeller extension shafts, and turbosuperchargers. Total engine weight would be 6,870 lb plus the extension shafts, the length and weight of which depended on the engine's specific installation.

The XH-9350-1 had a takeoff and military power rating of 5,000 hp at 2,200 rpm from sea level to a 25,000' critical altitude. Cruse power, depending on rpm, was 2,000–3,000 hp at 30,000'. The last SFC estimates found for a complete engine were given in August 1945 and were based on single-engine comparison tests with the XH-cylinder (on AF-4). It was believed a complete XH-9350 would have a SFC of less than .355 lb/hp/hr. However, with turbo-compounding, the XH-9350's SFC would be brought down to .320 lb/hp/hr. In addition, further tests and cylinder design improvements to increase efficiency had yet to be carried out.

Remote Gear Reduction Units

The XH-9350 employed two remote gear reduction units. The first was a two-speed gear reduction unit that connected, via shafts, between the engine and the final contra-rotating gear reduction unit. The two-speed gear reduction unit was used to keep the propeller rpm within the range of maximum efficiency for its size. With the XH-9350 running at cruise speed (low rpm), the two-speed unit allowed a direct drive

(1:1) between the engine and contra-rotating gear reduction unit. With the engine running at takeoff, military, or climb power (high rpm), the two-speed unit provided a 1.428:1 (.700) reduction. The reduction was achieved through the use of six planetary pinions. The speed change was accomplished through the use of a wrapping spring clutch made by L.G.S. Spring Clutches, Incorporated. The two-speed unit was approximately 37" long, 22.6" in diameter, and weighed 560 lb. At least one unit was built.

The engine was coupled to the input shaft of the two-speed gear unit via a drive shaft. The unit's input shaft was coupled to a housing with a ring gear mounted inside. Fitted inside the ring gear was a carrier housing six planetary pinions. Attached to and passing through the center of the planetary carrier was an output shaft that extended to the end of the two-speed gear unit. Here, the output shaft was coupled to another drive shaft that led to the contra-rotating gear reduction unit. Inside the two-speed gear unit and between the output shaft and the planetary carrier was a sun gear shaft.

For direct drive (1:1) or low engine speed operation, the wrapping spring clutch held the sun gear shaft to the output shaft. This essentially locked these two shafts, the planetary carrier, and the ring gear together so that they all turned at the same speed as the input shaft (engine rpm).

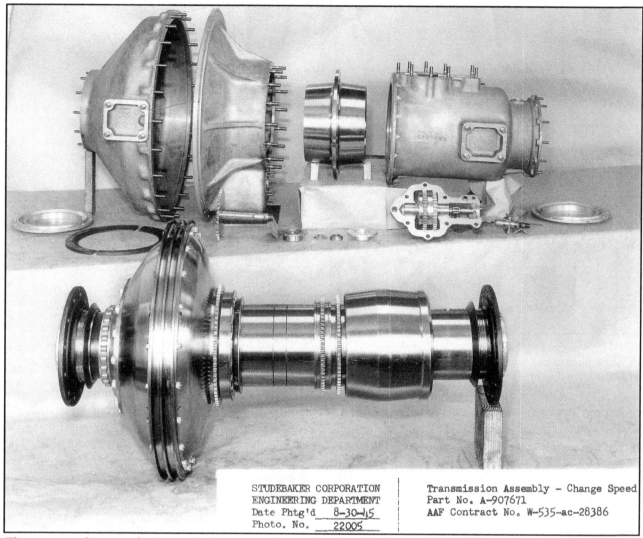

STUDEBAKER CORPORATION
ENGINEERING DEPARTMENT
Date Phtg'd _8-30-45_
Photo. No. _22005_

Transmission Assembly — Change Speed
Part No. A-907671
AAF Contract No. W-535-ac-28386

The two-speed gear reduction unit shown nearly completed on 30 August 1945. The housing is seen at top, with the internal rotating assembly below. (BL)

For reduction drive (1.428:1) or high engine speed operation, the wrapping spring clutch held the sun gear shaft to a stationary member within the two-speed gear unit. The stationary sun gear shaft forced the planetary carrier and attached output shaft to rotate at a reduced rpm compared to the ring gear and input shaft. Thus, the input shaft rotated 1.428 times for every single rotation of the two-speed gear unit's output shaft.

To change speeds, the wrapping spring clutches altered the rpm of the sun gear shaft so that it was either rotating at the same speed as the output shaft (1:1) or was held stationary (zero rpm) and allowed gear reduction (1.428:1) to occur. The wrapping spring clutch allowed the sun gear shaft to make a slow and smooth rpm transition that did not cause any stress or shock on the engine, drive shafts, contra-rotating gear reduction unit, or propellers.

The second remote gear unit was the contra-rotating gear reduction that would be connected to the two-speed gear unit via a drive shaft. A 10-pinion spur gear carrier would reduce the single rotation input by 2.4:1 (.417) and enable dual-rotation output shafts. The input shaft had a gear with 90 teeth that meshed with 18-tooth pinions in the carrier. The pinions rode on a fixed ring gear with 126 teeth that was attached to the inside of the dual-rotation unit's housing. The pinion carrier was attached to the inner propeller shaft.

Each of the 10 pinions in the carrier shared a shaft with a larger gear that had 36 teeth. The outer side of these larger gears rode in a 126-tooth ring gear that was attached to the rear of the outer propeller shaft. Since the larger 36-tooth gear had twice as many teeth as the 18-tooth pinion, it allowed the outer shaft to rotate at the same speed but in the opposite direction as the inner shaft. The ratio of 126 gear teeth for each

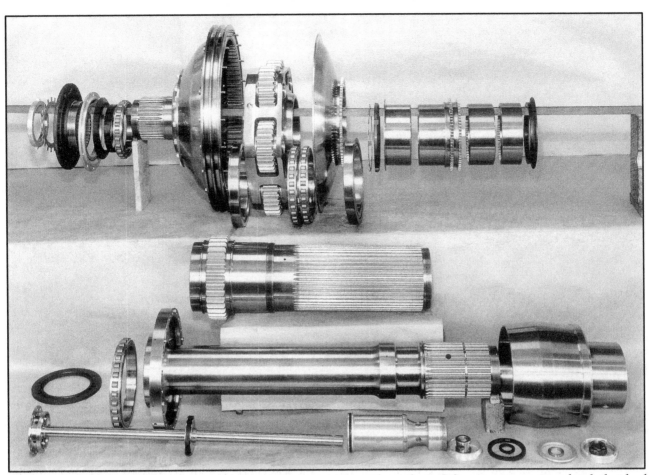

The internals of the two-speed gear unit's rotating assembly, without the L.G.S. wrapping spring clutch that had not arrived by the end of August 1945. The completed unit was delivered to Wright Field in July 1946. (BL)

propeller shaft and 90 gear teeth on the input shaft created the 1.4:1 (.714) reduction.

The output was contra-rotating 60L-80 propeller shafts, in which the SAE #60 spline shaft rotated inside the SAE #80 spline outer shaft. The inner shaft rotated counter-clockwise, and the outer shaft rotated clockwise (when viewed from the rear). The contra-rotating gear reduction unit was approximately 65" long, 27" wide, and 35" tall. It weighed 730 lb. Parts for the contra-rotating gear reduction were made, but it is doubtful that one was ever fully assembled.

Accessories not essential to engine operation were mounted on the back side of the contra-rotating gear reduction unit. These accessories included the propeller governor, a power take-off, generators, and vacuum and/or hydraulic pumps. Combined, the two remote gearboxes provided a 2.4:1 (.417) reduction for low engine speed operation and a 3.427:1 (.292) reduction for high engine speed operation. This configuration allowed for a 500 rpm propeller speed at 1,200 rpm engine speed (cruise power) and a 640

rpm propeller speed at 2,200 rpm engine speed (takeoff/military/climb power). The propeller size depended on application, but for the B-36, a 20' 8" eight-blade contra-rotating propeller was recommended.

Both the two-speed reduction unit and the contra-rotating gear reduction had their own oil pump and supply. At 2,200 rpm, oil flowed through the two-speed reduction unit at over 16 gpm and through the contra-rotating gear reduction at over 53 gpm.

The shafts connecting the remote gear reduction units had a 6.0" outer diameter and a 5 11/16" inner diameter, making the shaft wall 5/32" thick. The shaft was estimated to weigh 10 lb per foot. The length of the shafts depended entirely on how the engine was installed in a particular aircraft.

MX-232/XH-9350 Cancellation

The MX-232 project and the order for one XH-9350-1 engine were cancelled in October 1945. The

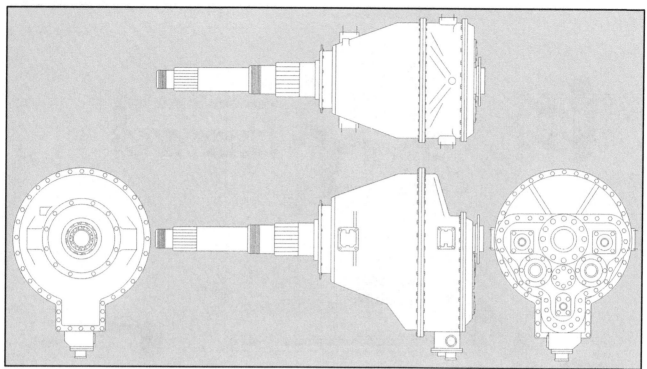

The remote contra-rotating propeller gear reduction unit incorporating SAE #60L-80 spline shafts that were approximately 33.25" long. A number of accessories were driven from the back of the unit. The original drawing was dated 27 April 1943. (A)

cancellation was initiated to curtail 1946 expenditures and saved $2,550,872 in the post-war economy. At the time of cancellation, the MX-232/XH-9350 project had cost $1,454,661.43.

Not included in the savings from cancelling the XH-9350 was the estimated $2 million needed to construct proper facilities to test a complete engine. Studebaker, backed by the AAF, was moving ahead in planning these facilities and acquiring equipment. The XH-9350 program was to be moved from the Motor Machining and Assembly Plant on Sample Street to the Aviation Division Aircraft Engine Plant on Chippewa Avenue, the site of the Wright R-1820 production.

Over the course of the MX-232 program, the single-cylinder test engines had run 4,735.5 hours, of which 2,770 hours were with an 8.0" bore cylinder. The twin-cylinder engines ran for 112.25 hours. The XH-cylinder had accumulated 211.5 hours in single-cylinder testing and 112.25 hours on the twin-cylinder engines, for a total of 323.75 hours. The grand total was 4,847.75 hours run under power for all test engines. In addition, a valve test rig had run for 292

hours, and extensive coolant pump tests had been run. Work was progressing on various test fixtures for the two-speed gear unit and contra-rotating gear reduction unit. Clay model mockups had been constructed on much of the complete XH-9350 engine. It is believed that all parts of the MX-232/XH-9350 program were eventually scrapped.

On 6 December 1945, thousands of various tracings, drawing, and sketches were sent to the Power Plant Laboratory at Wright Field. These covered the current engine's design, obsolete designs, alternate designs that were considered, and the engine test equipment designs. Wright Aeronautical had expressed an interest in the XH-9350 project. Wright obtained a number of MX-232/XH-9350 files that it returned to Wright Field on 16 April 1946 with apparently no further action being taken.

Despite the project's cancellation, work on the two-speed reduction gear unit continued. The unit was completed in June 1946 and delivered to Wright Field on 15 July 1946. Unfortunately, no records have been found regarding the testing or ultimate disposition of this unit.

Studebaker MX-232 Test Engines Hours Run						
	AF-1	AF-2	AF-3	AF-4	AF-5	AF-6
First Run	Feb-43	Mar-43	Jul/Aug-43	Oct/Nov-43	Jun-45	Jul-45
Up to Dec-43	226.00	225.00	48.00	108.00		
Jan-44						
Feb-44	14.00	75.00	24.25	76.00		
Mar-44						
Apr-44	113.00	165.00	22.75	26.00		
May-44						
Jun-44	181.50	185.00	135.00	69.00		
Jul-44	79.50	43.25	21.00	81.00		
Aug-44	75.00	43.25	27.00	30.00		
Sep-44	67.25	35.50	89.25	84.00		
Oct-44	73.75	0.00	67.75	*66.50		
Nov-44	96.50	0.00	**29.50	54.75		
Dec-44	116.00	72.50	34.50	95.75		
Jan-45	0.50	81.45	33.75	91.75		
Feb-45	92.25	94.50	10.25	61.25		
Mar-45	96.75	4.25	42.50	55.25		
Apr-45	64.75	Storage	47.25	12.75		
May-45	77.25		104.00	74.25		
Jun-45	90.25		13.25	35.75	3.25	
Jul-45	83.75		Stopped	73.00	5.00	11.25
Aug-45	87.25			79.00	0.00	27.75
Sep-45	77.75			53.00	0.00	49.00
Oct-45	21.00			0.00	0.00	16.00
Total	**1,734.00**	**1,024.50**	**750.00**	**1,227.00**	**8.25**	**104.00**

Total hours single-cylinder test engines:	4,735.50
Total hours 8.0" single-cylinder test engines:***	2,777.00
Total hours twin-cylinder test engines:	112.25
Total hours all test engines:	**4,847.75**

All figures are approximate. Blank rows indicate no data for that month. The month following the blank gives the accumulated hours from data point to data point.

*AF-4 was converted to an 8.0" cylinder in October 1944. The engine ran for 474 hours with the 7.0" cylinder.

**AF-3 was converted to an 8.0" cylinder in November 1944 and accumulated 4.5 hours with an 8.0" cylinder that month. The engine ran 460 hours with the 7.5" cylinder.

***This figure includes the 290.0 and 753.0 hours respectively run by AF-3 and AF-4 when fitted with an 8.0" cylinder.

Studebaker H-9350-1 Engine Estimated Specifications as of February 1945

Type: 24-cylinder, liquid-cooled (70% ethylene glycol and 30% water), horizontal (flat) H configuration aircraft engine with two crankshafts, fuel injection, and turbosupercharging

Bore:	8.0"
Stroke:	7.75"
Displacement:	9,349.4 in^3
Compression Ratio:	8.0:1
Takeoff and Military Power:	5,000 hp at 2,200 rpm, 0–25,000', 37 inHg, and .50 SFC
Normal Power:	4,000 hp at 2,000 rpm, 0–30,000', 33 inHg, and .48 SFC
90% Normal Power:	3,600 hp at 1,930 rpm, 30,000', 33 inHg, and .47 SFC
80% Normal Power:	3,200 hp at 1,860 rpm, 30,000', 33 inHg, and .47 SFC
70% Normal Power:	2,800 hp at 1,775 rpm, 30,000', 32 inHg, and .47 SFC
Cruise power:	3,000 hp at 1,600 rpm, 30,000', 38 inHg, and .37 SFC
	2,000 hp at 1,350 rpm, 30,000', 30 inHg, and .37 SFC
	1,500 hp at 1,100 rpm, 30,000', 27 inHg, and .38 SFC
	1,000 hp at 900 rpm, 30,000', 24 inHg, and .38 SFC
Maximum Altitude:	40,000'
Engine Length:	109"
Engine Width:	105"
Engine Height:	40"
Engine Weight:	5,580 lb
Fuel:	100/130 PN
Firing Order:	

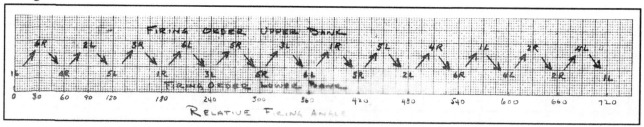

Two-Speed Gear Unit Length and Weight:	37" and 560 lb
Two-Speed Unit Output Speeds:	1:1 (no reduction) and 1.428:1 (.700 reduction)
Gear Reduction Length and Weight:	65" and 730 lb
Gear Reduction Ratio:	2.4:1 (.417 reduction)
High Engine Speed Final Propeller Reduction:	3.427:1 (.292 reduction)
Low Engine Speed Final Propeller Reduction:	2.4:1 (.417 reduction)
Propeller Extension Shaft Length and Weight:	Approximately 9.5' and 95 lb for tractor installations
Complete Engine Length:	Approximately 325" (27.1')
Complete Engine Weight:	Approximately 6,965 lb (not including turbosuperchargers, intercoolers, associated ducting, radiators, or coolant)

Late testing of XH-cylinders indicated the SFC at cruise power for the complete H-9350 engine would be lowered to .355 lb/hp/hr. With this SFC, the engine would burn 118 gph of fuel producing 2,000 hp in cruise conditions. Fuel flow for the H-9350 at takeoff producing 5,000 hp and with a SFC of .50 lb/hp/hr SFC would be 416 gph.

5. XH-9350 in Development

This chapter does not give a running narrative of the MX-232/XH-9350 program. Rather, it gives a month-by-month synopsis based on existing reports, photographs, and drawings. The information may be contradictory at times, but it is reported as it has been found. Any omission or lack of information is due to the fact that some reports have not been found, leaving gaps in certain time periods or subject matters.

March 1942

On 3 March, Roy E. Cole, Vice President of the Studebaker Corporation, wrote Col. Edwin R. Page, Chief of the Army Air Force's (AAF) Power Plant Section at Wright Field, a proposal outlining the development of the desired long-range aircraft engine. The engine would use fuel injection, liquid-cooling, two-speed contra-rotating propellers, and turbo-superchargers (exhaust-driven superchargers). The proposal was divided into nine items:

1) Design, construct, and conduct performance tests on at least four cylinders differing in bore, sized from 6.0" to 8.0". In addition, several stroke lengths would be tested to determine the best combination for low fuel consumption. A summary report of these tests would be completed 10 months after the contract date. Cost: $531,800.

2) Design and construct two complete two-cylinder test engines using the data from item 1. Endurance tests on the engines would be run to verify the durability of the cylinders, pistons, and connecting rods. A summary report of these tests would be completed five months after item 1 (at least 15 months after the contract date). Cost: $245,000.

3) Perform design studies for the complete engine layout. The studies would be made at the same time as items 1 and 2 and were to be completed 10 months from the date of the contract. Cost: $50,000.

4) Design and develop various engine components, including the reduction gears, fuel injectors, ignition system, coolant pump, turbosupercharger, accessory section, complete engine valve train, oil pumps, and other items. No time frame for completion was given, but it was to be completed before item 5. Cost: $700,000.

5) Design and complete detail drawings, including installation and assemblies, of a complete engine. Construct six complete engines for testing as outlined in items 6–9. The first engine would be completed just eight months after item 1 (18 months after the contract date), and the remaining engines would be completed as required. Cost: $1,837,000.

6) Perform developmental and calibration runs of one complete engine. This would be completed 6–12 months after item 5 (24–30 months after the contract date). Cost: $170,000.

7) Perform a 50-hour development test of one complete engine. This would be completed 6–12 months after item 6 (earliest possible completion would be 30 months after the contract date, and the latest would be 42 months). Cost: $270,000.

8) Perform a 50-hour military test of one complete engine. This would be completed 6–12 months after item 7 (earliest possible completion would be 36 months after the contract date, and the latest would be 54 months). Cost: $125,000.

9) Deliver three complete engines to the government: one for a type test and the other two for flight tests.

Rather optimistically, Studebaker forecasted the first engine would be assembled and ready for testing just 18 months after the contract date. If Studebaker's forecasted timeline were followed, the engine would take to the air no earlier than 36 months after the contract date. Cole stated the following in his proposal:

It must be understood that this project is one which has never been attempted and is reaching out into a field in which there has been very little research. Therefore, while every effort will be made to attain the objectives as proposed, there is no guarantee that these specifications can be met.

Studebaker gave the total cost for proposal items 1–8 as $3,928,800 (about $61,914,450 in 2018 USD).

On 18 March, Authority for Purchase No. 224892 was submitted to cover the first phases of development for the engine, now set at 5,000 hp. In addition, a request was made to classify the project as "Confidential." The engine project was given "Confidential" status on 23 March, and "Materiel, Experimental" Project Number MX-232 was assigned. An updated Authority for Purchase, utilizing the same number as before, was issued on 10 April. It described the engine project in detail and stated clearly that no comparable engine had ever been developed in the United States, and no developmental shortcuts to expedite the project or lessen its cost could be taken.

June 1942

Contract W-535-ac-28386 would cover the initial phases of engine development. It was written on 25 June and approved on 10 July. The agreement was a fixed-price contract, and it covered items 1–4 from the Studebaker proposal, for a total of $1,526,800 (about $23,618,190 in 2018 USD). It should be noted that Studebaker had wanted a cost-plus-fixed-fee contract but went along with the Power Plant Laboratory's request for a fixed-price contract.

Contract W-535-ac-28386 consisted of 14 items to cover engine development up to but not including the construction of a complete engine. However, the specific time frame for completion of the contracted items has not been found. With the contract approved, Studebaker moved forward with preliminary design and component testing of the 5,000 hp aircraft engine. The 14 items of contract W-535-ac-28386 (test engine "names" are in parenthesis) were as follows:

1) 6.5" single-cylinder test engine (AF-2),
2) 7.0" single-cylinder test engine (AF-4),
3) 7.5" single-cylinder test engine (AF-3),
4) 8.0" single-cylinder test engine (AF-1),
5) twin-cylinder test engine (AF-5),
6) twin-cylinder test engine (AF-6),

7) full-scale engine design,
8) propeller two-speed and contra-rotating gear reduction units,
9) fuel injection,
10) coolant pump,
11) ignition system,
12) accessories section,
13) multi-cylinder valve and cam drive unit, and
14) oil pump.

September 1942

A valve-lift test machine was in operation. It consisted of a partially assembled 164 in^3 Studebaker Champion inline six-cylinder engine modified to cycle various cam lobe, lifter, and valve spring designs through compressed and uncompressed phases. The tests had started by at least May 1942 and were focused on the PV (Pressure-Velocity) factor, which is a product of the specific load (or pressure) and the sliding speed (or velocity).

December 1942

Various drawings from December 1942 show the engine in an "X" and "H" configuration. All of the drawings list the engine as having 24 cylinders and displacing 8,750 in^3. In addition, the engine was "for submerged wing mounting," meaning it would be installed within the wing of an aircraft. Written on the drawings are a bore of 8.0" and a stroke of 7.25". These values would achieve the 8,750 in^3 displacement (actual displacement would be 8,746.2 in^3).

The "X" engine configuration featured a "tubular steel crankcase," but no specifics regarding this structure have been found. Each side of the engine had one camshaft situated near the top of the Vee formed by the upper and lower rows of cylinders. The camshaft actuated each cylinder's two valves through roller tappets, short pushrods, and rockers. Only the exhaust valve is shown on the drawing, and it is angled at 25° to the cylinder's centerline.

The combustion chamber was of a wedge design, and the pistons had domed tops. Side-by-side connecting rods of the master and articulated type were used, resulting in staggered cylinders on each side of the engine. The cylinders were mounted with 40° side bank angles and 140° top and bottom angles. The 24-cylinder X-8750 engine was listed as 29.125" tall and 73" wide. The engine's length was not recorded.

Left—Photograph from September 1942 of the Studebaker Champion engine that was converted into a valve lifter test machine. (NARA) Right—Various broken and damaged cam drive and lifter parts. (NARA)

The horizontal "H" engine configuration had an upper and lower crankshaft with a single overhead camshaft for each side of the engine. The cylinders had two valves, both angled at 25°. The camshaft was positioned above and between the two cylinder rows and acted directly on the inner valves (exhaust) of each cylinder row via roller tappets. The outer valves (intake) for each row were actuated by roller tappets, short pushrods, and rockers. The drawing shows cupped pistons, a hemispherical combustion chamber, and side-by-side connecting rods. The 24-cylinder H-8750 engine was listed as 34.875" tall and 73.5" wide. The engine's length was not recorded.

At some point in 1942, preliminary design work on a cylinder head was undertaken. The head was fairly similar to the heads that were ultimately used on the 6.5" and 8.0" cylinders. However, the early head had only two spark plug bosses.

January 1943

A preliminary drawing of a four-valve head arrangement with a flat combustion chamber was dated 26 January. Although not noted on the drawing, the diameter of the intake ports was approximately 2.76", and the diameter of the exhaust ports was approximately 2.64". The valves were actuated via roller tappets by dual overhead camshafts. The intake and exhaust ports were positioned on separate sides of the cylinder head, with one spark plug located below each port. It is not clear if provisions existed for more than the two spark plugs. A cupped piston was

illustrated in the drawing, but no fuel injection boss was shown.

February 1943

On 5 February, the MX-232 project received an AA-1 priority rating to help expedite the program. The project was run out of Studebaker's Motor Machining and Assembly Plant (Building 72 on Sample Street). Single-cylinder testing had begun as well as valve tappet tests and flow tests on the cylinder ports. One test room was complete, and another was to be finished before the next single-cylinder engine. The third room would be ready shortly after the second, with most of the parts and equipment already on hand. Some of the existing Studebaker shop equipment was not suited to machine the large engine components of the MX-232 project, and new equipment was on order.

The AF-1 engine with an 8.0" bore, 7.625" stroke, and 6.8:1 compression ratio (CR) had been assembled and had undergone early motoring tests in which the engine was turned by the dynamometer (dyno) without the engine producing any power. The engine's displacement was 383.27 in³. Teardown indicated the big end of the connecting rod was scuffed from deflection of the crankshaft cheeks. The crankshaft was modified with additional and larger cap screws to decrease its deflection. A new crankshaft was designed with a 4.75" diameter crankpin replacing the original 4.0" version. In addition, the flywheel was re-machined, which reduced its weight from 840 lb to 650 lb. The AF-1 engine was being reassembled to begin power tests. A second 8.0" cylinder was being

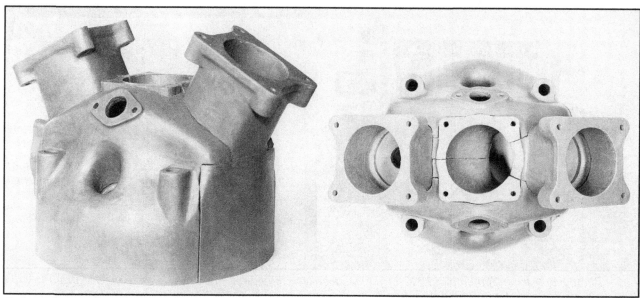

Side and top views of an early cylinder head design clay model produced in mid-1942. The design is similar to what was actually used on the test engines. However, the early design had only two spark plug bosses. Note the four holes for the cylinder hold-down through bolts. (AC)

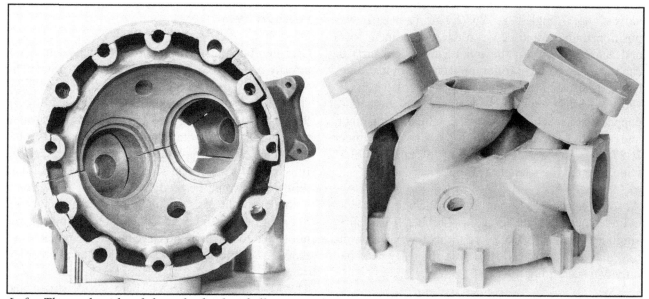

Left—The underside of the cylinder head illustrates the hemispherical combustion chamber. The stud holes around the head were used to attach the cylinder head and barrel together. (AC) Right—Clay cylinder head model with the water jacket partially removed. The exhaust port is on the right. (AC)

assembled and slightly modified to allow a cupped piston to be used. This would be compared to the domed piston already in service.

The AF-2 engine with a 6.5" cylinder was being assembled, with about 95% of the parts on hand. The remaining parts were expected in March. About 70% of the parts for the AF-3 (7.5" bore) engine and 60% for the AF-4 (7.0" bore) engine were on hand.

Work was ongoing to determine the general layout of the complete engine; both 24- and 32-cylinder "H" and "X" configurations were considered. Weight and size were the main factors in determining the superior configuration. Two types of "X" configurations were being evaluated: 45° side bank angle with 135° top and bottom, and 30° side bank angle with 150° top and bottom (differing from the December 1942 drawing with 40° and 140° angles). In addition, an alternative four-valve cylinder head was being designed as a

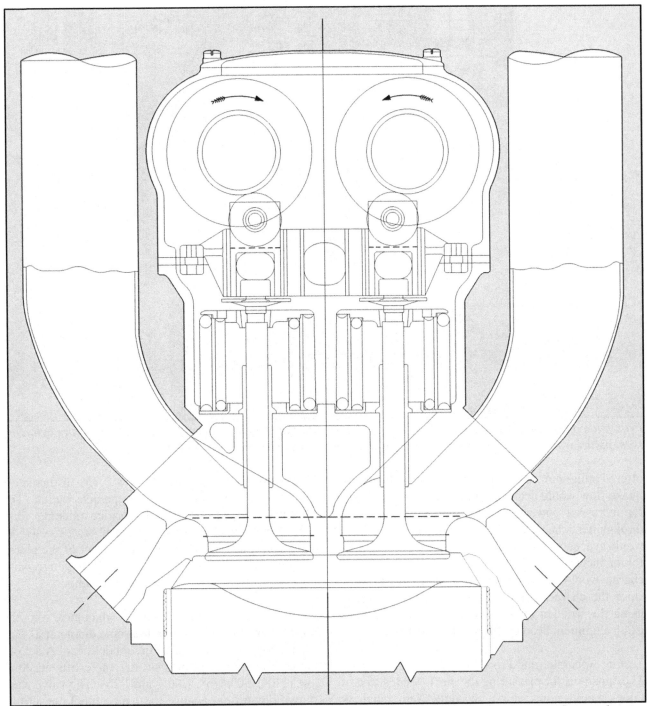

Reproduction drawing originally dated 26 January 1943 of a four-valve cylinder head with a flat combustion chamber. The valves were actuated by dual overhead camshafts. The larger intake valve is on the right. (A)

possible improvement over the current two-valve head.

A memo dated 18 February 1943 listed the engine's expected output as 4,000 hp at normal power and 5,000 hp at takeoff. Estimated fuel consumption was given as .36 lb/hp/hr at 55% of normal power (2,200 hp); .38 lb/hp/hr at 80% of normal power (3,200 hp); .53 lb/hp/hr at 100% of normal power (4,000 hp); and

.58 lb/hp/hr at 125% of normal power or takeoff power (5,000 hp).

March 1943

8.0" Bore Head Air Flow Tests
Air flow tests of the 8.0" bore head were reported 19 March. For this test, wooden models were used to develop intake and exhaust ports and valves that

Front side of the cylinder head air flow test apparatus with the smooth approach orifice to which the cylinder head model would attach. Note the inclined draft gauge attached to the box. (NARA)

offered minimum restriction of air flow. Increased intake flow would decrease pumping losses and allow for increased power and economy. Less resistance through the exhaust valve meant that the spent charge would evacuate the cylinder faster, leaving more space for the incoming fresh air charge. The gain in fresh air charge would allow operation at a leaner mixture, since the charge would be less diluted. The results using the wooden models were compared to results using aluminum head castings with steel valves.

Testing Apparatus and Procedure

The apparatus for measuring the air flow consisted of three major units. First, a draft fan rated at approximately 1,500 cfm at 3,500 rpm was used to draw air through the system. It drew air into the second part: a smooth approach orifice with a draft gauge to measure air flow. The approach orifice was attached to the third part: a model cylinder head and valve combination that was readily adaptable to test various minor modifications. The draft fan was operated at a constant speed. The rate of flow was controlled by changing the area of two openings in the side of the pipe that connected the fan and the orifice chamber.

The smooth approach orifice was 3.75" in diameter and 5.5" long with a 1.25" approach radius. To eliminate velocity effects, the orifice opening was placed in the wall between two chambers 22" x 47" x 47" in size, and baffles were put in front of the pipes leading from the chamber. A 72" draft gauge was connected to each side of the orifice chamber.

For the intake valve, the 3.75" diameter smooth approach orifice, which was the same diameter as the intake port, was attached to the model head. A set of gauge blocks was used to set the valve lifts at .20", .30", .40", .50", .75", 1.00", and 1.25". The valve was drawn down tight against the gauge block, ensuring exact duplication of valve lift. The model cylinder head was attached to a 50" straight tube with a diameter equal to the cylinder bore of the head. Inside this tube were a series of straightening vanes to eliminate turbulence. At the lower end of the tube was an annulus for measuring the static pressure of the air flowing through the tube. The drop below atmospheric pressure in this tube was equal to the drop resulting from the flow of the air through the head.

To measure the flow for the exhaust valve, A 48" straight pipe with a cross-section matching the exhaust

The draft fan used to draw air through the air flow test apparatus. The box contained baffles to prevent the flow of air directly between the draft fan and the smooth approach orifice. (NARA)

port was connected between the exhaust port opening and the orifice chamber. A similar annulus was provided in the tube next to the model head. The large tube simulating the cylinder bore was left attached to the head.

The test started at the minimum lift value (.20"), and each gauge block was inserted until the maximum lift value (1.25") was reached. A check run was then made for each lift, starting at the maximum value and decreasing to the minimum lift. For each lift, the opening in the pipe connecting the fan to the orifice chamber was set on seven fixed positions, giving seven rates of flow. Minimum flow at minimum lift was 100 cfm, while maximum flow at maximum lift was 800 cfm. The maximum flow was equivalent to the required air flow of an 8.0" bore cylinder with an average piston speed of 2,300 fpm.

Intake Results
The intake port was positioned at the center of the head. Flow on the wooden model was increased 10% by widening the combustion chamber bore from 8.0" to 8 19/32", changing the valve seat angle from 45° to 30°, and revising the valve seat insert so that it approximated the spherical shape of the combustion chamber. The finished aluminum head flowed 5.2% less than the wooden model. This decrease stemmed

from the sharper edges on the machined steel valve and insert. No appreciable flow difference was seen with different port passage contours in the region of the valve guide boss.

Exhaust Results
The exhaust port was positioned at the side of the head. Flow on the wooden model was increased 14.9% by increasing the combustion chamber bore from 8.0" to 8 19/32", increasing the radius at the rim of the valve head from 1/8" to 3/16", and, as with the intake valve, revising the valve seat insert so that it approximated the spherical shape of the combustion chamber. The finished aluminum head flowed 10% less than the wooden model. As with the intake port, this decrease stemmed from the sharper edges on the machined steel valve and insert. As with the intake port, the different port passage contours in the region of the valve guide boss had no appreciable effect on the flow.

Cylinder Results
The first cylinder head design matched the bore (8.0"), but there was not sufficient room around the valves for the valve inserts. The valve seat angle was at 45°. The flow number (a flow coefficient based on the average of several factors including valve lift and the corresponding crank interval) was measured at 88.8

for the intake and 90.0 for the exhaust. The second cylinder head design had its diameter increased to 8 19/32" so that the combustion chamber hung outside of the bore. The valve seat angle was changed to 30° and allowed room for the valve inserts. The flow coefficient was measured at 92.6 for the intake and 99.3 for the exhaust.

Modifications during the tests included using different valve seat angles, spacers between the head and barrel, flush versus projecting valve seats, various valve rims, different variations of blending the cylinder bore to the head, various port roof contours, various valve seat throats, and various valve guide boss heights.

An attempt was made to make a visual study of the air flow characteristics through the cylinder head. Air was forced through each port, past the valve, and into the cylinder. An 8.0" diameter glass cylinder was inserted between the cylinder head and the cylinder bore. Titanium tetrachloride was used to generate smoke, but considerable difficulty was encountered, and no worthwhile observations were made.

Since smoke was ineffective, sparks were resorted to as a means of determining the air distribution. The sparks were made with fine sawdust and a beekeeper's smoker. The sawdust was ignited in the beekeeper's smoker, and when it was burning properly, compressed air was blown through the smoker. This carried the burning particles into the port, past the valve, and through the glass cylinder. In general, the sparks appeared to swirl in a counter-clockwise direction on leaving the valve, as viewed from the head end. These particles appeared to have enough inertia to strike any projecting part, such as the exhaust valve. They also appeared to bombard the sides of the glass due to the angle they assumed on leaving the valve.

May 1943

After the 8.0" cylinder head air flow tests, the decision was made to compare the results with a cylinder head that had already been developed. A Wright cylinder, model G-200 (6.125" bore), was obtained from the Studebaker Aviation Division Aircraft Engine Plant (on Chippewa Avenue), where the Wright R-1820 engines were currently being built under license. The air flow was measured for various lifts of both the intake and the exhaust valves. For the intake, Studebaker's wooden head and ports model showed better air flow at various low valve lifts than the

Wright cylinder. But above a .14" lift, the Wright cylinder showed less resistance through the ports. Overall, the Wright head showed about 1% better flow. For the exhaust, the Wright head had about 5% less resistance than Studebaker's.

6.5" Bore Head Air Flow Tests
Air flow tests were completed on the 6.5" cylinder head, again using wooden models and a complete aluminum head with steel valves. The tests were compared with the 8.0" head. It was theorized that the results would be dimensionally similar. Additionally, tests were conducted reversing the ports: using the side exhaust port as the intake and the center intake port as the exhaust. The apparatus and procedure were the same as for the 8.0" bore test. Maximum air flow was 650 cfm, equivalent to a 2,800 fpm average piston speed for a 6.5" bore cylinder.

Intake Air Flow Results
The original 6.5" bore cylinder head had .5" port radii. Tests showed the flow to be equivalent to that of the 8.0" bore head. However, the radii were considerably smaller proportionally than those of the larger head. The inner port radii were increased in .125" increments up to 1.25" to find the optimal radii. Each change was flow tested.

For the center port (true intake), flow was increased 8.4% by changing the radius between the port bottom and the seat insert from .5" to 1.0"; the optimal radius was 1.0". An aluminum head was made with the 1.0" radius. Tests showed that the aluminum head was within 1% of the wooden head and 5.5% better than the best intake flow of the 8.0" cylinder head wooden model. The side intake (true exhaust) was optimized at a 1.125" inner port radius, yielding a 7.6% improvement over the original .5" radius. The side intake port gave slightly better (less than 1%) flow than the center port.

Exhaust Air Flow Results
The exhaust port was tested in the same manner as the intake port. Flow through the side opening (true exhaust) port was increased 4.1% by changing the radius between the seat insert and the port bottom from .5" to 1.0" and changing the valve seat angle from 30° to 45°. This flow was 5% less than the best exhaust flow obtained with the 8.0" bore wooden model head. The finished aluminum head checked within 1% of the wooden model, and flow was 4.5% less than the best exhaust flow obtained with the 8.0" bore head.

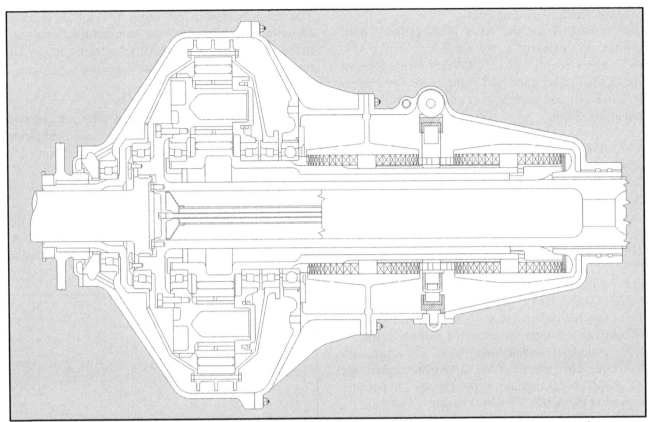

Reproduction drawing of the two-speed gear reduction unit originally dated 23 June 1943. As can be seen on page 145, the finished unit was very similar to this early drawing. (A)

Using the center port (true intake) for exhaust, the best flow was 1.1% less than the best side exhaust port flow. The optimal radius was between 1.0" and 1.125", the flow being basically equal between the two. The change in inner port radius produced a gain of 4.4% over the original design. The 45° valve seat produced an 8% gain over the best flow with a 30° valve seat.

Recommendations
It was recommended that improved flow could be obtained by

- lowering the port wall's radius along the axis of the valve stem for both side and center ports and continuing this radius in the seat insert using a curved surface for the insert throat,

- filling the straight portion of the port bottom on the side port so that the surface was normal to the plane of the port opening, and

- filling the concave portion of the inner port wall on the center port to approach a plane contour between the opening and the radius at the seat insert.

June 1943

Propellers
Work to define the propeller arrangement was undertaken during this time period. Although the exact specifics would vary by application, a clear image of the propeller setup began to emerge by mid-1943. A two-speed propeller arrangement would be used with single or contra-rotating propellers. In a single propeller configuration, a 3.75" diameter (No. 50) shaft size would be used with the propeller rotating at 800 rpm for high speed and 700 rpm for low speed.

However, more emphasis was placed on a contra-rotating setup. This would have a 5.125" (SAE #60) inner shaft and a 6.375" (SAE #80) outer shaft. Each shaft would weigh around 1,400 lb and would be able to handle future engine power increases above 5,000 hp. By 18 June, dimensions for an "H" engine configuration were given as 73.5" long, 66" wide, and 34.875" tall, but an "X" configuration was still being considered.

Single-Cylinder Test Engines
The crankshaft for the AF-4 (7.0" cylinder bore) engine was compared to the crankshaft for the AF-2 (6.5" bore) engine. At a 3,500-fpm average piston speed, the 7.0" bore and 7.625" stroke AF-4 engine ran at 2,760 rpm, and the 6.5" bore and 7.25" stroke AF-2 ran at 2,900 rpm.

The 7.0" bore cylinder had a gas pressure of 1,100 psi, or 42,300 lb of force total. Its inertial force was 20,410 lb (19.75 lb x 2,760 rpm), for a difference of 21,890 lb. At 20,000 lb, deflection at the crankshaft cheeks was .0164" and estimated to be .0179" at 21,890 lb.

The 6.5" bore cylinder had a gas pressure of 1,100 psi, or 36,400 lb of force total. Its inertial force was 18,850 lb (17.5 lb x 2,900 rpm), for a difference of 17,550 lb. At 20,000 lb, crankshaft deflection was also .0164". The expected deflection at 18,850 lb was .01545", which was less than the expected deflection for the 7.0" cylinder's crankshaft. With its crankshaft deflection 16% greater at the same piston speed, the AF-4 (7.0" bore) engine was not expected to perform as well as the AF-2 (6.5" bore) engine.

For the AF-1 (8.0" bore) single-cylinder engine, a deflection comparison of a 7.25" stroke, one-piece crankshaft versus a three-piece crankshaft was conducted. With the same load, the one-piece crankshaft was about 280% more rigid than the three-piece crankshaft. In other words, the three-piece crankshaft showed a .012" deflection at 14,200 lb of force, whereas the one-piece required 40,000 lb of force to give the same deflection. A defection of .017" would require 20,000 lb of force on the three-piece crankshaft and 56,400 lb for the one-piece crankshaft. The one-piece 7.625" and 8.0" stroke crankshafts exhibited virtually the same deflection as the one-piece 7.25" stroke crankshaft.

The flywheel on the AF-1 (8.0" bore) engine running a three-piece crankshaft with a 7.625" stroke (383.27 in^3) started to wobble at 1,800 rpm. Although it had not been run, it was believed a one-piece crankshaft would give less wobble, even at 2,500 rpm. Attempts were made to increase the rigidity of the three-piece crankshaft. A three-piece crankshaft was tried with six additional dowels, but the increase in rigidity was only slightly over 10%.

A 7.25" stroke crankshaft for AF-1 (8.0" bore) was Magnafluxed and showed cracks before it was ever run in the engine. After running for 53 hours, cracks in the pin journals became visible to the naked eye.

The crankshaft also lost about 15% of its rigidity. However, the crankshaft was released for further use in the engine because even with the cracks, it was still more rigid than the three-piece crankshaft.

Four-Valve Head
A drawing of a four-valve head arrangement was dated 30 June. It featured a hemispherical combustion chamber with intake port diameters approximately 3.23" and exhaust port diameters approximately 2.73". The valves were angled 25° and were actuated via roller rockers by a single overhead camshaft. Four spark plugs were positioned between the valves in the lower combustion chamber, and the fuel injection boss was positioned near the center of the combustion chamber.

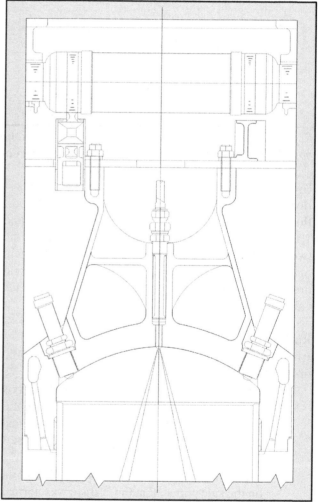

Reproduction drawing originally dated 10 June 1943 of the four-valve cylinder head with a hemispherical combustion chamber. The fuel injector is at the center of the combustion chamber, and spark plugs are positioned at the sides. The single camshaft is at the top of the drawing. (A)

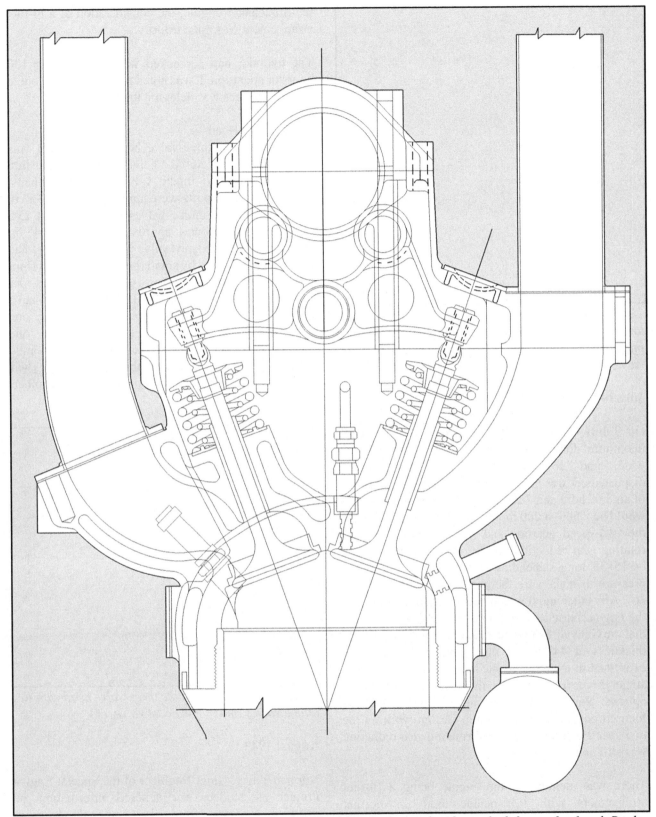

Reproduction drawing originally dated 30 June 1943 of the single overhead camshaft four-valve head. Rocker arms driven by the camshaft actuated the valves. The larger intake valve is on the right. The coolant outlet is on the right side of the cylinder head. (A)

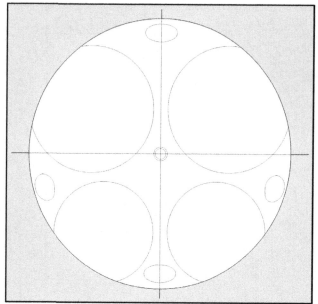

The combustion chamber of the four-valve head. The larger valves are intake valves. At the center is the fuel injector. A spark plug is positioned between each valve. (A)

July 1943

On 9 July, the complete engine grew a little, with maximum dimensions listed as 104.5" long, 66.5" wide, and 36" tall. The approximate engine displacement was given as 8,750 in³ with 24 cylinders of an 8.0" bore and 7.25" stroke. The engine's weight would be 5,500–6,000 lb, with an additional 465 lb for the two-speed gearbox and 440 lb for the contra-rotating gear reduction box. Propeller shafts were to be 15–30' long, depending on installation. There was pressure to make sure the engine was no taller than 36". Any taller and it would become difficult to install the engine buried in an aircraft's wing. It was noted that the Convair B-36 Peacemaker bomber had a wing thickness of 44" at the outer engine. Interest was expressed in interchangeable nose sections and right-angle drives to maximize the engine's installation options. Single-cylinder testing continued and was focused on low boost operation. Design work on the two-speed gear unit and contra-rotating gear reduction was still underway.

There was mention of the engine being a bi-fuel arrangement with 100 octane used for normal operation and "super fuel" (115/145 PN) used for takeoff. This is the only reference made regarding bi-fuel. Fuel of 115/145 PN was under development at the time and went into production around May 1945. Given the current status and ongoing development of the Studebaker engine, the consideration of a bi-fuel arrangement was not a priority.

The cylinder had a cracked water jacket after 100 hours of operation. It was noted that crankshaft trouble with all engines was delaying the program.

Three-Valve Head

A drawing of a three-valve head arrangement was dated 20 July. It featured a hemispherical combustion chamber with two intake valves and one exhaust valve. The intake ports were approximately 3.175" in diameter, and the intake valves were angled at 15°. The exhaust port was approximately 3 33/64" in diameter, and the exhaust valve was angled at 20°. The valves were actuated by small rocker arms driven from a single overhead camshaft with three lobes per cylinder (two intake lobes flanked the single exhaust lobe). The head had three spark plug bosses: one positioned between the intake valves and one positioned between each intake valve and the single exhaust valve. A boss for the fuel injector was positioned near the center of the combustion chamber, between all three valves.

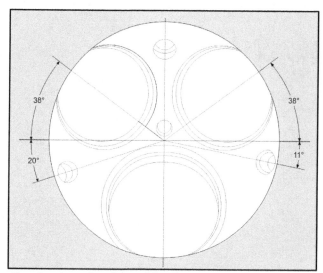

Combustion chamber of the three-valve head with two intake valves and one exhaust valve. (A)

August 1943

Norman Tilley, Chief Engineer of the Special Engine Project at Studebaker, gathered information on cylinder pressure from the National Advisory Committee for Aeronautics (NACA) and researched how the NACA measured cylinder pressure. Tilley was also interested in engine performance and detonation rating of fuels. The gathered information had an emphasis on hemispherical combustion

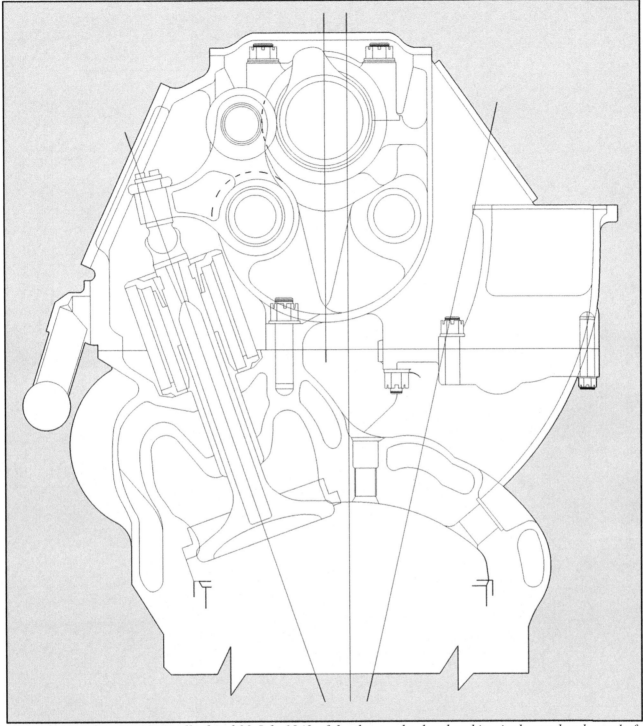

Reproduction drawing originally dated 20 July 1943 of the three-valve head and its single overhead camshaft. The single exhaust valve is pictured. (A)

chambers and detailed intake temperature, intake pressure, and cylinder CR.

Engine Starter

The question of how to start the big Studebaker engine was brought up during the summer of 1943. Representatives from Eclipse Aviation believed that

2,000 lb-ft of torque would be required to start the engine but advised having a starter capable of 3,000 lb-ft. No available starters produced the needed torque. The best course of action was to use two Eclipse model 715X2A starters of 1,500 lb-ft each. However, the 715X2A starter was not in production and was only available in limited quantities.

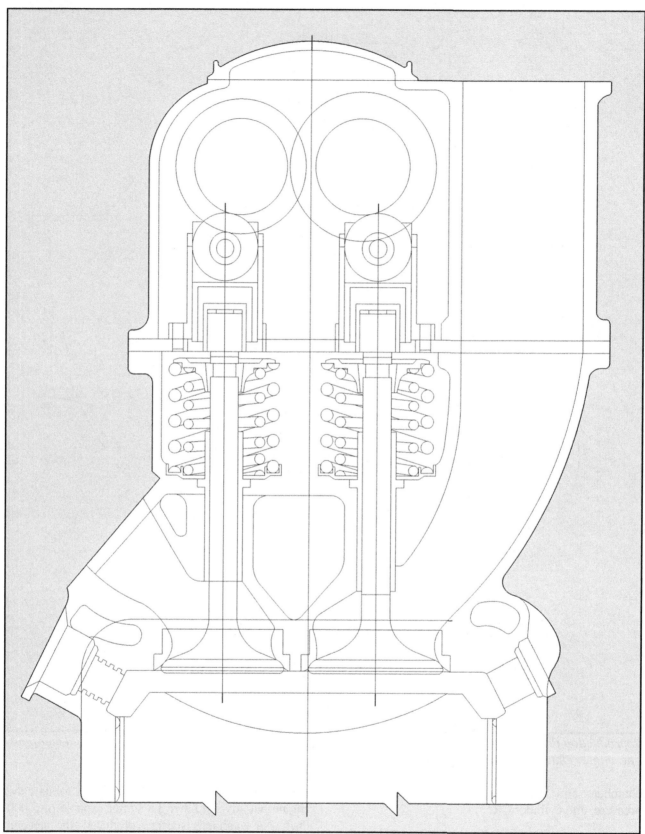

Reproduction drawing originally dated 4 September 1943 of the four-valve head with a flat combustion chamber. The larger intake valve is on the right. (A)

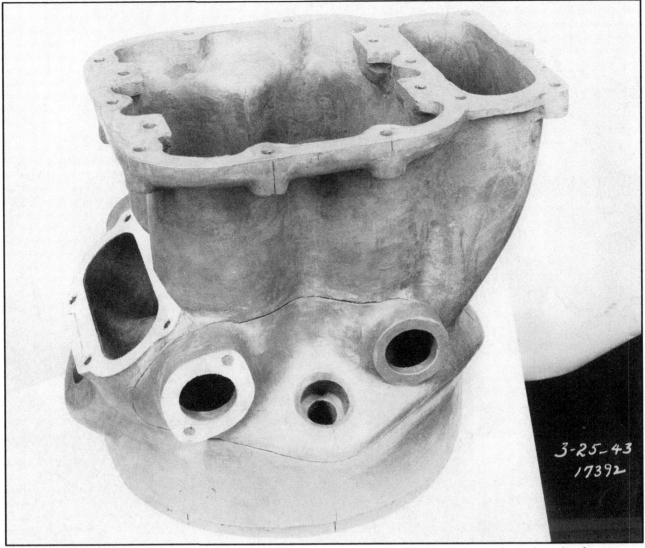

A clay model of the four-valve head photographed on 25 March 1943, over five months before the drawing on the previous page was made. This style of cylinder head was under consideration for quite some time. A camshaft housing would have bolted atop the cylinder head. (AC)

On 3 August, the decision was made to use two standard Army Air Force starters, and on 17 September, these starters were defined as Jack & Heintz model JH-10. However, Eclipse Aviation believed the JH-10 starters would only provide 2,000 lb-ft and that it might not be enough under extreme conditions. The engine was again listed as displacing 8,750 in³ at this time. On 20 September, the starter discussion continued; two left or right hand rotating Jack & Heintz JH-5E units were proposed.

September 1943

Four-Valve Head
A drawing of a four-valve head arrangement with a flat combustion chamber was dated 4 September. This

appears to be a refinement of the cylinder head originally drawn in January 1943. A clay mockup of this design was photographed on 25 March 1943. The intake port diameters were approximately 2.85", and the exhaust port diameters were approximately 2.36". The valves were actuated via roller tappets by dual overhead camshafts. The drawing indicates the camshaft bearing journals were staggered so that they overlapped, making the cylinder head as narrow as possible. The intake port was integral with the cam box that mounted to the top of the cylinder head. Like the four-valve hemispherical head, four spark plugs were positioned between the valves in the lower combustion chamber, and the fuel injection boss was positioned near the center of the combustion chamber.

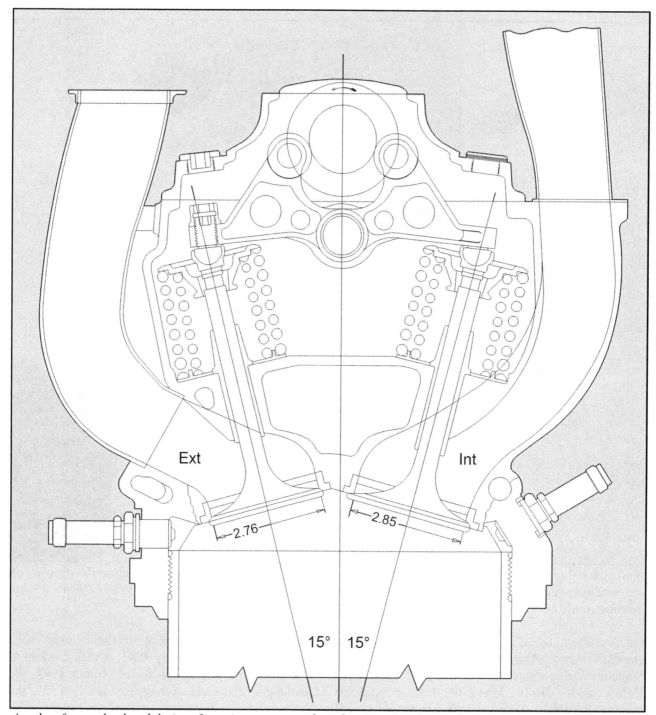

Another four-valve head design, featuring a pent roof combustion chamber and a single overhead camshaft. (A)

Another four-valve head, with a pent roof combustion chamber, is detailed in a drawing with an obscured date. One version shows the valves angled at 15° with intake port diameters of 2.85" and exhaust port diameters of 2.76". A second version shows the valves angled at 25° with 2.98" intake port diameters and 2.84" exhaust port diameters. In both designs, the valves were actuated via roller rockers by a single overhead camshaft. Again, four spark plugs were positioned between the valves in the lower

combustion chamber. The location of the fuel injection boss is not shown.

7.5" Bore Head Air Flow Tests
The same flow tests were performed on the 7.5" bore cylinder head that were done on the 8.0" and 6.5" heads. The 7.5" head's intake flowed slightly better than the 8.0" head's intake. For intake, the side port (true exhaust) flowed 4.7% better than center port (true intake). There were no flow differences in the

exhaust flow tests. Minimum port flow at minimum valve lift was 100 cfm. Maximum port flow at maximum valve lift was 730 cfm (equivalent to 2,400 fpm average piston speed for a 7.5" bore cylinder). All other results mirrored the 8.0" head.

Modifications included adjustments to the valve seat angle, inner port contour, various blends of the cylinder bore to the head, oval port contours of reduced cross sections, valve guide boss contours, various port surface heights, intake port size, port width, and inner port shapes. It was noted that a smaller intake port could be used; the flow actually increased slightly with a smaller port.

B-36 and Propeller Gear Ratios

On 9 September, a request was issued for design studies of the Studebaker engine installed in the B-36 bomber. The request was made to determine the range improvement that resulted from the installation of four Studebaker engines in place of the six Pratt & Whitney R-4360s. Studebaker inquired to the Materiel Command (MatCmd) regarding which gear ratios were desired for a 5,000 hp engine operating at 2,400 rpm. Studebaker proposed a 3:1 reduction for high-speed operation, which would give a propeller speed of 800 rpm. After takeoff and climb to 20,000', cruising power would be about 67% of takeoff power, or an engine speed of 1,600 rpm. Using a second gear ratio of 2:1 for low engine-speed operation would again give a propeller speed of 800 rpm. Studebaker proposed reducing power as the flight progressed by maintaining maximum engine torque for best fuel economy. Of course, speed would drop directly in proportion to power.

MatCmd concluded that the requirements of an airplane in which this engine would be used had not been determined sufficiently to permit a study of airplane operating characteristics and a choice of propeller gear ratios. It was estimated to be two to three years before the engine would be installed in an aircraft, and since the two-speed gearbox and contra-rotating gear reduction box were both external from the engine, postponing the gearing work would have no effect on engine development. Thus, the propeller gear ratios were not seen as an immediate priority, and a decision on gearing was left open for the time being. Also, development of gear reduction units had the potential to delay engine development, and engine development needed to take precedence. With other companies developing coaxial and two-speed gearboxes, the option of utilizing units from another manufacturer might be possible by the time the engine

was ready. However, it was acknowledged that no known units were being developed that could handle 5,000 hp.

MatCmd recommended that requirements of an airplane that would use this type of large engine be more clearly defined. It requested that Studebaker provide, as soon as possible, minimum specific fuel consumption (SFC) data over a complete range of operating speeds and powers to determine curves for minimum SFC versus engine speed. This information would be used to determine the aircraft requirements for the use of the engine. No issues were raised with Studebaker's proposal of starting cruise at 67% power (3,333 hp at 1,600 rpm) and of dropping power while still using constant torque to maximize economy. MatCmd also stressed that engine service could require application of 90–100% normal power rating for up to five hours on each flight mission.

Later in the month, the Propeller Lab at Wright Field replied with some propeller specifications. Based on 5,000 hp and a propeller speed of 800 rpm, a 21' eight-blade, contra-rotating unit on SAE #60-80 splines was desirable. The inner shaft (forward) blade would use SAE #60 splines, and the outer shaft (rear) blade would use SAE #80 splines.

Cylinder Deflection Tests

AF-1 (8.0" bore) cylinder deflection and stud elongation tests were conducted. With the piston at top dead center, the cylinder was pressurized to 600; 800; 1,000; and 1,200 psi. At 1,200 psi (or 60,000 lb), the studs on the non-flywheel side elongated .006", and the studs on the flywheel side stretched .007". Cylinder dome deflection was .000" at center, .001" on the non-flywheel side, and .0006" on the flywheel side. The cylinder barrel deflected more in line with the crankshaft than at right angles and had more movement on the side opposite the flywheel. From the center of the dome, the non-flywheel side moved .006" at the 14.25" mark and .0010" at the 7.125" mark. On the flywheel side, the cylinder barrel moved .005" at the 14.25" mark and .0010" at the 7.125" mark. The exhaust side moved .002", and the intake side moved .0004". The intake cam housing moved .002" vertically and .0012" horizontally, while the exhaust cam housing moved .0005" vertically with no horizontal movement detected.

Cylinder deflection vertically and horizontally was measured at various loads to determine the relative travel between the cylinder barrel and coolant jacket's lower flange. They were practically the same,

The 8.0" bore AF-1 cylinder undergoing deflection tests. The cylinder is attached to the test engine, and the intake side of the cylinder is shown. Note the added supports between the intake cam drive pad and the tab on the side of the cylinder head. (AC)

indicating .009" at a load of 60,000 lb. Tests of diametral changes in the cylinder bore were run at 60,000 and 90,000 lb. These tests indicated that general stiffening of the cylinder barrel was desirable. The lower 6.0" of the cylinder increased in diameter by .0025", but the upper 8.0" decreased in diameter by .0010", giving the cylinder a slight conical shape (with a .0035" variance). Flanges present on the outside of the barrel tended to bring the value back toward zero. It was noted that excessive piston ring wear had been encountered in engine operation. It was believed that changes in bore shape were occurring due to the loads encountered in actual operation, similar to those experienced during the deflection tests. The cylinder head, barrel, and jacket assembly were under a load of approximately 50,000 lb due to initial stud tension. Explosion pressures of 1,200 psi gave a load of 60,000 lb.

The load of the cylinder stud on the barrel was reduced by approximately 14,000 lb due to the added .007" elongation under a 1,200 psi load. The cylinder barrel operated between 36,000 and 50,000 lb of compression loads, while the studs carried 50,000–96,000 lb of tensile loads. The stud elongation was thought to have caused the failure of two cylinder hold-down studs. General cylinder stiffening was recommended.

AF-2 (6.5" bore) cylinder deflection and stud elongation tests were conducted in the same manner as those for AF-1. At 1,200 psi (or 60,000 lb), the studs elongated .005". The cylinder dome deflected nothing at center, .0006" on the non-flywheel side, and .0003" on the flywheel side. The exhaust side of the cylinder barrel moved .0008", and the intake side moved .002". From the center of the dome, the non-flywheel side moved .005" at the 13.25" mark and .0012" at the 6.625" mark. On the flywheel side, the cylinder barrel moved .0028" at the 13.25" mark and .0011" at the 6.625" mark. The intake cam housing moved .0005" vertically and horizontally, while there was no movement detected from the exhaust cam housing. Again, general cylinder stiffening was recommended.

Tests were conducted on AF-2, with a 6.5" bore, 7.25" stroke (240.58 in"), and a 6.16:1 CR. The test cylinder's average SFC was .376 lb/hp/hr, and fuel to air ratio was .055 or 18:1. SFC at maximum power was .440 lb/hp/hr, with air consumption at 5.95 lb/hp/hr. It was estimated that a 24-cylinder engine would produce 4,300 hp at 2,400 rpm and 3,750–4,000 hp at 2,100 rpm. At 2,400 rpm, indicated mean

effective pressure (IMEP) was 210, and brake mean effective pressure (BMEP) at 90% mechanical efficiency was calculated to be 188.5. At 2,100 rpm, IMEP was 192, and BMEP at 90% mechanical efficiency was 172.5. The engine's average piston speed was 2,900 fpm at 2,400 rpm.

October 1943

By 4 October, the complete engine had an estimated military and takeoff rating of 5,000 hp at 2,400 rpm and a normal rating of 4,000 hp at 2,100 rpm. Two General Electric (GE) CH-5 turbosuperchargers (at 260 lb each) were to be used. This would give the Studebaker engine a critical altitude of 30,000' for military power and 37,000' for normal power.

Studies of the coolant pump, ignition systems, accessory section, "X" versus "H" configuration, and engine weight reduction were underway. The 8.0" bore cylinder head was being modified with a new valve seat insert to increase flow. The new casting was expected in early November. A new 6.5" cylinder would be ready for tests on AF-2 in December.

November 1943

On 3 November, Tilley requested a ten-month extension of the contract. The program was taking longer than expected because of test cylinder failures and the time taken for repairs. It took four months to complete mixture ratio runs for the 8.0" bore cylinder. The actual testing time was only two weeks; the rest of the time was spent on repairs. The 6.5" cylinder was delayed three months by the redesigning and building of a new cylinder head and associated parts. The extension requested by Tilley was granted.

Further recommendations regarding the propeller gear reduction ratios were received from the Propeller Lab. The criteria used was for a 20', eight-blade, contra-rotating propeller intended for an aircraft cruising at 30,000' with an engine producing 5,000 hp at 2,400 rpm and 4,000 hp at 2,100 rpm. The recommended ratios were .26–.28:1 for high engine speed operation and .46–.49:1 for low engine speed operation. The ideal ratios were noted as .271:1 and .472:1 respectively.

December 1943

The comparative studies between the "X" and "H" engine layout continued, but it was determined that a fork-and-blade connecting rod arrangement for the

Photos taken 18 December 1943 of the damaged 8.0" bore cylinder. The cylinder head is on the left, and the cylinder barrel is on the right. The cylinder suffered a severe coolant leak while running on the test engine. (AC)

"H" engine was superior to the side-by-side connecting rods. The fork-and-blade rods required less crankpin length and would decrease the overall length of the engine by approximately 8.75". A shorter engine would also decrease the engine's weight, as less material was necessary for the engine's crankcase. To incorporate the fork-and-blade connecting rods, the arrangement of the "H" engine was updated to have a center-to-center cylinder distance of 9.25", down from the original 11".

Work was ongoing to determine the propeller contra-rotating gear reduction ratios and the two-speed gearbox layout. Requirements for the coolant pump had been outlined as 700 gallons per minute (gpm) flow rate at takeoff, with a 35° F temperature rise. This would give an inlet velocity of 18 feet per second (fps) and a manifold velocity of 40 fps at takeoff. Cruise conditions called for a 420 gpm flow rate, which would give an inlet velocity of 11 fps and a manifold velocity of 24 fps.

Studies continued on other components, such as ignition, fuel injection, oil pumps, and valve and camshaft drives. The single-cylinder test engines had revealed a longitudinal deflection of the cylinder barrel, and efforts were underway to correct it. Another area of study was the propeller drive shafts and their deflection under power.

Twin-cylinder test engine design was being delayed by some of the developmental issues with the single-cylinder test engines. The single-cylinder engines had experienced issues with the water jacket cracking around the cylinder head. The cylinder was being

redesigned to allow more flexibility between it and the head.

Single-Cylinder Test Engines
The AF-1 (8.0" bore) test engine was configured with a 7.25" stroke crankshaft. It displaced 364.42 in³ and had a CR of 6.8:1. The engine had accumulated 226 hours under power but was on its second cylinder. The first cylinder had lasted 193 hours before it experienced severe coolant leaks from cracks in the water jacket surrounding the head. The faulty cylinder was replaced with a new cylinder containing the second design head. Performance between the two different head designs was practically identical.

The AF-1 test engine had been run with up to 45 inches of mercury (inHg) of absolute dry manifold air pressure (MAP) at 2,400 rpm, mostly on the second test cylinder and using only four spark plugs. This cylinder began to exhibit the same cracks in the water jacket as the first cylinder. In addition, a hold-down bolt broke and fell into the crankcase, damaging several parts of the engine. A bolt retainer was supposed to prevent such an occurrence, but it was not effective.

The damaged parts were repaired, and the engine runs were continued. Both tappets exhibited cracks around their crowns and were replaced at 200 hours. Maximum IMEP was 289 at 45 inHg MAP and 2,400 rpm, and SFC was .430 lb/hp/hr. The best SFC was .330 lb/hp/hr at 1,200 rpm and 30 inHg MAP (137 IMEP). It was noted that a 1–2% decrease from maximum power gave an increase in economy by as much as 10%. It was also noted that the engine was not very responsive to spark advance; + or - 5° degrees gave no difference in power.

The AF-1 test engine was then run with a CR of 8.0:1, despite the cracked water jacket. After a few runs were made, the testing was stopped because of coolant leaking into the combustion chamber, between the cylinder barrel and head. The barrel was removed and was found to be coated with carbon. The barrel and head connection was a shrink fit, and the carbon deposits indicated that the fit was inadequate. It was believed that the head had separated from the seal when a cylinder head hold-down stud failed during an earlier test. It was estimated that it would be at least a month before AF-1 was ready to run again.

Preliminary comparisons of 6.8:1 CR versus 8.0:1 CR indicated that at 1,200 rpm and 30 inHg MAP there was an 8% improvement in SFC and IMEP with the higher CR. With a 6.8 CR, IMEP was 147 and SFC was .330 lb/hp/hr. With an 8.0 CR, IMEP was 159 and SFC was .305 lb/hp/hr.

The AF-2 (6.5" bore) engine was still awaiting a new cylinder. This engine also had a 7.25" stroke crankshaft, giving a total displacement of 240.58 in³. The engine had accumulated 225 hours of run time.

The AF-3 (7.5" bore) engine was running with a 6.75" stroke crankshaft, giving a total displacement of 298.21 in³. The engine was running at 6.8:1 compression and had accumulated 48 hours. Power output was low compared to AF-1 and AF-2. Tests showed the valve lift was not sufficient, and a new camshaft was being machined. All other parts looked good and had little wear.

The AF-4 (7.0" bore) engine had accumulated 108 hours. It was running a 6.75" stroke crankshaft that gave the test engine a displacement of 259.77 in³. The engine was running a 6.8:1 CR and was experiencing leaks in the cylinder head water jacket. AF-4 was lacking power compared to AF-1 and AF-2. A new high-lift camshaft was being machined. It was noted that the engine ran very smoothly after it was rebalanced in November.

January 1944

A single crankshaft design had been investigated for the complete engine. Part of the single crankshaft design considered was a connecting rod arrangement where four articulated rods were on one crankpin. These articulated rods would approximate true motion by means of a link connected to an eccentric boss on one of the link rods. This design showed severe load reversals when passing over top center.

However, a single crankshaft engine with various forms of connecting rods was found to be impractical for the 5,000 hp engine. This eliminated the "X" configuration, so the focus shifted to a 24-cylinder "H" engine with two crankshafts using 7.5" or 8.0" bore cylinders. An engine utilizing the smaller bores of 7.0" or 6.5" would require 32 cylinders to reach the target of 5,000 hp. The complete engine to fulfill the MX-232 project was, at that point, regularly referred to as the XH-engine, for eXperimental Horizontal engine and because its ultimate displacement was still not known.

Studebaker felt it was still four months away from determining which cylinder would be optimal for the 5,000 hp engine. The company was working on detailing a schedule and requirements for complete XH-engine construction and testing, but that could not be accomplished until the most suitable cylinder size was known. It was expected to take 10–14 months to procure the dynamometer equipment and 6 months for installation. It was also estimated that the design of the 5,000 hp engine would be done by May 1945 and a complete test engine built by May 1946. Therefore, to avoid holding up the program, work on the test cell for the complete XH-engine needed to be started no later than July 1944.

For complete XH-engine testing, the plan was to use one of the test cells at the Studebaker Aviation Division Aircraft Engine Plant on Chippewa Avenue. These cells were used in testing the Studebaker-built Wright R-1820 engines. The cell would need to be modified to support the 5,000 hp engine. Otherwise, an entirely new test cell would need to be built. Exactly what equipment Studebaker would need for the completed engine was under investigation. It was noted that the equipment should not be limited to 5,000 hp, because more power was expected as the engine was developed.

February 1944

Air flow tests were conducted on the first cylinder of the third head design. Compared to the first design, the third design showed a 5% increase in intake flow and a 3% increase in exhaust flow. However, the expected improvement was around 10%. The third design head model was inspected and found to have a .055" clearance between the valve and cylinder barrel at .36" valve lift. The cast aluminum head had even less clearance, only .008". In fact, there were indications that the valve had actually rubbed on the cylinder bore when the cylinder was running on the engine. The clearance was opened up to 0.046", but the cylinder was needed back on the engine, and no further flow tests were made. In May 1944, another test was done using the second cylinder of the third head design. Clearance was noted as .035", and there was a 9% improvement in flow over the first head design.

Layout and weight analyses of the "H" engine design continued. Study of the contra-rotating gear reduction with a ratio of 2.5:1 indicated it would weigh twice as much (500 lb additional) as a 2.0:1 gear ratio. A ratio of 2.3:1 was also studied and found to be nearly as heavy as the 2.5:1 ratio. Considering the weight gain, it was questioned whether the ratios over 2:1 would produce any net advantages.

Based on the propeller speed calculations from Wright Field, studies were done to determine the speeds of the two-speed gear unit. Calculations were done based on an 8,750 in³ engine with an 8.0:1 CR. Cruise power of 3,025 hp was estimated at 1,500 rpm and 40 inHg MAP. These settings would give a fuel consumption of about .355 lb/hp/hr. Takeoff power of 5,000 hp was estimated at 2,200 rpm and 37 inHg MAP. From these estimates, it was determined that the cruise gear ratio should be .435:1, and the takeoff/climb/normal power gear ratio should be .290:1. However, all estimates showed a BMEP that was possibly above the detonation margin for the proposed 8,750 in³ engine. It was thought that the overall displacement could be increased to avoid the risk of detonation.

Studies were also being undertaken to compare a separate gearbox for all the accessories versus having the accessories driven directly off the engine. The design of the camshaft and valve drive was held up until the engine layout was finalized. Work on the twin-cylinder test engines was still waiting for tests of the redesigned cylinders on the single-cylinder test engines to be completed. It was believed that development of the twin-cylinder engines would continue in April.

Single-Cylinder Test Engines
The AF-1 (8.0" bore) engine indicated a SFC of .31 lb/hp/hr during a mixture run at 1,200 rpm. This engine was operating with the second cylinder of the original design and experienced coolant leaking in the cylinder while running at 8.0:1 compression, 1,600 rpm, and 30 inHg MAP. The cylinder was

reconditioned and went back on test. It quickly developed new coolant leaks and was replaced by a new, redesigned cylinder. The new cylinder was being broken in and tuned up at 6.8:1 compression. A new cupped piston was being designed and was projected to be ready in March. The engine had run 240 hours.

The AF-2 (6.5" bore) engine had been reassembled and was on the dyno. The engine had run 75 hours with the new cylinder, bringing its total time to 300 hours. The engine was first run at 6.16:1 compression up to 2,400 rpm and 30 inHg MAP. The engine was rebuilt with 8.0:1 compression. During a run at 2,400 rpm and 35 inHg MAP, a piston ring stuck and scratched the cylinder. The engine was repaired, and the oil jet in the top of the connecting rod that sprayed the underside of the piston was enlarged. The 8.0:1 compression runs were expected to be completed by the end of the month. The engine would then be rebuilt with its stroke decreased from 7.25" to 6.375". The .875" shorter stroke would reduce the engine's 240.58 in³ displacement to 211.54 in³.

The AF-3 (7.5" bore) engine was being run on a tune-up program when a counterweight bolt broke at 67 hours. The engine was repaired and placed back in operation. At 72.25 hours, the exhaust lever follower broke. Inspection revealed the intake lever follower was cracked. This was the only engine that used lever-type cam followers. The parts were redesigned, and the engine was undergoing repairs. The high lift cam would be installed, and tests were expected to resume in the near future.

The AF-4 (7.0" bore) engine was now producing comparable power to the 6.5" and 8.0" cylinders. The power increase was a result of continued tune-up work on the original camshaft. However, during a mixture run at 2,000 hp and 35 inHg MAP, the testing was stopped because of coolant leaking into the cylinder. The cylinder, which had accumulated 158.5 hours, was rebuilt and the new high lift camshaft installed. Additional engine runs were made, but the cylinder continued to leak. Many attempts were made to prevent the leaks but without success. The cylinder was being reconditioned and was expected to be back under test in March. The engine had accumulated 184 hours under power.

The Aircraft Laboratory Memorandum Report ENG-51-4261-4-10 was released on 14 February 1944. It was a design study of the XB-36 airplane with four 5,000 hp Studebaker engines. Unfortunately, a copy of this report has not been found.

March 1944

Notes from March indicated some analysis of g-loading on the engine. Typically, bombers had a 3g expected load with a 1.5-times safety factor that brought the ultimate load to around 5g. The Boeing B-29 Superfortress was noted as having a 6.3g ultimate load. The Studebaker engine would have +6/-4g as an overall design load.

Around this time, Tilley had quickly sketched a push/pull design for the XH-engine. The upper crankshaft would be geared to a propeller shaft extending through the leading edge of the wing, and the lower crankshaft would do the same but for the trailing edge of the wing. No further information has been found regarding this concept.

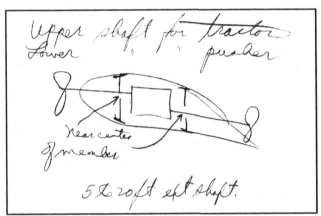

Tilley's sketch of the XH-engine in a submerged wing installation push/pull configuration. (NARA)

AF-1 (8.0" bore) with a 7.25" stroke, 6.8:1 CR, and four plugs was run in tests comparing the first head design with the third head design. IMEP improved 8% at 1,200 rpm and 4% at 2,400 rpm. SFC also improved across all speeds, except 1,200 rpm, with the highest gain being 8% at 2,000 rpm. These results mirrored the air flow test from the previous month, after the valve clearance had been opened up.

On 28 March, the British Air Commission Technical Branch at Wright Field requested a few reports on the Studebaker 5,000 hp engine. It is not known which specific reports were requested or if they were provided to the British.

April 1944

Theoretical vibration studies for an "H" engine of 8,750 in³ were underway. A main concern was to keep the engine's height under 36". A ring type oil manifold located below the cylinder had been designed. This manifold would spray four continuous streams of oil toward the underside of the piston to cool it. The manifold had already been installed in the AF-3 (7.5") and AF-2 (7.0") engines and was being built for the AF-1 (8.0") and AF-2 (6.5") engines.

Single-Cylinder Test Engines
The AF-1 (8.0" bore) engine was still running a stroke of 7.25" and displacing 364.4 in³. Compression had been reduced from 8.0:1 down to 6.8:1 for further mixture ratio runs. Runs were made as low as 1,000 rpm and 20 inHg MAP. The engine was running with a new third-design cylinder, and after 37 hours, a crack developed in the water jacket of the head. Testing continued until the leak became excessive at 95 hours on the new cylinder. Another new cylinder was fitted, and it cracked in the same place after 19 hours. The engine was still under test and had been run up to 2,400 rpm and 40 inHg MAP. A third cylinder of the new design was being built. The runs at an 8.0:1 CR would be restarted later in the month. A cupped type piston was being designed and was expected by May 1944. The engine had accumulated 353 total hours.

The AF-2 (6.5" bore) engine was under test, and a new third-design spare cylinder had been prepared. Testing with a stroke of 7.25" (240.6 in³) and a CR of 8.0:1 had been completed. Previously, the engine was running a 6.375" stroke (211.5 in³) and at an 8.0:1 CR. Runs up to 2,400 rpm and 30 inHg MAP were completed. However, delays were experienced due to excessive tappet wear. A thicker tappet coated with Colmonoy was reported to solve the issue. The engine had accumulated 465 hours total, with 240 hours on the third-design cylinder.

The AF-3 (7.5" bore) engine had a 6.75" stroke crankshaft, giving a total displacement of 298 in³. The engine had a 6.8:1 CR and was using the old cylinder. A new third-design cylinder had been completed, and a second unit was being built. During tests, numerous coolant leaks occurred. The cylinder was reconditioned, but small leaks continued. These smaller leaks did not prevent further testing. The engine had accumulated a total of 95 hours.

The AF-4 (7.0" bore) engine was running a 6.75" stroke (260.8 in³) and a 6.8:1 CR. The engine had completed runs up to 2,400 rpm and 30 inHg MAP before a rocker broke. The cylinder was awaiting valve train repairs and was still using the old cylinder. As with AF-3, a new third-design cylinder had been completed for AF-4, with a second cylinder under construction. The engine had accumulated 210 hours.

With all the delays, it was felt that single-cylinder testing to determine bore, stroke, and CR for a prospective complete XH-engine would not be completed until May. These variables were needed before construction of the twin-cylinder test engines could continue. This lack of information held up construction of the twin-cylinder engines.

May 1944

The AF-1 (8.0" bore) engine with a 7.25" stroke and 6.8:1 CR completed evaluative tests to determine the best valve timing and spark plug position on the third-design head. This head had 45° valve angles (rather than 30°) and six 18 mm spark plug holes (rather than four 18 mm and two 14 mm in the center). The best exhaust valve timing occurred with the exhaust opening at 55° before bottom center (BBC) and closing at 60° after top center (ATC). The best timing for the intake valve occurred when it opened at 20° before top center (BTC) and closed at 60° after bottom center (ABC). Retarding the intake valve opening increased power at higher speeds but decreased the IMEP at lower speeds. The best spark plug combination was two center and two exhaust plugs firing. This combination was used for all subsequent tests. Tests were started using a CR of 8.0:1.

AF-2 (6.5" bore) was being repaired. AF-3 (7.5" bore) and AF-4 (7.0" bore) were running under tests.

June 1944

Single-Cylinder Test Engines
The AF-1 (8.0" bore) engine with a stroke of 7.25" (364.42 in³) had completed mixture runs up to 2,400 rpm and 45 inHg MAP at both 6.8:1 CR and 8.0:1 CR. The engine achieved a SFC of .320 lb/hp/hr at 1,200 rpm and .322 lb/hp/hr at 1,600 rpm, both at 35 inHg MAP. It was believed a complete 24-cylinder engine utilizing the 8.0" bore and 7.25" stroke would have a SFC of .36 lb/hp/hr. A new third-design cylinder was also being machined. A valve spring failed during tests. A redesigned unit with dampening action to eliminate the possibility of valve surge was on order.

The engine was rebuilt with an 8.0" stroke (402.12 in³) and 6.8:1 CR. In this configuration, the engine was run up to 2,400 rpm and 30 inHg MAP. With the 8.0" stroke, the engine exhibited IMEP increases of 6% at 1,000 and 1,200 rpm; 2% at 1,600 and 2,000 rpm; and

a 1% decrease at 2,400 rpm. The engine was run 14.5 hours with the 8.0" stroke and 534.5 hours total.

The AF-2 (6.5" bore) engine had completed its mixture runs. It was run up to 2,400 rpm and 45 inHg MAP with strokes of 6.375" (211.54 in³) and 7.25" (240.58 in³) and CRs of 6.16:1 and 8.0:1.

The 7.25" stroke consistently had better (4–10%) SFC than the 6.375" stroke. In addition, the 8.0:1 CR had better (8–14%) SFC than the 6.16:1 CR. The best SFC, measured at .310 lb/hp/hr, was achieved at 1,600–2,000 rpm with the 7.25" stroke and 8.0:1 CR. Overall, higher rpm resulted in better SFC. The 8.0:1 CR had 8–15% better IMEP than the 6.16:1 CR. The highest IMEP of 228 psi was achieved with the 7.25" stroke and 8.0:1 CR at 2,400 rpm and 40 inHg MAP. At these settings, the cylinder was producing around 175 hp. However, the tests were limited because of detonation issues.

The 6.5" bore cylinder had an operating speed of 2,400 rpm and a 40 inHg MAP detonation limit. With these constraints, 32 cylinders would be needed to create an XH-engine with a 5,000 hp output. A 32-cylinder engine with a 6.5" bore and a 7.25" stroke would displace 7,698 in³. It was estimated that a complete XH-engine could achieve a SFC of .360 lb/hp/hr. The cylinder tests required three cylinder assemblies and 650 hours of operation. The first cylinder was used for 225 hours, the second for 303.5 hours, and the third for 121.5 hours.

As an experiment, the test engine was run up to 2,600 rpm with both the 6.375" and the 7.25" stroke. No issues were encountered at the higher speeds. In addition, preliminarily tests were done to compare performance using four and six spark plugs. It was found that four plugs did not reduce the engine's performance over using six plugs. A cupped piston was installed, and the engine was prepped for new tests.

The AF-3 (7.5" bore) test engine with a stroke of 6.75" (298.21 in³) had accumulated 230 total hours and was used in mixture runs up to 2,400 rpm and 45 inHg MAP. During an 8.0:1 CR test at the leanest mixture, the intake valve broke while at 2,400 rpm and 30 inHg MAP. The loose valve then damaged the piston crown and subsequently jammed between the piston and exhaust valve; it bent the exhaust valve and broke out the exhaust valve seat insert. A large hole was punched in the cylinder head between the two valves. The head showed signs of a previous crack prior to

The 6.5" cylinder atop the AF-2 test engine. The exhaust port can be seen on the right. Note the three spark plugs installed in the cylinder and the double nuts securing the hold-down through bolts. Another three spark plugs were installed on the opposite side of the cylinder. Coolant flowed into the fitting at the bottom of the cylinder and exited the fitting mounted to the triangular pad just above the spark plugs. (NARA)

The opposite side of the 6.5" cylinder and AF-2 test engine, completely assembled and ready for test runs.

failure. A new cylinder was ready for replacement, but a new piston needed to be made and wouldn't be ready for two weeks.

The AF-4 (7.0" bore) test engine with a stroke of 6.75" (259.77 in³) was making mixture runs up to 2,400 rpm and 30 inHg MAP with a 6.8:1 CR. At 2,400 rpm and

20 inHg MAP, the exhaust rocker arm broke. The rocker arm was redesigned and testing resumed. After 10 additional hours of operation, the cylinder head water jacket was cracked and leaking coolant. The engine was being rebuilt with the redesigned head and redesigned cam followers and rocker arms. The engine had accumulated 279 hours.

GE Dyno Proposal and Propeller Tests
Studebaker had requested that GE issue a proposal for dynos to test the complete XH-engine and the propeller gearboxes. Studebaker's request was for dynos with and without contra-rotating shafts. The single shaft needed to absorb 8,000 hp; run from 1,800 to 2,400 rpm; and be able to have 2,000 hp available for motoring. The duel shaft needed to absorb 4,000 hp on each shaft and run from 600 to 1,200 rpm. The same 2,000 hp motoring requirement was requested but with the added capabilities of using a single shaft at speeds under 1,800 rpm and dual shafts under 600 rpm. The dyno needed to operate at a constant torque.

On 15 June, GE responded with two dynos to be used in conjunction with each other. Dyno one was intended for both single and contra-rotating use over a speed range of 600 to 2,400 rpm. It was built of synchronous turbine-generator parts and allowed for 2,000 hp of motoring. Dyno one weighed 71,000 lb and was 15.5' long.

Dyno two was solely for contra-rotating use and had a maximum rpm of 1,200 rpm. It was a synchronous machine of the salient pole type and did not allow motoring. Dyno two weighed 38,000 lb and was 11.2' long. It would be coupled to dyno one, making the combination 109,000 lb and 26.7' long.

XH-Engine Development
In late June, Tilley requested another extension on the engine. He also requested a Junkers Jumo 211 engine and a Packard 2A-2500 crankshaft, both for study and deflection tests. The Jumo and Packard engines were both V-12s and probably the largest inline engine examples available. The Jumo 211 had a 5.91" bore and a 6.5" stroke, and the Packard had a 6.375" bore and a 6.5" stroke. Tilley hoped these examples could aid in designing the 5,000 hp engine's crankshafts. At the time, the Studebaker XH-engine was to have a crankshaft with a main bearing diameter of 4.75" and a crankpin diameter of 4.25". The twin-cylinder test engine's crankcase was being fabricated and would have three main bearings, while the single-cylinder engine's crankcase had two.

Design of the complete XH-engine's layout was advancing, and there was debate as to exactly where the propeller shaft should be geared to the engine. The new thought from Studebaker was to have the shaft offset either to the left or right but aligned horizontally with the centerline of the engine. The Studebaker team thought this arrangement would be superior for installing the engine buried in a wing, compared to the previous design of having the shaft either above or below the engine centerline and in line with the upper or lower crankshaft. Studebaker asked that Wright Field determine the ideal position for the propeller shaft. In addition, a comparison of single versus contra-rotating propellers was requested.

Regarding propeller performance, analysis indicated the heavier 2.4:1 reduction gear would be more efficient over a 10,000-mile range than the lighter 2.0 gear. At 2,200 rpm engine speed, a propeller speed of around 650 rpm was desired for climb and high speed at military power, resulting in a 3.4:1 reduction.

At this time, the final engine was estimated to weigh 6,400–7,000 lb. Cylinder valve layout was still being considered. MatCmd suggested a three-valve cylinder head with one exhaust valve and two intake valves. One intake valve was located above the head's horizontal axis, with the other valve below. At this point, Stanwood W. Sparrow was added to the engine project.

July 1944

In July, various drawings to illustrate the propeller shaft placement options were sent to Wright Field for evaluation. Studebaker also received the Jumo 211 engine and a Packard 1A-2500 crankshaft that Tilley had requested for studies. (Tilly had requested a 2A-2500 crankshaft, but it appears a 1A-2500 crankshaft was sent. Most of the reports simply say it was a "Packard 2500" crankshaft. There does not appear to be a difference between the crankshafts.)

Single-Cylinder Test Engines
Oil consumption for the AF-1 (8.0" bore) with a 7.25" stroke (364.42 in³) had been mostly below .02 lb/hp/hr. When it was running an 8.0:1 CR at 2,000 rpm and 30 inHg MAP, oil consumption was .014 lb/hp/hr. Now that the cylinder had the 8.0" stroke (402.12 in³), it was experiencing high oil consumption as a result of blow-by. The 8.0" stroke running 6.8:1 CR at 1,600 rpm and 25 inHg MAP was consuming .033 lb/hp/hr of oil. To decrease oil consumption, new piston rings were installed. The top ring was chrome

plated, and the other rings were tin plated. A study of the three-valve cylinder head indicated that oil consumption would increase to above .030 lb/hp/hr.

With the 8.0" stroke, AF-1 was finishing runs at 2,400 rpm when a connecting rod bolt broke, allowing the big end bearing to spin. Upon inspection, the connecting rod was found to be cracked. The rod was repaired to finish the runs, and a new rod was being made in case the old one failed. AF-1 had 614 total hours.

The AF-2 (6.5" bore) engine was running a 7.25" stroke (240.58 in³) and 8.0:1 CR. It was under tests to compare a cupped piston versus a domed piston. Initial tests showed the cupped piston had a very slight advantage. The engine had accumulated 693.25 hours.

The AF-3 (7.5" bore) engine was running with a 6.75" stroke (298.21 in³) and 8.0:1 CR, but it was running rough at the higher compression ratio. An issue with the valve action was believed to be causing the roughness. This engine had new connecting rod bearings because of a piston seizure. Additionally, the valve struck the piston, breaking the head off the valve. Oil consumption was below .01 lb/hp/hr, and the engine had 251 total hours.

The AF-4 (7.0" bore) engine was running a 6.75" stroke (259.77 in³) and 6.8:1 CR. It was undergoing mixture runs up to 2,400 and 40 inHg MAP. The cylinder suffered a cracked jacket, and it was believed that the ports were wobbling. Rocker arm support bracing was added to eliminate or lessen wobble. The engine had 360 total hours.

August 1944

Single-Cylinder Test Engines
The AF-1 (8.0" bore) engine was mistakenly rebuilt with an 8.7:1 CR. The Studebaker team decided to test the configuration and then return it to an 8.0:1 CR. Since the 8.0" cylinder had shown the best performance (SFC and power), it was proposed that development should focus on the 8.0" bore and that tests on the other cylinders should be halted. The other test engines could be reequipped with 8.0" bore cylinders. The AF-1 engine had 689 total hours.

The AF-2 (6.5" bore) engine had completed all tests and was now being used to compare a domed piston versus a cupped piston. For this engine, there was little weight difference between the two types of pistons. But, for the 8.0" piston, the domed weighed 19.8 lb,

whereas the cupped was 6.8 lb lighter, at 13.0 lb. For a complete XH-engine, the difference represented a weight savings of 13.6 lb for each crankpin and 81.6 lb overall. AF-2 had accumulated 736.5 hours.

It was discovered that the AF-3 (7.5" bore) engine had faulty cams that gave greater valve acceleration than the spring force and permitted valve float above 2,000 rpm. This was thought to have caused the previous failure on this cylinder, in which the valves stayed open and caused a general failure. New cams had been designed and were to be made as soon as possible. Another issue was that the top two compression piston rings stuck under tests. As a result, the piston ring grooves were opened up. AF-3 had run 278 hours.

AF-4 (7.0" bore) was disassembled for inspection and for bracing the rocker arm housing; rocker arm vibration was cracking the cylinder jackets. The engine had been noisy, and inspection revealed that the front main bearing liner had been pounded out. An extensive crack was found in the crankshaft (at the crankpin) and was the cause of the engine running rough. AF-4 was being rebuilt with a 7.625" stroke crankshaft (293.21 in³). It had run 390 hours total.

XH-Engine Development
Overall, tests for the XH program indicated that fuel economy improved as bore and stroke increased. The effect of a longer stroke on engine fuel economy was more pronounced and indicated that the stroke should be greater than the bore. However, these tests were solely indicated SFC, and the final results were likely to differ when compared to the brake SFC for a complete XH-engine.

On 16 August, Power Plant Laboratory requested cost estimates for three complete XH-engines. Studebaker estimated the first engine would cost $1,945,000, and the two subsequent engines would be $1,216,500 each. The total estimate for all three engines was $4,378,000. This figure did not include engine testing or the equipment required for engine testing, which Studebaker would need financial assistance to purchase. Paul M. Clark, General Counsel for Studebaker, said that a cost-plus-fixed-fee contract should be used to cover the complete XH-engines. He suggested a fixed fee of $1.00. A cost-plus-fixed-fee type of contract was in effect for the Studebaker-built Wright engine production. Because Studebaker's work on the MX-232 project was on a fixed-price contract and was over budget, any work on a complete XH-engine would carry an appreciable contingency fee if the contract was not cost-plus-fixed-fee.

Late in August, the Power Plant Laboratory felt the proposed Studebaker XH-engine's weight was excessive and advised that every effort should be made to make the engine lighter. It was felt that the weight would limit the engine's use to only long-range bombers. It was also found that for a pusher configuration, the two-speed gearbox and contra-rotating gear reduction were too heavy for installation in the rear portion of the wing. It was requested that Studebaker look into ways to reduce the weight of these components.

The Power Plant Laboratory also advised that tests be discontinued on the 7.0" and 7.5" cylinders as soon as possible. The department felt that there was no useful purpose in studying four cylinder sizes simultaneously and that testing should focus on the 6.5" and 8.0" cylinder, with the main focus on the 8.0" cylinder. The Lab noted that the study of the other cylinder sizes resulted in serious delays of the overall program.

The height of the engine was under scrutiny. In order to stay at 36" height, an engine with an 8.0" bore and 7.25" stroke (8,746 in3) would have only a 3.0" sump,

which was considered insufficient. An engine with an 8.0" bore and 8.0" stroke (9,651 in3) would be over the 36" height goal. One possible way to minimize the engine's height was to phase the crankshafts together. This allowed the crankshafts to have the absolute minimum distance between them, thus decreasing the engine's height. However, if there were some type of a failure in which the crankshafts came out of phase, they would collide and destroy the engine. Given the issues at hand, it was felt that a stroke of more than 7.25" would not allow the engine to stay under the 36" height goal.

A new cylinder design that featured a conventional flange and stud mounting was designed to replace the four long hold-down studs that were currently used. This change required an extensive redesign of the cylinder, and Studebaker was requested to get the new cylinders in the test program as quickly as possible. It was believed that this cylinder would be used on the complete XH-engine. Most documents refer to this cylinder as the "multi-cylinder" because it would be used on the complete multi-cylinder engine, rather than on the single-cylinder test engines. Occasionally,

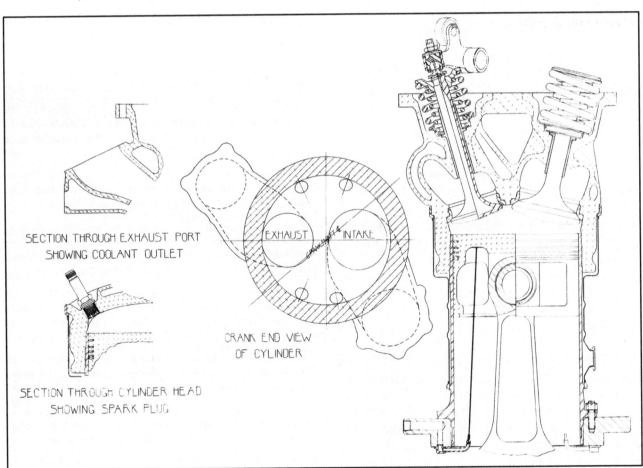

The XH-cylinder was a refinement of everything that had been learned with all the previous cylinder testing. The long through bolts were eliminated, and the camshaft drive and valvetrain were simplified. (NARA)

it was referred to as the XH-cylinder, because it would be used for the XH-engine. For clarification, this cylinder will be referred to as the XH-cylinder.

The twin-cylinder test engines were being constructed with the ability to run the new-design XH-cylinders. The test engines were being built of steel plating welded together. The twin-engines were to incorporate as many final cylinder parts as possible, to allow the best developmental application for the complete XH-engine.

The Power Plant Laboratory wanted updated engine specifics so it could better forecast aircraft designs to utilize the Studebaker engine. The Lab also recommend a comparison study of a 32-cylinder engine with a 6.5" bore (7,698 in^3 displacement with a 7.25" stroke) and the 24-cylinder engine with an 8.0" bore (8,746 in^3 displacement with a 7.25" stroke).

A three-valve cylinder head design was laid out, but there was very little material left in the center of the head. However, by cocking the valves 5° off the cylinder centerline, the arrangement appeared workable, but it complicated the camshaft arrangement and drive.

Cost proposals for Dynos to test the complete XH-engine had been received: GE quoted $300,000, and Dynamatic quoted $200,000. In addition, the cost to build the test facilities was estimated to be $1,000,000.

Crankshaft Deflection
As a design reference for the complete XH-engine's crankshaft, the deflection of a Jumo 211 crankshaft was evaluated. Also, a Packard 1A-2500's crankshaft was tested. While it may be unrelated, at 40,000 lb, the Packard's crankpins were more rigid than the Jumo's, but the Jumo's crank cheeks were more rigid than the Packard's. Further strain tests on both the crankpins and cheeks indicated the Jumo 211's crankshaft exhibited roughly 2/3 the deflection of the Packard's crankshaft.

Based on the Jumo 211 crankshaft test results, the decision was made to increase the XH-engine's crankshaft main journal and crankpin diameters by .25" in. The main journals were now 5.0" in diameter, and the crankpins were now 4.5" in diameter. The twin-cylinder engines were being modified for this larger crankshaft design.

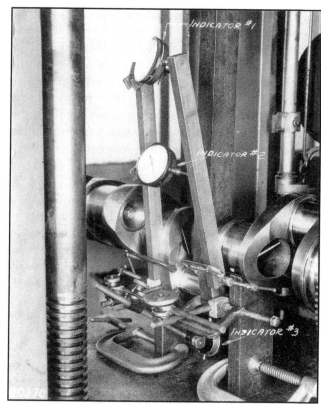

The Packard 1A-2500 V-12 engine crankshaft undergoing deflection tests. (AC)

Jumo 211 Flow Tests
Flow tests on Jumo 211 cylinder heads were compared to the 8.0" cylinder head. The Jumo 211 head had over-head valves with two intake ports, one exhaust port, and a flat combustion chamber. The intake valves on the Jumo 211 made up 24.5% of the cylinder bore area, while the intake ports for the 8.0" cylinder made up 25%. The exhaust ports of the 8.0" cylinder made up 14.9% of the cylinder bore area for the Jumo 211 and 21.2% for the 8.0" cylinder.

Corrected for the difference in valve size, the 8.0" cylinder head had superior intake efficiency at lower lifts, but the Jumo 211 was up to 21% more efficient at higher intake valve lifts. It was found that very little flow interference existed between the two intake ports in the Jumo 211's head. Once corrected for the different valve size, the 8.0" cylinder's exhaust valve flow was found to be 8% more efficient than that of the Jumo 211. The 8.0" cylinder actually had a mass flow 50% greater than the Jumo 211's flow.

The Jumo 211 had a much higher intake rate than exhaust rate; the exhaust flow was only 54.5% of the intake flow. The 8.0" cylinder flow rates were very similar, with the exhaust flowing at 97.5% of the intake.

Propeller Gear Reduction

Propeller gear reduction layouts were under study, and three tentative conclusions had been reached:

1) A planetary reduction in which the drive was through the sun gear, with the internal gear held and the planet carrier driven, appeared to be moderately light compared to some other arrangements. This would give 2.4:1 (.417) reduction.

2) A two-speed gear unit would provide a direct drive (1:1), or a further reduction of 1.4:1 (.712). This would give overall reductions of 2.4:1 (.417) for low engine speed operation and 3.36:1 (.298) for high engine speed operation. The 1.4:1 (.712) reduction, instead of the previous 1.5:1 (.667), permitted reducing the number of planetary pinions from eight to six, and this design was being detailed.

3) The spur gear design for obtaining contra-rotating propeller shafts appeared to be heavier than the bevel gear design.

Propeller Drive

On 17 August, Wright Field responded to Studebaker's June inquiry regarding the location of the propeller drive. Wright Field stated that the main design focus should be on propeller shafts taken from outboard of the engine but on its horizontal centerline, rather than on shafts taken from above or below the engine's centerline. It was acknowledged that this change would necessitate left- and right-hand engines, but the extra effort was considered worthwhile to allow the propeller shaft to pass through the center of the wing spar. Wright Field also requested that development continue on propeller shafts taken from above and below the centerline. It was felt that these arrangements would allow for the greatest number of engine installation options and configurations. The Aircraft Laboratory stated that it was continuing to study installation of the Studebaker engine in very large bombers. The Lab wanted to know the weight of different power take-off (PTO) gear arrangements and the current fuel consumption estimates under a variety of conditions.

September 1944

AF-1 Cylinder Test Procedure

The AF-1 (8.0" bore) engine had completed its performance characteristics tests and had run for 756.25 hours. For these tests, the engine was run with a 7.25" and 8.0"stroke (364.42 in^3 and 402.12 in^3 respectively), both with 6.8:1 and 8.0:1 CR. Tests were done from 1,000 to 2,400 rpm and 25–45 inHg MAP.

Power runs were made at 1,000; 1,200; 1,600; 2,000; and 2,400 rpm with maximum power air/fuel mixtures and best power spark plug advance at 30 inHg MAP. Various intake and exhaust valve timings were used to determine the best over-all power valve timing. With this timing, the intake air tank was raised and lowered to obtain the optimal induction length over the speed range tested. The optimal induction system length was around 41" from the surge tank to the intake valve seat.

With the best valve timing and tank height set, the ideal number and position of spark plugs was investigated. The best results were achieved with four spark plugs: two located toward the exhaust valve and two in the upper, near-center holes. This spark plug configuration was used during all mixture ratio runs. However, it was believed that satisfactory results could be obtained with fewer spark plugs.

AF-1 SFC Results

At 30–35 inHg MAP, a 6–14% gain in SFC was seen from 6.8:1 CR to 8.0:1 CR with the 7.25" stroke, and a 4.5–9% gain was seen with the 8.0" stroke. The best SFC achieved was with the 8.0" stroke and 8.0:1 CR. The 8.0" stroke showed a 3–4% SFC improvement over the 7.25" stroke, but the 8.0" stroke's piston speed was 10.3% higher. The lowest SFC was recorded as .292 lb/hp/hr at 2,400 rpm and 25 inHg MAP, recording an IMEP of 138.

AF-1 with an 8.0" stroke and 8.0:1 CR had a better SFC than AF-2 (6.5" bore) with a 6.325" stroke and 8.0:1 CR. The difference ranged from 8 to 25%, with an average of 19%. With both test engines at a 7.25" stroke (364.42 in^3 and 240.58 in^3 respectively), the 8.0" bore had a 6.5% better SFC. However, detonation was more likely, and this limited test results to under 40 inHg MAP for the 8.0" stroke and 8.0:1 CR configuration.

AF-1 Power Results

The maximum IMEP achieved was 289 psi at 2,400 rpm, 45 inHg, 7.25" stroke, and 6.8 CR. This represented around 319 hp for the 364.42 in^3 cylinder. Because of detonation, the higher CR and stroke configuration was not able to obtain a higher IMEP (timing was retarded to lessen detonation). With an 8.0" stroke (402.12 in^3) and 6.8:1 CR, the maximum IMEP was 277 (338 hp) at 2,400 rpm and 45 inHg MAP. At this power and configuration, SFC was .413

B/s = 1.000

Engine AF-1 8"x8"=402.1 cu.in. 8.0:1 C.R.

	MAX. POWER						MAX. ECONOMY			
R.P.M.	I.M.E.P.	#F/I.H.P.HR.	#A/HR.	#A/CU.FT.	"HG	R.P.M.	I.M.E.P.	#F/I.H.P.HR.	#A/HR.	#A/CU.FT.
1000	135	.371	373	.0535	25	1000	116	.322	379	.0543
1200	140	.375	442	.0529		1200	116	.315	450	.0538
1600	150	.373	632	.0566		1600	124	.300	639	.0571
2000	157	.372	800	.0573		2000	134	.294	815	.0584
2400	164	.350	950	.0567		2400	138	.292	950	.0567
1000	164	.403	462	.0663	30	1000	137	.328	465	.0666
1200	173	.411	551	.0659		1200	144	.319	560	.0669
1600	183	.373	770	.0689		1600	154	.306	780	.0698
2000	190	.362	982	.0703		2000	160	.300	980	.0701
2400	193	.352	1155	.0690		2400	171	.300	1160	.0693
1000	188	.422	553	.0791	35	1000	155	.332	562	.0805
1200	198	.408	672	.0804		1200	162	.328	680	.0811
1600	213	.395	940	.0840		1600	175	.317	945	.0845
2000	227	.370	1180	.0845		2000	181	.308	1200	.0860
2400	230	.350	1370	.0818		2400	191	.300	1380	.0824
1000	208	.438	660	.0945	40	1000	171	.351	660	.0945
1200	218	.432	788	.0940		1200	180	.344	793	.0946
1600	232	.417	1095	.0980		1600	192	.320	1100	.0984
2000	244	.394	1360	.0975		2000	190	.328	1380	.0989
2400	247	.395	1600	.0955		2400	199	.316	1610	.0961

lb/hp/hr. With an 8.0" stroke and an 8.0:1 CR, the maximum IMEP was 247 (301 hp) at 2,400 rpm and 40 inHg MAP, but detonation was experienced. At this power and configuration, SFC was .395 lb/hp/hr.

Up to 2,000 rpm, IMEP increased with the longer stroke but decreased at 2,400 rpm because of deteriorating volumetric efficiency. However, below the detonation limit, IMEP was higher at lower MAP for the 8.0:1 CR than for the 6.8:1 CR. As an example, at 2,000 rpm and 35 inHg MAP, the 7.25" stroke and 6.8 CR combination had an IMEP of 216 (199 hp), while the 8.0" stroke and 8.0 CR combination had an IMEP of 227 (232 hp).

AF-1 Conclusion

Studebaker believed that 24 cylinders of an 8.0" bore operating at 2,300 rpm with a maximum of 40 inHg MAP would fulfill the desired engine requirements.

Detonation issues aside, the test showed a peak of 338 hp. This occurred with the 8.0" stroke, displacing 402.12 in^3. Using these numbers, a 24-cylinder engine of 9,651 in^3 would have an output of around 8,100 hp (indicated). At 90% mechanical efficiency, the engine would produce around 7,290 hp.

The tests required seven cylinders and totaled 754 hours of engine operation. Two pistons were used, one for 730 hours and the second for 24 hours. The AF-1 engine was now being rebuilt with a 7.25" stroke and 8.0:1 CR. Three 8.0" bore cylinders were on hand.

Status of Other Engines

The AF-2 (6.5" bore) engine had a 6.0" stroke crankshaft (199.10 in^3) and 8.0:1 CR. It was undergoing repairs of its cracked crankcase. It had accumulated 772 hours.

The AF-3 (7.5" bore) engine was on test with an 8.0" stroke crankshaft (353.43 in^3) and 8.0:1 CR. Once runs were complete, the 7.5" cylinder would be put in storage, and AF-3 would be modified to run an 8.0" cylinder. The engine had run 367.25 hours.

The AF-4 (7.0" bore) engine had just completed tests with a 7.625" stroke crankshaft (293.44 in^3) and 8.0:1 CR. The 7.0" cylinder would be put in storage, and AF-4 would be modified to run an 8.0" cylinder and a 7.625" stroke (383.27 in^3). This combination was as near to the expected 8.0" x 7.75" (389.56 in^3) of the complete XH-engine as the available parts would allow. The engine was expected back in operation in October. AF-4 had 474 hours of run time.

Twin-cylinder test engine construction was still underway. Dies were released for the construction of the connecting rods and new lighter pistons. The first of the two twin-cylinder engines was expected to be completed by the end of the year.

XH-Engine Development

Tilley stated that the present data indicated an 8.0" bore and a 7.75" stroke as the probable size for the final XH-engine design. Each cylinder would displace 389.56 in^3, and a complete 24-cylinder engine would displace 9,350 in^3. This was the first time a displacement of 9,350 in^3 was mentioned. Fuel economy improved as the bore was increased and was best with a stroke longer than the bore. But given the height limit of the engine, it was not possible to have a longer stroke.

Weight of the latest 8.0" piston had been reduced to 11.25 lb, but it was not known if this piston would stand up to the operating temperatures and pressures of the engine. The 8.0" piston that was currently in use weighed 16 lb. Studebaker requested information from MatCmd on SAE #70-90 spline contra-rotating propeller shafts that were to replace the SAE #50-70 spline shafts then being considered. Studebaker was actively investigating coolant pumps to eliminate air bubbles, as a high degree of aeration occurred under preliminary tests.

An exhaust cooling shroud would need to be .375"-thick to accommodate 2.5–3.0" diameter pipes coming from the cylinder head and 1.0"-thick for a 6.0" diameter collector pipe. These figures were needed for the design of the new cylinder. Its configuration was being worked out in drawings and clay models. The cylinder would have a new head pattern, and a new screwed and shrunk on construction process would be used to attach the head to the barrel. The new cylinder eliminated the four long hold-down bolts that went through the head and all the way into the crankcase. Rather, a conventional mounting flange would be used. The flange-and-stud mounting called for sufficient strength and stability in the screwed and shrunk head attachment so that all the cylinder head loads could be taken through the barrel. The new design was not expected to be ready for testing until early spring 1945.

For the new cylinder, two types of cam gear were being considered. One was a conventional, two-valve head with direct-acting valve gear. The second used the same type of rocker arm, but the valves were set on an angle of approximately 45° to reduce the width of the cam housing. In this case, it was necessary to use a "dumb-bell" link to transmit motion from the rocker to the valve stem. Studies were being done on the geometry needed to reduce the side loads on the valve stem guide. The position of this valve setup looked very promising, and it allowed for a narrower cam box with better oil drainage. The XH-9350 would have two GE torque meters, one mounted to the front of each of the upper cylinder's cam boxes.

Studebaker had only one AAF verification test observer. He spent most of his time at the Aviation Division Aircraft Engine Plant (Chippewa Ave), where the Wright engines were being produced, not at the Motor Machining and Assembly Plant (Building 72 on Sample Street), where the MX-232 program was underway. This caused some delays when the observer was needed during the tear-down of MX-232 test engines. The suggestion was made to have the observer on site at the Sample Street location for two half-days twice a week.

October 1944

Single-Cylinder Test Engines
The AF-1 (8.0" bore) engine had completed tests with an 8.0" stroke (402.12 in^3) and 8.0:1 and 8.7:1 CRs. The 8.7:1 CR was a result of a misassembled cylinder, and tests were done to see how the cylinder tolerated the increased compression. At 2,000 rpm and 30 inHg MAP, 6.8:1 CR had an IMEP of 182; 8.0:1 CR had an IMEP of 190; and 8.7:1 CR had an IMEP of 196. The engine was now running a 7.25" stroke crankshaft (364.42 in^3). AF-1 had been run up to 40 inHg MAP and 2,000 rpm using a cupped piston for tests. The engine had accumulated 830 hours.

Compression Ratio Comparison with AF-1					
8" Bore, 8" Stroke, at 30 inHg MAP					
Comp. Ratio	IMEP at RPM				
	1000	1200	1600	2000	2400
6.8	158	164	176	182	182
8.0	164	173	183	190	193
8.7	171	178	187	196	195

AF-2 (6.5" bore) with a 7.25" stroke (240.58 in^3) and 8.0:1 CR had completed tests with domed and cupped pistons. The engine ran for 122 hours up to 2,400 rpm and 40 inHg MAP to complete the piston tests. There was no appreciable difference in power, fuel consumption, detonation, spark advance, or compression pressure between the two piston types. AF-2 had 772 total hours.

The AF-3 (7.5" bore) engine with an 8.0" stroke (353.43 in^3) had received new camshafts. Upon disassembly, the cam followers were found to be worn and were replaced. AF-3 was finishing oil circulation performance tests, with valve spring dampening tests to follow. The engine would then be switched to an 8.0" cylinder and an 8.0" stroke. The AF-3 engine had run 435 hours.

The AF-4 (7.0" bore) engine had completed performance tests with 6.75" and 7.625" stroke crankshafts (259.77 in^3 and 293.44 in^3 respectively) and with 6.8:1 and 8.0:1 CR. These tests were done

over 1,000–2,400 rpm and 25–45 inHg MAP. The engine had run for 540.5 hours.

SFC increased 3–10% with the larger stroke and higher CR. The best SFC of .300 lb/hp/hr was achieved with the 7.625" stroke and 8.0:1 CR at 25 inHg MAP and 2,400 rpm. SFC of the 7.0" cylinder was 3–5% better than that of the 6.5" cylinder, but it was 5–9 % worse than the 8.0" cylinder. The 8.0" had the best SFC thus far.

A maximum IMEP of 272 was recorded at 2,000 rpm with 45 inHg MAP, a 6.8:1 CR, and a 6.75" stroke. With a 7.625" stroke and 8.0:1 CR, a maximum IMEP of 255 was recorded at 40 inHg MAP and 2,400 rpm. The IMEP was higher at lower MAP for the 8.0:1 CR than for the 6.8:1 CR.

A maximum of 227 hp was achieved with the 7.625" stroke and 8.0:1 CR at 40 inHg MAP and 2,400 rpm. However, detonation limited tests to 40 inHg. With a maximum of 40 inHg MAP, 32 7.0" bore cylinders operating at 2,100 rpm would fulfill the desired 5,000 hp engine requirements. A 32-cylinder engine with a 7.0" bore and 7.625" stroke would displace 9,390 in^3.

The tests required three cylinders and totaled 474 hours. The first cylinder was of the first design and ran for 256 hours. The second and third cylinders were of the second design and ran for 159 and 59 hours respectively. Cylinders two and three suffered cracks in the water jacket, causing coolant to leak into the cylinder. Both were repaired.

It was noted that AF-4 was not capable of running at 2,400 rpm and 45 inHg MAP. Attempts were made, but the engine vibrated so severely that it caused various lines to fracture. Several weeks were spent trying several modifications to allow continued testing, but the results were not successful. Ultimately, runs at 2,400 rpm and 45 inHg MAP were abandoned. Subsequent tear-down of the engine revealed that the 6.75" stroke crankshaft was cracked at the crankpin and cheek intersection on the non-flywheel side. The damage to the crankshaft could not be practically repaired, so no runs were made at an 8.0:1 CR and a 6.75" stroke. The engine was rebuilt with the 7.625" stroke crankshaft to complete testing.

After testing, AF-4 was converted to run an 8.0" cylinder with a 7.625" stroke crankshaft (383.27 in^3). This configuration was now under test and experiencing pre-ignition, which had eroded the exhaust valve. The engine had also overheated, and

The 7.0" cylinder on the AF-4 test engine in October 1944. The 7.0" cylinder was the only cylinder of the MX-232 program that had a direct camshaft drive with a fixed valve duration. (NARA)

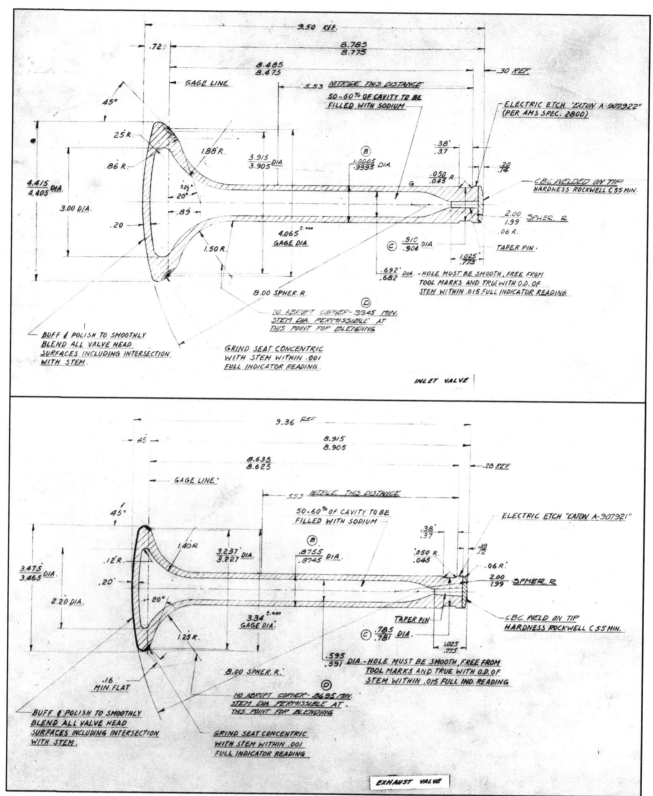

Drawing of the intake valve (top) dated 12 October 1944 and the exhaust valve (bottom) dated 14 October 1944. Although these may not be the final versions of the valves, the drawings do represent the basic valve configuration used in the XH-cylinder. Note that both valves were hollow and cooled by sodium. (NARA)

the cylinder head failed. AF-4 was being repaired and would run again soon.

Twin-Cylinder Test Engines
The crankcase for the first twin-cylinder test engine was on the boring mill having the mains machined.

On 4 October, it was requested that the "Confidential" status of the Studebaker engine (MX-232) be reduced to "Restricted." The security decrease would allow for more program access by subcontractors and overall quicker development. The request was approved on 26 October.

The contra-rotating propeller gear reduction unit with a 2.0:1 reduction and SAE #60-80 shafts had a forecasted weight of 850 lb when using bevel gears. The unit's weight decreased to 780 lb if spur reduction gears with a 2.4:1 reduction were used, again with SAE #60-80 shafts. If SAE #70-90 shafts were used, the unit's weight decreased again, to 732 lb. A 10-pinion reduction gear appeared sufficient to handle 2,200 psi of tooth pressure. The design for the two-speed gear unit was sent to Merz Engineering in Indianapolis, Indiana for analysis.

Test Cylinder Valve Comparison					
Cylinder:	6.5	7.0	7.5	8.0	XH-8.0
Intake Dia	3.15625	3.5	3.75	4.0	3.9375
Exhaust Dia	3.15625	3.5	3.6875	3.6875	3.25
Intake Lift	0.750	0.799	0.865	0.900	0.900
Exhaust Lift	0.750	0.799	0.865	0.900	0.820
Intake Dur	250°	252°	258°	250°	250°
Exhaust Dur	260°	276°	258°	260°	260°

November 1944

As of 1 November, Studebaker had spent $752,807.09 on the MX-232 project and estimated another $1,361,960.00 was needed to complete its contractual obligations. This would amount to a total expense of $2,114,767.09. The original contract value was $1,526,800, leaving Studebaker to pick up the remaining $587,967.09. The largest cost overruns were with the two-speed and contra-rotating gear reduction units (266% over budget), 8.0" single-cylinder test engine (237% over budget), and XH-engine design (217% over budget). Those three items together accounted for $528,083.56 (90%) of the over-budget expenses.

Three test engines were now running the 8.0" bore cylinder: AF-1, AF-3, and AF-4. There was an issue

with the 8.0" cylinder head cracking where the thick section between the valves transitioned to the normal cylinder head section. It was found that the cylinder was defective and that the section was not thick enough; it should have been 1.3" thick but was only 0.9" thick. The casting pattern was updated to avoid this defect in future cylinders.

Tests of the oil jets used to cool the pistons showed that no cooling was needed under 1,200 rpm and 30 inHg MAP. Some oil was needed at 35 inHg MAP, and a considerable flow (2.5 gpm in total) of cooling oil was needed at 40 inHg MAP. Oil flow to the jets would be automatic: above 30 inHg MAP, oil would flow to the jets, but there would be no oil flow under 30 inHg MAP.

A cam lobe and valve spring test rig was set up to observe valve spring surge at various speeds. This rig was built because a number of valve springs had failed during the test program. It was found that the valve springs came into resonance at a number of cam speeds. A harmonic analysis of the cam would be made to see if the issue could be eliminated by changing the cam lobe contour. The rig would be modified to test the angled valve position and rocker arm incorporated in the latest cylinder design. The new XH-cylinder was expected to be ready by February 1945.

Domed and cupped piston tests had been nearly completed. Flat top pistons were now under test, and preliminary results indicated that they would be the best choice. The flat top piston was lighter and gave slightly better performance.

Test Engines
Test engine AF-1 was running with an 8.0" bore, 7.25" stroke (364.42 in³), and 8.0:1 CR. Tests comparing domed and cupped pistons up to 2,400 rpm and 30 inHg MAP had been completed and had taken 93.5 running hours. Both types of pistons showed the same results at 30 inHg MAP, but the cupped piston showed an increased tendency toward detonation, and pre-ignition was encountered above 40 inHg MAP. The detonation and pre-ignition issues resulted in the cupped piston showing a loss in maximum power and economy above 40 inHg MAP. The two pistons exhibited the same explosion pressures up to 2,000 rpm at 40 inHg MAP. Beyond that, the cupped piston showed explosive pressures about 100 psi higher as a result of detonation. Four spark plugs were used for these tests: two in the center position and two toward the exhaust side of the cylinder. Further piston tests

with an 8.0" stroke were scheduled. AF-1 had accumulated 926.5 hours.

The AF-2 engine with a 6.5" bore and 6.0" stroke (199.10 in^3) was not run. The engine had 772 total hours.

The AF-3 engine was configured with an 8.0" bore, 8.0" stroke (402.12 in^3), and 8.0:1 CR. The cylinder was leaking coolant and was being repaired. The engine had accumulated 464.5 hours.

The AF-4 engine was configured with an 8.0" bore, 7.625" stroke (383.27 in^3), and 8.0:1 CR. Pre-ignition issues and coolant temperatures of 300° F had caused the cylinder dome to crack between the valve seats. The cylinder was being repaired. AF-4 had run for 595.25 hours.

The twin-cylinder test engine's crankcase was being assembled. Both of the twin-cylinder test engines would be built to use the new XH-cylinders and were expected to be ready in April 1945.

XH-Engine Development

Preliminary data on the complete XH-9350 engine was given, reporting it to be a 24-cylinder, liquid-cooled, horizontal H engine with upper and lower crankshafts. Combining gears at the front of the engine would join the two crankshafts to a power output shaft. The engine would have an 8.0" bore, 7.75" stroke, and 8.0:1 CR. The engine would be fuel injected and turbosupercharged. It would not have a geared supercharger.

The XH-9350 would weigh 6,400–7,000 lb. The engine's dimensions were given as 40" tall, 90.5" wide, and 101.75" long not including accessories. With induction, the engine was 135.5" long, plus another 102" for the contra-rotating drive gearboxes and shafts. As installed, the combined length of the engine, driveshafts, and gear boxes would be over 20' long.

With two GE CH-5 turbosuperchargers, the engine's takeoff and military power was 5,000 hp at 2,200 rpm, with an estimated critical altitude of 34,000'. The XH-9350's normal power was 4,000 hp at 2,000 rpm, with an estimated critical altitude of 36,500'. Minimum SFC cruise power was given as 1,750 hp at 1,200 rpm to 2,700 hp at 1,750 rpm. Other SFC figures were given as .364 lb/hp/hr at 3,000 hp and 1,800 rpm, and .356 lb/hp/hr at 2,450 hp and 1,600 rpm.

The Propeller Lab recommended a 20' 8" eight-blade, contra-rotating propeller for the engine if it were to be used in the B-36. Design for the contra-rotating gear reduction and two-speed gear unit was almost complete. The propeller shafts were to be SAE #60L-80 splines with a GE strain gauge on the extension shaft. The final propeller gear reduction would be 3.427:1 for takeoff, climb, and military power and 2.4:1 for cruise power. A remote accessory gearbox for all non-engine items would be driven from the contra-rotating gear reduction. Epicycle (planetary) reduction gears were also being examined.

The Linde Air Products Company was working on a proposal for a vapor separator to combat bubbles in the XH-9350's cooling system. Studebaker returned the Jumo 211 engine to Wright Field on 23 November.

December 1944

Test Engines
The AF-1 test engine was waiting on a new 8.0" bore cylinder assembly, which was expected in January 1945. The engine was now running an 8.0" stroke crankshaft (402.12 in^3). It was still being used to test different piston types. The engine had a total of 1,042.5 hours.

The AF-2 engine was running with a 6.5" bore, 6.0" stroke (199.10 in^3), 8.0:1 CR, and a domed piston. The engine was being used to test valve overlap effects on economy and to possibly explain the relatively poor economy of the 6.375" stroke (211.54 in^3) compared to the 7.25" stroke (240.58 in^3). The engine had 844.50 hours.

The performance report for the AF-3 engine with the 7.5" bore cylinder was issued. For testing, AF-3 ran with a 6.75" and 8.0" stroke (259.77 in^3 and 353.43 in^3 respectively) and with a 6.8:1 and 8.0:1 CR. Tests were done over 1,000–2,400 rpm and 25–45 inHg MAP.

AF-3 had issues with detonation and pre-ignition more so than the other engines. Initially, four spark plugs located symmetrically in the head (the two center plugs were not fired) gave the best results with a 6.8:1 CR and were used during all mixture ratio runs. However, the detonation characteristics of this spark plug combination were not as favorable as when the two center plugs were fired alone. During some of the mixture ratio tests with an 8.0:1 CR, it was necessary to run with the two plugs alone to avoid detonation. The 8.0" stroke was slightly more likely to detonate.

The 7.5" AF-3 engine undergoing tests. AF-3 had the lowest run time of the single-cylinder test engines in the MX-232 program. Exhaust from the cylinder was collected in the large manifold on the left. (NARA)

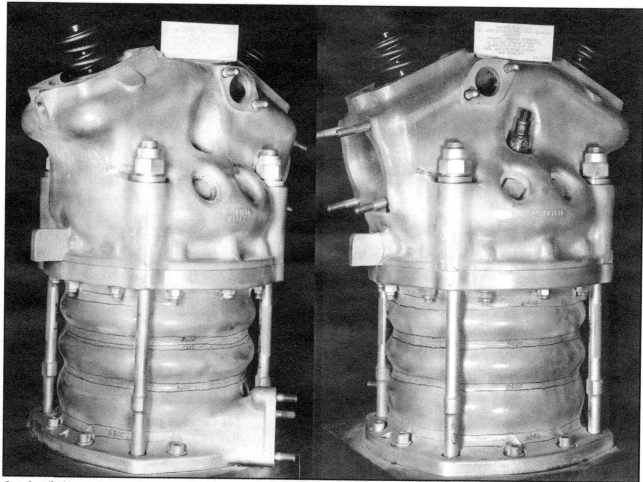

Intake (left) and exhaust (right) sides of the 7.5" cylinder. The photos were taken by ALCOA as the company performed strain tests on the cylinder in December 1944. The markings on the cylinder indicate specific pressure levels encountered in that area. Note the numerous studs joining the cylinder head to the cylinder barrel. (NARA)

With the 6.75" stroke, a SFC gain of 5–10% occurred with the 8.0:1 CR over the 6.8:1 CR. A further 2.5–4% gain in SFC occurred with the 8.0" stroke compared to the 6.75" stroke. However, mean piston speed was 18.5% higher. The best SFC was .310 lb/hp/hr and was achieved at 2,000 rpm, 25 inHg MAP, and with an 8.0:1 CR.

A maximum IMEP of 280 was recorded at 2,000 rpm with 45 inHg, a 6.75" stroke, and a 6.8:1 CR. An IMEP of 253 was the highest recorded for the 8.0" stroke and 8.0:1 CR. This was reached at 40 inHg MAP and 2,000 rpm, with higher MAP limited because of detonation. The 8.0:1 CR registered higher IMEP at lower MAP compared to the 6.8:1 CR. A peak of 260 hp indicated was recorded, meaning a 24-cylinder engine would have 6,245 hp indicated or 5,620 hp with a 90% mechanical efficiency.

Studebaker reported that with 40 inHg MAP and 8.0:1 CR, 24 cylinders of a 7.5" bore operating at 2,400 rpm would fulfill the desired engine requirements. A 24-cylinder engine with a 7.5" bore and 8.0" stroke would displace 8,482 in^3. Three cylinders were required to complete the tests, and the engine ran for 460 hours. The first cylinder was of the first design and ran for 112 hours. The second and third cylinders were of the second design and ran for 118 and 230 hours respectively. Cylinder one failed because of cracks in the water jacket of the head. Cylinder two was destroyed when the intake valve was struck by the piston, most likely a result of the intake valve separating from the stem. Cylinder three was operational.

Once tests were concluded, AF-3 was converted to run an 8.0" cylinder. The engine was then used for piston cooling oil flow tests, which were stopped because of cylinder head failures. The engine was being rebuilt with a 7.25" stroke crankshaft and a special cylinder that was 1.3" shorter than the regular cylinders. The shorter cylinder was for testing a short connecting rod

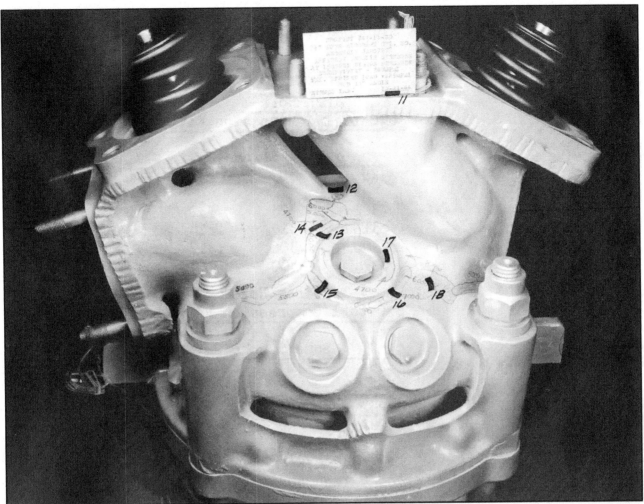

The 7.5" cylinder with its water jacket removed. Note the passageways that allowed coolant to flow up from the barrel and into the head. The cylinder was used during ALCOA's strain tests. (NARA)

11.75" in length (center-to-center length from crankpin to piston pin) rather than the normal 14.75". AF-3 had accumulated 499 hours.

The AF-4 engine was being assembled with a new 8.0" cylinder and a 7.625" stroke crankshaft (383.27 in³). Testing the effect of coolant temperature on performance required three cylinder assemblies and two pistons. The third cylinder was of the short-barrel type. Parts were being made to adapt the shorter, 8.0" cylinder for use with the 7.625" stroke crankshaft because all other 8.0" bore cylinders had failed. When ready, it would be used to test oil circulation to the piston. The engine had run for 691 hours.

To prevent the failures that had occurred in testing, the 8.0" cylinder's head design was revised with thicker metal between the spark plugs and valves. Flat top pistons, like the one planned for the final engine, had been designed and were being built. The piston would be used with the new XH-cylinder head that had the

combustion chamber flush with the inside diameter of the cylinder barrel rather than the outside diameter.

Design of the twin-cylinder engine was nearly complete, and cylinder construction would begin soon. The crankcase, crankshaft, gears, and other parts were being built. It was anticipated that the first twin-cylinder engine would be running in late April 1945.

XH-Engine Development
Complete XH-engine and final cylinder design were nearing completion. The new XH-cylinder would weigh 71 lb, or 1,704 lb total for a complete 24-cylinder XH-engine. Current weight estimates were 5,400 lb for the bare engine, 550 lb (240 lb was clutch mechanism) for the two-speed gearbox, 700 lb for the contra-rotating gear reduction unit, and 10 lb per foot for the propeller shaft.

Engine accessories would be driven from the front of the engine, and their drive layout was nearing

THE STUDEBAKER CORPORATION

Minimum Specific Fuel Consumption - Pounds/I.H.P.Hr.

8-Inch Bore
8.0 to 1 Compression Ratio

Tank Air Press.*	Bore/Stroke Ratio = 1.000				
	25	30	35	40	Avg.
1000 r.p.m.	.322	.328	.332	.351	.333
1200 "	.315	.319	.328	.344	.326
1600 "	.300	.306	.317	.320	.311
2000 "	.294	.300	.308	.328	.308

7-1/2-Inch Bore
8.0 to 1 Compression Ratio

Tank Air Press.*	Bore/Stroke Ratio = .938				
	25	30	35	40	Avg.
1000 r.p.m.	.345	.333	.345	.349	.343
1200 "	.343	.328	.332	.359	.341
1600 "	.320	.321	.330	.321	.323
2000 "	.310	.312	.320	.321	.316

7-Inch Bore
8.0 to 1 Compression Ratio

Tank Air Press.*	Bore/Stroke Ratio = .918				
	25	30	35	40	Avg.
1000 r.p.m.	.382	.348	.342	.392	.366
1200 "	.348	.340	.341	.346	.344
1600 "	.333	.322	.323	.389	.342
2000 "	.319	.313	.324	.317	.318

6-1/2-Inch Bore
8.0 to 1 Compression Ratio

Tank Air Press.*	Bore/Stroke Ratio = .897				
	25	30	35	40	Avg.
1000 r.p.m.	.382	.366	.362	----	.370
1200 "	.368	.342	.361	.350	.355
1600 "	.347	.332	.328	.377	.346
2000 "	.310	.333	.330	.360	.333

* Intake tank air pressure in inches of mercury dry air pressure.

Cylinder fuel consumption comparison from a report dated 4 December 1944. (NARA)

completion. This included the layout of the spur combining gears for the two crankshafts and the drives for camshafts, magnetos, starter, and front-end oil scavenge pump. The rear accessory drive layout was completed, which included provisions for a rear-end power connection to a crankshaft and the drives for the fuel injectors, fuel pumps, pressure oil pump, and rear scavenge oil pump. Layout for a drive from the contra-rotating gear reduction for a PTO accessory drive box was also complete. The two-speed gear unit could also have a right-angle PTO drive. The generator would need to run at 7,600 rpm, which would be 3.8 times engine speed at 2,000 rpm.

The 10-pinion spur gear reduction and contra-rotating drive layout was anticipated for January 1945, with construction to follow. Two two-speed gear units were being built and were expected in June 1945. Bendix was working on fuel injectors. The complete 24-cylinder unit with a speed density control, air valve, and discharge nozzles was estimated to weigh 85 lb.

The coolant pump was finished, and a pump test rig was being built. Scintilla Magneto, GE, and P.R. Mallory were working on proposals for the high-altitude ignition system. The design for the valve and cam drive unit was complete. The final cam outline was awaiting single-cylinder tests.

Contract items 1–4 (single-cylinder test engines) were completed. Items 5 and 6 (twin-cylinder test engines) were being constructed. Items 7 (full-scale engine design), 10 (coolant pump), and 11 (ignition system) would be completed soon. One portion of item 8 (two-speed propeller gear drive) was being built, with completion about three months off. The other portion (dual-rotation gear reduction) was not completely designed. Item 9 (fuel injection) had a 12–18 month promise, which was in line for the complete XH-engine build time frame. Items 12, 13, and 14 (accessories section, multi-cylinder valve and cam drive unit, and oil pump) would be delayed, as they were not fully designed and were partially dependent on single-cylinder tests.

XH-Engine Cost and Procurement

On 27 December, an engine purchase meeting was held in Gen. Franklin O. Carroll's office at Wright Field, Ohio. Representing Studebaker were Tilley, Cole, and Clark. Representing the AAF were Gen. Carroll, Gen. Laurence C. Craigie (who was the first US service member to fly a jet), Col. Howard Z. Bogert, Col. Ralph L. Wassell, Col. Pearl H. Robey,

and Opie Chenoweth (Chief Civilian Engineer of the Power Plant Laboratory).

Studebaker stated that at the time of the original contract, it was not interested in making money from the project. John W. Schwinn, Procurement Executive of the Aircraft Production Section, had originally wanted a cost-plus-fee contract because of the nature of the project. However, Chenoweth was opposed and felt a fixed-price contract would be more efficient. Studebaker went along with the fixed-price contract covering the engine program but had no experience with this type of contract.

Currently, Studebaker estimated it would spend around $587,967.09 over the amount for which the company had been contracted. The contracted amount was $1,526,800, and Studebaker estimated $2,114,767.09 would be spent to complete the contract. Studebaker was fully prepared to take the loss and fulfill its contractual obligations but would, of course, like to be reimbursed. The next phase was to build complete XH-engines, and Studebaker wanted to see the project through to completion but on a cost-plus-fee contract. Cole said the new contract could be cost-plus $1.00 fee because Studebaker was not interested in making a profit on the engine.

The AAF did not want six engines, as optioned in the original contract, but it did want three engines. Studebaker estimated it would cost $4.4 million for the three engines and an additional $2 million for test facilities and equipment. Gen. Carroll said the AAF did not want Studebaker or any other contractor losing money. The AAF would find a way to reimburse Studebaker for the money spent, convert the contract to cost-plus-fee, and cover the total project cost at an estimated $8–9 million. Gen. Carroll said that he wanted to move forward with an order for three engines.

Col. Robey asked Tilley if the project justified the cost. Tilley replied that it all depended on whether or not the AAF wanted the engine. Col. Robey clarified that he wanted to know if Tilley and Studebaker thought the project was going to be successful and were interested in building such an engine. Tilley said he felt the project would be successful in producing the type of engine the AAF had requested and that Studebaker would want to complete the project. Gen. Carroll asked Cole if Studebaker would be interested in manufacturing the engine. Cole said that Studebaker would be extremely interested in producing the engine from an engineering standpoint, but Studebaker was primarily interested in manufacturing cars and trucks and would not be interested in manufacturing such an engine or entering the aircraft engine market. Cole said that Harold S. Vance, Studebaker's Chairman of the Board, would make the final decision.

Gen. Carroll stated that he felt Studebaker would have an interest in producing the engine on a commercial basis. Cole and Tilley stated they felt the engine had no commercial possibilities at the present time. Tilley pointed out that it was a long-range engine and that the airlines could not afford to transport the fuel required to make the long flight. The airlines would rely on smaller aircraft making shorter flights. Tilley said the engine should be considered solely for military applications.

Col. Robey asked if the project was a one-man operation. Cole and Tilley explained that this was not the case and that if something happened to Tilley, the project would continue. Clark said that Studebaker would fulfill all contractual obligations regardless of the war situation. If the complete XH-engine was being built and the war ended, the company would proceed as the AAF wished. However, whether or not Studebaker would be interested in building additional engines for the AAF or for another corporation after development was complete was a decision that would need to be made at that time.

Gen. Carroll wanted to move forward with the project and wanted to know what Studebaker's attitude toward the engine would be if the war ended in 1945, before the engine was built. Cole responded, again, that Studebaker would continue and complete the project. Gen. Carroll pressed to expedite the project to completion as soon as possible. Col. Robey asked if there was anything the AAF could do to help expedite the project, whether it be material, manpower, or anything else. Tilley suggested that they could use some specialized draftsmen. Col. Robey said that he would see if he could find additional draftsmen for Studebaker. The AAF seemed very enthusiastic about the project and eager to proceed with the construction of complete XH-engines.

Studebaker was to cut off the old fixed-price contract and be re-contracted on a cost-plus-fee contract. Studebaker would seek reimbursement for the money it had spent in excess of the original contract. It was decided that both Studebaker and the Engineering Division would collect the facts and present them to the proper officials who could legally facilitate changes to the contract.

January 1945

At the beginning of 1945, the government started its effort to reimburse Studebaker for the cost overruns the company had accrued on the MX-232 project. In addition, the AAF set up a streamlined billing process to aid with any cost audits of claims made by Studebaker.

Single-Cylinder Test Engines

The AF-1 engine was configured with an 8.0" stroke (402.12 in^3) and 8.0:1 CR. It was waiting on a new head to continue piston tests and would then begin fuel injection tests. AF-1 had accumulated 1,043 hours.

The AF-2 engine was equipped with a 6.5" cylinder, 6.0" stroke (199.10 in^3), and 8.0:1 CR. Mixture runs were made to test the difference in cylinder performance with a fuel nozzle placed 2.5", 6.0", and 14.0" above the intake port flange. The 6.0" position had been used for all prior tests with this engine. Most tests results were within 2%, and all results were within experimentation error. Fuel bar height as tested had no effect on maximum power or SFC. The tests took 24 operating hours. AF-2 was currently being used to determine the best spark plug number and locations. The engine had accumulated 925.75 hours.

The AF-3 engine was running the short 8.0" cylinder, a 7.25" stroke crankshaft (364.42 in^3), an 8.0:1 CR (one report lists 7.9:1 CR), and using a domed piston. The short and long connecting rod comparison tests took 44 operating hours, and runs were made up to 2,400 rpm and 30 inHg MAP. It was determined that there was no real difference in engine power between the short and long connecting rods. All results were within the range of experimentation error, mainly a 2% or less difference in maximum power, fuel consumption, friction pressure, explosion pressure, exhaust temperatures, and compression pressures. The engine had accumulated 532.75 hours.

The AF-4 engine running an 8.0" cylinder, 7.625" stroke (383.27 in^3), and 8:1 CR was used for mixture runs to compare a Bendix fuel injection system with a carburetor. The fuel injection used 30° bulb-type injectors that worked best in the inlet spark plug location on the flywheel side of the engine. The engine's domed piston was causing pre-ignition and was replaced with a cupped piston. Examination of the piston's welded dome revealed a loose flap of metal which may have created a hot spot resulting in the pre-ignition. The engine was being set up with a new cylinder for cupped versus domed versus flat piston tests. The head of the new cylinder blended to the inner diameter of the cylinder barrel. AF-4 had accumulated 782.75 total hours.

The Aluminum Company of America (ALCOA) had now made a forging die for the 8.0" piston that would cut down on the costs involved to machine pistons. Previously, the pistons were machined from aluminum blanks. Three new pistons were on their way to Studebaker's plant (these were not made with the new ALCOA die). The new XH-cylinder design would not be ready for runs until late April. The XH-cylinder had angled valves, new cam followers, and a screwed and shrunk on cylinder head.

XH-Engine Development

Scintilla and GE were working on ignition systems for the complete XH-engine, with the latter exploring a high-tension system and a high-frequency, low-tension system. These systems were to be tested running six, four, and two spark plugs.

Torsional vibration studies of the XH-9350 engine and its remotely connected two-speed and contra-rotating gear reduction units were underway. Because of the two crankshafts and various propeller shafts, the harmonic dampers needed to be carefully worked out in order to avoid trouble due to excessive amplitudes in the operating range of the engine. Attempts to construct simple dummy systems to anticipate the vibrations for the complete XH-engine had not been successful. It was felt that a more complex test was needed, as the vibration analysis would be very beneficial to the development of a complete XH-engine.

The PTO drive, generator drive, and hydraulic and vacuum pumps were all to be driven off the rear of the contra-rotating gear reduction unit. This configuration would save weight over using a remote box and would keep all accessories within the diameter of the contra-rotating gear reduction unit.

February 1945

XH-9350-1 Specifications

A report issued on 1 February 1945 gave the specifics for the Studebaker XH-9350-1 engine. It listed the engine as a liquid-cooled, flat H with extension shafts and provisions for a two-speed drive of contra-rotating propellers. Takeoff and altitude power was obtained

with turbosuperchargers, which could possibly be used for compound operation (no descriptive information has been found regarding turbo-compounding). The engine was designed to operate up to an altitude of 40,000' with low SFC over a wide power range to enable long-range operations of over 30 hours non-stop. The engine's configuration allowed submerged installation for either pusher or tractor configurations.

The basic engine was forecasted to weigh 5,357 lb, with an additional 120 lb for fuel injection equipment (injector, speed density control unit, air valve, 24 discharge nozzles, and piping), 100 lb for an ignition system, 730 lb for the contra-rotating gear reduction and associated drives, 560 lb for the two-speed gear unit, and 3 lb for accessory drive covers, giving a total weight of 6,870 lb. This weight figure did not include propeller extension shafts, and no mention was made of the turbosuperchargers.

The XH-9350-1's takeoff and military power was given as 5,000 hp at 2,200 rpm with .50 lb/hp/hr SFC from sea level to 25,000' critical altitude. Normal power and SFC was given as follows:

- 4,000 hp at 2,000 rpm with .48 lb/hp/hr SFC at sea level up to 30,000',
- 3,000 hp at 1,600 rpm with .37 lb/hp/hr SFC at 30,000', and
- 1,000 hp at 900 rpm with .38 lb/hp/hr SFC at 30,000'.

The engine's oil consumption was not to exceed .025 lb/hp/hr, regardless of the power setting. Oil temperature would be 185° F, and oil would flow at 580 lb/min with 22,000 btu (520 hp) heat rejection. The two-speed gear unit would have an oil flow of 87 lb/min and 920 btu (22 hp). The contra-rotating gear reduction would have an oil flow of 290 lb/min with 3,080 btu (73 hp). The engine's coolant would be a 70/30 mix of ethylene glycol and water. For normal operation, coolant would be at 250° F and flow at 640 gpm, rejecting 47,000 btu (1,110 hp) per minute.

For military power, engine oil temp increased to 203° F with a 640 lb/min flow and 27,000 btu (646 hp) heat rejection. The two-speed gear unit's flow increased to 120 lb/min and 1,270 btu (30 hp). The contra-rotating gear reduction oil flow increased to 400 lb/min and 4,250 btu (100 hp). The engine's coolant had the same temperature, but the flow increased to 700 gpm, and heat rejection increased to 56,000 btu (1,320 hp) per minute.

The XH-9350-1 engine had a length of 102" without a starter and 109" with a starter. The contra-rotating gear reduction had a length of 65", and the two-speed gear unit was 37" long. The engine was 80" wide or 105" wide with intake and exhaust manifolds. The engine's height was 36" without sump and 40" with sump.

The propeller shafts would be SAE #60L-80 splines. When viewed from the non-propeller end, the inner shaft rotated counter-clockwise, and the outer shaft rotated clockwise. The contra-rotating gear reduction had a fixed 2.4:1 reduction. Ratios for the two-speed gear reduction were 1:1 and 1.428:1. When the two-speed and contra-rotating units were combined, the engine had a 2.4:1 reduction for cruise conditions and a 3.427:1 reduction for takeoff and military power. For tractor installations, about 9.5' of extension shafting would connect the engine to the remote gear units.

A Bendix fuel injection system would be used unless a better alternative was found. An electric starter would allow operation down to -22° F. Accessories for normal engine operation would be on the engine. All others accessories, (generators, vacuum pump, hydraulic pump, etc.) would be on the contra-rotating gear reduction drive. Driving the accessories from the gear reduction allowed for a steadier drive speed based on propeller rpm. Direct engine speed (before the two-speed unit) would vary in the different phases of flight.

The spark plugs would be fired by low-tension magnetos. The XH-9350's preliminary firing order, based on vibration studies, was as follows: Bottom 1 Left, Top 6 Right, B4R, T2L, B5L, T3R, B1R, T6L, B3L, T5R, B5R, T3L, B6L, T1R, B3R, T5L, B2L, T4R, B6R, T1L, B4L, T2R, B2R, and T4L. The No. 1 cylinders were at the non-propeller end of the engine. The upper crankshaft would rotate counter-clockwise, and the lower crankshaft would rotate clockwise. The upper right cylinder would fire 30° degrees behind the lower left cylinder. Given the configuration of the engine, all orders of vibration were cancelled out except for the 12th.

To determine spark plugs and maintenance access, Studebaker was building mockups of the XH-9350's cylinder assemblies, cam housings, and various manifolds and piping.

Test Engines
The AF-1 engine was configured with an 8.0" cylinder, 8.0" stroke (402.12 in³), and 8.0:1 CR. Mixture runs to compare Bendix fuel injection with a standard carb were continuing. The cylinder was removed twice before the 2,000 rpm test run to correct sticking of the top piston ring. The ring's side clearance on the domed piston was increased, and the ring was chamfered. The second (from the top) piston ring broke after 20.25 hours, and the top ring broke after 45.5 hours. A cupped piston was installed to keep the engine in use while the domed piston was repaired. The engine had run 1,135.25 hours.

The AF-2 engine was being used for valve timing tests with a 6.5" cylinder, 6.0" stroke (199.10 in³), and 8.0:1 CR. Valve timing for maximum power did not coincide with timing for the best SFC. As valve overlap was increased, air/fuel was lost through the exhaust port—especially when the intake pressure was greater than the exhaust backpressure. With valve overlap, increasing exhaust backpressure increased economy. Tests were run because of the high fuel consumption noted when AF-2 had a 6.375" stroke (211.54 in³) crankshaft. The high consumption occurred because the 6.375" stroke tests were for maximum power and used a valve overlap that caused higher fuel consumption.

Later in the month, AF-2 was involved in mixture runs with various spark plug combinations. The engine started to run rough, and air bubbles were found in the coolant. The cylinder was removed, but no cracks were found in the water jacket. The engine was rebuilt with a new cylinder. Power runs with various valve timing and mixture runs were made. All six spark plugs were in place for these tests. The engine had accumulated 1,020.25 hours.

The AF-3 engine had an 8.0" cylinder, 7.25" stroke (364.42 in³), and 8.0:1 CR. It was waiting for a new domed piston so that the comparison runs using the 14.75" and 11.75" connecting rod lengths could be finished. The engine had run a total of 543 hours.

The AF-4 engine had an 8.0" cylinder, 7.625" stroke (383.27 in³), and 8.0:1 CR. Mixture runs to compare injection with carburation were still underway. Valve spring clatter was occurring above 2,350 rpm, and new springs were installed. Testing of the cupped piston was concluded, and a domed piston was installed. This was the same piston that had experienced pre-ignition issues the previous month. The piston had an aluminum band welded around its top, and the piston ring grooves were cut into this band. The original weld had rough spots on the top which were believed to have caused the pre-ignition. The piston was sent to ALCOA's Cleveland, Ohio plant and was re-welded.

Tests were underway when a connecting rod bearing seized at 2,000 rpm. The bearing had run 127.25 hours and seized because of a clogged oil hole. The AF-4 engine had run a total of 844 hours.

The twin-cylinder test engine had been fully designed, detailed, and released. Parts, including cylinders and various spare parts, were being made for two of the twin-cylinder test engines. Installation drawings of the twin-cylinder engine were started to determine the intake and exhaust flow and what needed to be changed in the test room, since it was set up for single-cylinder test operations. Machining started on various parts, such as connecting rods and cylinder barrels. One crankcase had been machined, and the other was 75% done. Two crankshafts were finished except for machining their splines and grinding their journals. One pair of camshafts was completed, and a second pair was undergoing machine work. The cylinder head pattern was expected to be done at the end of the month. The pattern would then be at the foundry by mid-March, and a casting was expected by April. Valves and bearings were expected by the end of March. The test fixture for the twin-cylinder valve drive mechanism was designed, detailed, and released for manufacture. The testing machine was designed for the cam housing group intended to serve one complete bank of the full-scale engine. The first twin-cylinder was expected to be done in May and the second in June.

XH-Engine Development
Studebaker and the AAF met in mid-February at the Studebaker plant to discuss the project's progress. Tilley and Clark represented Studebaker, and J. G. Blackwood of Air Technical Service Command represented the AAF. Both parties wanted a cost-plus-fee contract. Three single-cylinder engines were currently running (AF-1, AF-2, and AF-4). Tests were being run on different piston shapes and cylinder head shapes. One style of cylinder head joined the outside of the barrel, leaving a small recess. The other head style joined flush with the inside diameter of the barrel. The recessed cylinder head detonated earlier than the flush cylinder head. Detonation also occurred at a lower IMEP with the recessed head and cupped piston. The three test engines were predicted to be in operation until June to complete the current test programs.

Five 8.0" cylinder heads with increased material thickness at the upper spark plug bosses had been machined, three with their dome combustion chamber flush with outer diameter of the cylinder barrel, and two flush with the inner diameter of the barrel (cylinder bore). Three of the assemblies were complete, leaving one of each type waiting for cylinder barrels and final assembly. The 8.0" flat top piston machined from billet had been completed. Two 8.0" flat top pistons for the single-cylinder test engines were being made from die forgings.

The first 8.0" domed piston was reworked several times to use wider rings in an effort to keep the ring grooves in good condition. The original 3/32" grooves were widened, first to 1/8" and then to 5/32" for the top groove, and to 1/8" for the other two compression ring grooves. The wider rings were not as effective at preventing blow-by as the original 3/32" ring. The oil ring below the piston pin was not effective at controlling oil consumption, especially at high speed. Piston scuffing was now occurring daily. After two years and 892 hours of power operation, the first domed piston was reworked. The ring belt was cut away, and a new aluminum ring was shrunk on and welded to the piston crown. New ring groves were cut into the piston, and the oil control ring was relocated above the piston pin.

The second 8.0" domed piston failed by breaking out a piece of the ring land between the top and second rings. This failure occurred after 247 hours of operation. An aluminum band was shrink-fitted and pinned to the upper outer diameter of the piston, and then new first and second ring grooves were cut. This repair failed after 10 hours of running. A second repair was made by cutting away all the ring grooves and shrinking on and welding another band that had a groove around the top of the piston. After machining, the weld was found to be porous. Test operations showed the detonation margin was much lower than previously experienced with this piston. The piston was sent to ALCOA, where the old weld was cut out, and the same ring was re-welded to the piston. The piston was then machined to specifications and reinstalled in the engine, after which it worked satisfactorily.

The 8.0" cupped piston used in a cylinder head flush with the barrel's outer diameter showed a tendency to detonate more than the domed piston. It also had a lower detonation rating compared to the domed piston. However, the cupped piston used in a cylinder head flush with the cylinder barrel's inner diameter had shown an improvement over the domed piston. Piston tests were ongoing and expected to be completed in March.

For the single-cylinder test engines, adapters and drive couplings were designed, detailed, and released for the drive of a fuel injector from the ignition timer drive. There was not enough room for the fuel injector at its original location. In addition, an 8.0" flat top piston was designed, detailed, and released. The piston would be made from die forgings to allow its use in the 8.0" cylinders, with the combustion chamber wall flush with the cylinder bore. The cylinder would have an 8.0:1 CR and a 7.625" stroke.

The first XH-cylinder assemblies were expected in May and would be used to build up the first twin-cylinder test engine and one single-cylinder test engine. A test fixture for stress testing of the XH-cylinder was designed, and it was recommended that ALCOA do the tests. A wooden model of the new cylinder head was detailed and released.

Valve spring dampers to reduce spring surge were on test. They were installed in two test engines to see if spring life increased. The dampers eliminated the low-speed surge period and reduced the high-speed surge periods and amplitudes.

Front and rear accessory drive sections were still being designed. All accessories other than those needed for the engine were to be on the contra-rotating gear reduction unit. Layouts were completed for the contra-rotating gear reduction unit, which included drives for the generator, PTO, hydraulic pump, vacuum pump, and propeller governor. Per Blackwood, the drive ratio of the generator and PTO to the propeller shafts would be 12.83:1. Preliminary releases were made for principal forging and patterns and for manufacturing studies. Complete release for manufacture was expected in March.

Couplings for extension shafts were sketched, and discussions for angled drives were underway. The focus was on angled drives of the Rzeppa and Weiss types. The two-speed gear unit would use a wrapping spring clutch built by L.G.S. Spring Clutches, Incorporated (LGS) out of Indianapolis, Indiana. A test fixture for the two-speed gear unit's LGS spring clutches was designed, detailed, checked, and released. Studebaker was awaiting the arrival of sample LGS spring clutches, which were expected at the end of March. Two complete assemblies would be ready by June. Material was being procured for two contra-rotating gear reduction units.

The dyno used for coolant pump tests could only go to 2,500 rpm. Delivery of a high-speed dyno was delayed several months. In the meantime, a Studebaker car transmission was set up to allow the pump to turn faster.

In late February, Studebaker's engine development contract with the AAF was changed to cost-plus-fee basis retro-active to 31 December 1944.

March 1945

In March, the Power Plant Laboratory requested the estimated cost and delivery dates for three XH-9350 engines. This was to include designs, parts, and the testing required for run-in calibration. It also included performance checks and investigations on manifolding, torsional vibrations, spark advance, valve timing, turbosupercharging, fuel injection, and heat rejection tests on engine coolant and oil. All of the tests needed to be completed and all the information complied prior to a 50-hour development test. The Power Plant Laboratory requested the estimated number of test hours needed to accomplish this work and the estimated cost for necessary test facilities. The Lab also requested the estimated designs, parts, and testing required to accomplish a 50-hour military test.

Test Engines
The AF-1 engine with an 8.0" cylinder, 8.0" stroke (402.12 in^3), and 8.0:1 CR was being used for Bendix fuel injector and spark plug location tests. The injector was tried in every spark plug hole, with spark plugs in the other five positions. The same was done with just two spark plugs. During the tests, the main bearing was found to be worn. It had 1,000 hours and was replaced with the same type of bearing. Once the tests were complete, tests on different injector nozzle angles were begun. During these tests, the engine began to run rough, and it was found that the exhaust valve was not seating. The valve was lapped in for further testing. The AF-1 engine had 1,232 hours.

The AF-2 engine with a 6.5" cylinder, 6.0" stroke (199.10 in^3), and 8.0:1 CR was being used to test the effects of the number and position of spark plugs. All previous tests had been completed with six spark plugs. Separate tests were run with all six plugs, four lower plugs, and two vertical center plugs with one lower exhaust and one intake side plug. Compared to six plugs, the tests showed lower power at 30 inHg MAP but more power at 35 inHg MAP. SFC went up more at 30 inHg MAP than at 35 inHg MAP, but the difference was very small. Using only two spark plugs reduced power and economy typically by 1% but by no more that 2%. The best location for two spark plugs was in the upper, center position. With two plugs, the engine ran rough at lower air/fuel ratios (less than 0.050). During the tests, the engine was being motored at 2,400 rpm by the dyno when a connecting rod bearing seized. The bearing had 800 hours of power operation. It was being replaced with a new bearing, and AF-2 would soon be operational. The engine had 1024.5 total hours.

AF-3 had an 8.0" cylinder, 7.25" stroke (364.42 in³), and 8.0:1 CR. The engine had been rebuilt with a new domed piston for continuation of spark plug location and combination tests. The engine was run up to 2,200 rpm and 30 inHg MAP with just one spark plug, installed in the flywheel side upper location. The test was repeated with the plug in the five other locations: flywheel side exhaust, flywheel side intake, camshaft drive side upper, camshaft drive side exhaust, and camshaft drive side intake. The domed piston was removed after the tests and would be installed in AF-4 for detonation studies of different pistons. AF-3 had 585.5 total hours.

The AF-4 engine had an 8.0" cylinder, 7.625" stroke (383.27 in³), and 8.0:1 CR. The engine was being used for piston comparison studies when a connecting rod with 52.75 hours seized. A flat spot was ground next to the oil hole on the crankpin to increase oil flow to the bearing. Tests on the domed piston were completed, and a flat top piston was installed. Heavy detonation occurred at 1,200 rpm and 35 inHg MAP. The cylinder was removed, and the cooling oil jets were adjusted. The jets were directed to the middle portion of the piston, on either side of the piston pin, because the piston was thinnest at these two places. When using the domed piston, the jets were directed to the four areas on either side of the piston pin, between the piston wall and the piston pin boss. During inspection, it was noted that there was aluminum pick-up on the piston pin and that the piston pin was tight in both the piston and in the connecting rod bushing. A new bushing was installed and pinned in position in the connecting rod. After the runs were complete, detonation investigation runs were made.

The domed piston was reinstalled for detonation runs. It was noted that less oil was required to cool the domed piston and that the piston was less prone to detonation when there was no oil cooling. The flat top piston was then reinstalled, and the oil-cooling jets were directed to the four pockets on the underside of the piston. During the run-in, the balance drive idler shaft broke, and excessive backlash was noted at the crankshaft to cam driving gear. One spline on the cam-drive end of the crankshaft was found to be badly worn. The crankshaft was removed from the engine for reworking. AF-4 had accumulated 899.25 hours.

Two complete twin-cylinder test engine crankcases were ready and waiting on internal components. It was expected that a complete two-cylinder test engine would be assembled by 15 April.

XH-Cylinder

Air flow tests were conducted on a wooden mockup of the new 8.0" bore XH-cylinder head. The intake port was 4.3% less efficient (6.2% less flow) than the third design cylinder head, but the difference was expected to be recovered with straightening vanes in the intake approach orifice. The exhaust port was 2.6% more efficient than the third design cylinder head. The tests were done with and without straightening vanes in the approach orifice.

The valve seat inner diameters for the new XH-cylinder head were 3 15/16" for intake and 3.25" for exhaust. The third design head had a 4.0" intake and a 3 11/16" exhaust. All seats were at a 45° angle. The straightening vanes were two thin, flat plates that divided the approach orifice into quarters. With an 18" run to the intake port with straightening vanes, efficiency was 1.8% less than the third design head. For exhaust, the flow rate was down 18%, but efficiency was up 2.7%.

Tests were done with vanes on the valve head. It was thought that these vanes could reduce interference with separate streams of exhaust from opposite sides of the valve and would increase overall flow. Tests showed the vanes did not have the desired effect and that they reduced the flow by up to 6.5%.

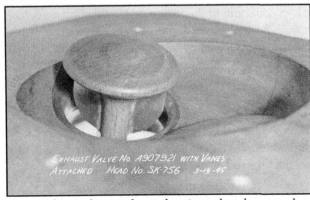

A wooden valve and combustion chamber mockup were used to test vanes added to the intake valve. Tests indicated the vanes did not improve air flow. (NARA)

129

XH-Engine Development

Studebaker was building full-scale mockups of the XH-9350's cylinder assemblies, cam housings, and various manifolds and piping to accommodate spark plugs and maintenance access. Some issues existed with the intake flanges not lining up perfectly, and modifications were planned.

Studies were underway to determine the best crankcase design for a complete engine. A method to properly support the cylinder hold-down flange had not been chosen. The flange was rigid at the attachment to the main bearing diaphragms, but the support was very poor between the rows of cylinders and at the lower side, where an oil sump was formed. A clay model would be made as soon as a design was found that appeared to be sufficiently rigid.

Layout of the crankshaft combining gears was being prepared. The gear configuration needed adequate support to resist excessive movement from thrust loads. Different expansion rates would occur between the crankshaft and the crankcase and needed to be considered. The cooling system setup was being tested to determine pump performance. Air bubbles were occurring in the system. To combat radiator pressure drop, a Linde Air Products system to maintain coolant in an expansion tank from 0 to 50,000' was being studied. Maximum coolant temp was revised to 120° C (248° F).

April 1945

Single-Cylinder Test Engines

The AF-1 engine with an 8.0" cylinder, 8.0" stroke (402.12 in³), and 8.0:1 CR was involved in fuel injection nozzle angle tests. A run at 2,200 rpm and 30 inHg MAP had to be terminated because of detonation. Examination of the cylinder revealed a damp condition in the intake port indicating a coolant leak. The cylinder assembly was removed from the engine and replaced by a new one with new valves and springs. The engine was back in service, but detonation occurred again, and the test was abandoned.

The cylinder jacket was given a Bakelite treatment to seal the intake port. The domed piston and its connecting rod were replaced by the cupped piston and its connecting rod. The domed piston was being used in a different engine. The best fuel injector cut-off was at 70° ATC, but 15° on either side affected economy by less than 2%. The injector in any spark plug hole varied maximum power and economy by

less than 3%. The best result was with the injector positioned in the intake spark plug hole on the flywheel side of the engine. However, the performance was about the same as with the intake pipe injection. Injector angle tests of 30°, 45°, 60°, and 90° were underway. AF-1 had accumulated 1296.75 total hours.

The AF-2 (6.5" cylinder) engine was stopped when the big end rod bearing failed the previous month after 800 hours under power. The engine was dismantled and placed in storage. The flywheel and cam drive were modified for use with the twin-cylinder engine. The connecting rod was being reground and refitted with a new big end bearing. Once the modifications were finished, the connecting rod would be placed in storage. Like the previous month, the engine had a total of 1,024.5 hours.

The AF-3 engine was running with an 8.0" cylinder, 7.25" stroke (364.42 in³), and 8.0:1 CR. The engine was testing a new forged flat top piston and undergoing spark plug number and position tests. During a run at 2,200 rpm, the oil return screen was clogged after 15 minutes. A piston pin lock ring had come off the flywheel side, broken into several pieces, and then shot peened both sides of the piston, which caused the piston rings to stick. The damaged parts were repaired, the cylinder bore honed, and the lock rings replaced by rings reworked to have 10–12 lb compression instead of 3–4 lb, as the original ring. Various lock rings were developed and tested to find one suitable for use in the engine. Time on the new piston and lock rings before the failure was 31 hours, almost all at 1,200 rpm. Spark plug position tests continued. The engine had 632.75 hours.

The AF-4 engine with an 8.0" bore, 7.625" stroke (383.27 in³), and 8.0:1 CR had just been repaired following the issues encountered the previous month. After further investigation, the detonation that occurred at 1,200 rpm and 35 inHg with the flat top piston was attributed to a shift in valve timing caused by a broken cam drive gear fixed support shaft. That failure was believed to have been caused by timing gear spline wear on the crankshaft, which permitted axial movement of the timing gear to the gear on the shaft that broke. These gears were helical. The shaft was replaced, and the crankshaft splines were repaired by chrome plating and regrinding. Testing was stopped for a month while the repairs were made. The big end connecting rod bearing failed after 200 hours of power operation, some of which was at 2,400 rpm. It was replaced by a used bearing with a central groove, which failed after 8.75 hours. The bearing failures were attributed to a loss of bolt stretch. The connecting rod cap bolts were replaced with new bolts with thicker heads. AF-4 would be used to test valve timing when assembled. AF-4 had run 912 hours.

For the single-cylinder engines, machining was started on a 7.75" stroke crankshaft using one of the two spare hammer forgings obtained for the twin-cylinder engines. Machining was also underway on the cylinder adapter, cam drive shafts, and spacers needed to permit use of the new XH-cylinder on the single-cylinder test engines. The final bore and stroke configuration of the XH-engine would be simulated when these components came together.

Valve spring damper tests were continued. Three engines were operating with valve spring dampers, and no valve spring failures had occurred. The first damper had run 150 hours in AF-1 when several fingers of the outer damper were found to be broken, but the damper was still effective. The dampers had been reworked and heat-treated several times. The metallurgy report indicated a more suitable steel could be used. The valve springs now had 235 hours of running time and were still intact. The other two sets of springs and dampers had run 10.5 and 76 hours respectively without failure.

Machining was completed on modified cam drive idler shafts and new connecting rod bolts with slots that did not extend into the cone seat of the bolt head. The cam drive idler shafts were revised with increased shoulder fillets to correct for failures that occurred in the test engines. Other work was done to maintain the three test engines that were then in service. This included the repair of the timing gear splines on the 7.625" crankshaft. But this work was delayed due to a strike at the Gear Grinding Company in Detroit, Michigan.

Twin-Cylinder Test Engines

For the twin-cylinder test engines, assembly drawings for the cylinder and engine were completed and released. Layouts were made, detailed, and released of the intake and exhaust piping, including surge tanks. A new ignition timer shaft was designed, detailed, and released. This permitted the use of one ignition timer per engine, when there were two spark plugs per cylinder, with 180–540° firing instead of two four-breaker units per engine. An XH-cylinder assembly with a head shrink ring and without a cylinder barrel jacket was released, constructed, and shipped to ALCOA for stress analysis.

Most parts for assembling one of the two twin-cylinder engines were completed. There were some delays in getting the crankshaft bearings. Assembly of the first twin-cylinder engine was started on 25 April and was waiting on the remaining parts. Assembly of the second twin-cylinder test engine was expected to start in May, and all the parts were expected to be available by then.

XH-Cylinder Tests

Machining was started on the XH-cylinder valve and cam drive test housing and on a fixture to test one valve drive and its springs. The test cylinder's cam and other parts were made. Flow tests of a wooden model of the new XH-cylinder ports and valves were completed. Air flow tests of the cast XH-cylinder were being started.

Tests of the XH-cylinder's steel coolant jacket upper shrink band were made. This band was .125" thick and had a .020" interface fit with a 10.7" diameter. The band was placed on an aluminum dummy head for tests. It showed no leakage with 0–25 psi and 25–250° F with ethylene glycol. A pull of 9,600 lb axially was required to separate the joint at room temperature. An earlier test at 0.015" interference showed seepage.

Another series of leakage tests using a dummy cylinder assembly were conducted. The tests used jackets and a cylinder barrel of the XH-type. First, straight ethylene glycol was used at 0–50 psi and heated to 70, 140, 190, and 250° F. A 50/50 water ethylene glycol solution was then used for tests at -40° F. Slight seepage occurred at the lower (jacket to cylinder barrel) joint, which decreased to only dampness with successive testing. No leak was observable at the -40° F tests. The shrink (or interference) fit at this joint was approximately .007" instead of .010" as planned. Examination of the joint after removal suggested just a thin line of contact area was occurring rather than a wide band of contact area. The interference fit was increased to a minimum of .014", and corrections to the stop were made to avoid the possibility of line contact in the final cylinder assembly. The jacket was .060" sheet steel, which expanded about .005" on the diameter when the gauge pressure was at 50 psi.

Despite numerous delays caused by various factors, both single-cylinder and twin-cylinder engines were expected to be running with the new XH-cylinders in May.

The XH-cylinder undergoing strain tests at ALCOA in May 1945. The XH-cylinder was normally attached to the crankcase via 24 studs. Note the strain gauges affixed to the cylinder. The exhaust port is on the left side of the cylinder. (NARA)

MX-232 Program Cylinder Comparison					
	6.5"	**7.0"**	**7.5"**	**Original-8.0"**	**XH-8.0"**
Compression Ratio (:1)	6.16/8.0	6.8/8.0	6.8/8.0	6.8/7.5/8.0/8.7	8.0
Cylinder Barrel Length (in)				14.53125	13.00
Diameter of Hold-Down Flange (in)				13.245	10.06
Cylinder Jacket Thickness (in)	0.030	0.030	0.030	0.030	0.018
Con Rod Length (center to center, in)				14.75	13.00
Con Rod Small End Width (in)				2.56	2.50
Crankpin Diameter (in)	4.00	4.00	4.00/4.75	4.00/4.75	4.50
Crankshaft Main Bearings		Two SAE 222 Spherical Rollers			
Crank Rotation Viewed From Flywheel		Counterclockwise			
Reciprocating Weight (lb)	16.90	20.61	21.62	31.67	24.73
Rotating Weight (lb)	18.40	18.40	20.77	20.74	20.58
Piston Pin Diameter (in)	2.00	2.25	2.13	2.75	2.50
Piston Pin Bearing Length (in)	5.75	5.56	5.86	6.81	6.00
Piston Boss Bearing Area (2, sq in)				8.24	7.60
Piston Head Type	Dome	Cup	Cup	Dome	Flat
Piston Skirt Bearing Length (in)	3.13	3.44		4.25	3.50
Piston Skirt Bearing Area (each side, sq in)	15.60	33.00	37.75	28.70	15.50
Piston Compression Ring Thickness (3, in)			0.09375		
Piston Oil Ring Thickness (2, in)			0.125		
Weight of Piston (no rings, lb)	7.68	9.52	11.05	15.91	11.72
Weight of Piston Rings (5, lb)	0.60	0.69	0.79	0.91	0.91
Weight of Piston Pin (lb)	3.76	4.11	4.37	7.60	4.20
Weight of Piston Lock Rings (2, lb)	0.04	0.06	0.05	0.12	0.02
Weight of Complete Piston Assem. (lb)	12.08	14.38	16.26	24.54	16.85
Weight of Complete Cylinder Assem. (lb)				83 (approx)	70.50
Cylinder Height (in)				26.60	21.75
Cylinder Hold Down Bolt Load (lb)	19,100	22,600	26,500	33,200	
Valve Seat Inside Diameter Intake (in)	3.15	3.50	3.74	4.00	3.9375
Valve Seat Inside Diameter Exhaust (in)	3.15	5.50	3.69	3.6875	3.25
Valve Seat Angle	45	45	45	45	45
Valve Lift Intake (in)	0.75	0.64	0.865	0.90	0.90
Valve Lift Exhaust (in)	0.75	0.64	0.865	0.90	0.82
Valve Spring Force Intake Open (lb)	708	521	504	1220	955-995
Valve Spring Force Intake Closed (lb)	450	193	162	440	185-225
Valve Spring Force Exhaust Open (lb)	708	521	504	1220	640-680
Valve Spring Force Exhaust Closed (lb)	450	193	162	440	140-180
Cam Rotation Viewed From Flywheel		Clockwise			

XH-Engine Development

A clay mockup of XH-9350's cylinder crankcase was started. A full-scale mockup of several cylinders with sections of cam housings and piping was continued for accessibility studies. Estimates were prepared for transverse and torsional deflections of the cam housing and for camshaft loadings and deflections. Preliminary detail drawings of the crankshafts were made. A report on crankshaft deflections was completed. Analysis work continued on torsional characteristics of the main power system, including vibration damper requirements. Layouts were nearly complete for the combining gears, camshaft drives, and accessory drives. Layouts of the rear-end group drives were started. Work continued on weight calculations, deflection estimates, and load and stress analyses of various parts, all focused on minimizing the engine's weight.

Installation drawings in 1/4 scale were made for the two-speed unit and for the contra-rotating propeller gear reduction unit. Patterns were completed, and some of the larger castings were received for the contra-rotating gear reduction unit and 2.4:1 reduction gear. The propeller drive shafts were forged, rough machined, heat-treated, magniflux inspected, and awaiting finish machining. Most of the material for the unfinished parts was on hand, with the reaming steel awaiting hammer forging. Design layout for a test fixture for the contra-rotating gear reduction and the two-speed gear unit were in process, along with a design report and weight estimates.

The first sample LGS spring clutches for the two-speed drive unit were lost to excessive distortion during heat-treating. Completion of the next set was promised for the week of 23 April. Work on the remaining parts for the two two-speed units was about 30% complete, and all parts were expected in June. A shift rod requiring longitudinal motion to select the reduction gear ratio would be provided on the two-speed gear unit.

The AC Spark Plug Division of General Motors Corporation was contacted regarding a high-frequency ignition system for the XH-9350. It recommended an engine-speed drive for the company's spark generator unit instead of the half-speed drive required by Scintilla and GE. Inquiries were sent out for equipment to run on the single- and twin-cylinder test engines.

Estimates for oil pump capacities were made, and layouts of the pumps were started. The coolant pump was changed from a belt drive to a transmission gear. Considerable work had been required to remove air from the coolant. After all other leaks had been nearly stopped, it was found that the de-aerator actually added air to the coolant system. Runs at 100° F to compare discharge head versus flow were made using water at various pump speeds. A 700 gpm flow occurred at 21 psi discharge at 2,800 rpm. Runs under altitude conditions were not yet possible due to air in the system. Work was being done to solve the aeration issue.

May 1945

Test Engines

All engines were now running 8.0" bore cylinders and 8.0:1 CR.

The AF-1 engine had an 8.0" stroke (402.12 in^3) and was being used to determine the cause of the detonation previously reported. Runs were made at 2,200 rpm and 30 inHg MAP with water pressurized to 20 psi used as the coolant. No detonation occurred. The same test was run but with ethylene glycol as the coolant, and light to heavy detonation resulted. After the runs, the cylinder was inspected, and several spots were found in the intake port where the coolant had leaked into the cylinder. The cylinder was honed out, and new piston rings were installed. Water was again used as coolant at 20 psi. AF-1 was now used for fuel injector location and nozzle tests. Once the injector nozzle tests were completed, new tests were begun with the coolant outlet temperature at 170° F to test detonation. After these tests, the cylinder head and barrel were replaced with a new head and a used barrel. The engine had 1,374 hours.

The AF-3 engine had a 7.25" stroke (364.42 in^3) and was used for spark plug position and combination tests. The engine had accumulated 736.75 hours.

The AF-4 had a 7.625" stroke (383.27 in^3) and was used for piston shape comparisons. While testing the flat top piston, the connecting rod bearing failed after 287.75 hours on the bearing. A new bearing of the same type was installed and testing resumed.

Performance tests of various combustion chambers with different piston types took 114.5 hours of engine operation. The tests were run up to 2,000 rpm at 40 inHg MAP and included mixture runs comparing compression pressure and explosion pressure. The results of the three piston types (domed, cupped, and flat) and the two combustion chamber types (flush

The XH-cylinder at ALCOA undergoing strain tests. The intake side of the cylinder is on the left, and the exhaust side is on the right. The centerline of where the camshaft would be is marked "CSℓ" atop the cylinder. (NARA)

outer diameter and flush inner diameter) were basically the same. Maximum power results for all the combinations showed very little variation (less than .5%). Best economy results showed slightly more variation, but it was still negligible. At 40 inHg MAP, the cupped piston did not experience the detonation issues with the flush inner diameter combustion chamber like it did with the flush outer diameter. The cupped piston was all around better with the flush inner diameter combustion chamber head. The dome of the domed piston had an 11.04" radius, and the cup of the cupped piston had a 7.0" radius. AF-4 was now running valve timing exploration tests and had 986.25 total hours.

The AF-5 twin-cylinder test engine used 8.0" cylinders with a 7.75" stroke crankshaft and 8.0:1 CR. Its displacement was 779.12 in³. All parts of the engine had been completed, and the engine was being assembled. Testing was scheduled to begin in early June.

XH-Cylinder Tests

Flow tests on two 8.0" XH-cylinder heads (#2 and #5) were completed. Results for the individual head castings were within 1% of each other and within 1% of the wooden mockup. ALCOA completed cylinder

stress tests on the new XH-cylinder. A crack emerged between 1,000 and 1,200 lb. The cause appeared to be from a core shift during casting, resulting in a thin spot about .125" thick. Another stress point was found around the spark plug bosses. Studebaker felt it could alter the head design slightly to eliminate this concentration. The new XH-cylinder design was expected to be running on single-cylinder test engines around mid-June.

XH-Engine Development

Preliminary tests on the coolant pump for the XH-9350 were completed and indicated the system would satisfy the design requirements. However, air leaking into the system at altitude conditions continued to be an unsolved problem. Studebaker was using a vapor separator to eliminate air from the coolant system. The National Carbon Company issued a report covering a number of coolant pump tests. Studebaker thought the report would be instrumental in the setup of a XH-9350 coolant pump test program.

Clay and wooden model mockups were being used to finalize the design of the XH-9350's crankcase. The test fixture for the rocker arms and valve actuating mechanism was designed and fabricated. This rig would be in operation soon and would test the wear

A photograph dated 13 June 1945 shows the two-XH-cylinders and internal components for the twin-cylinder test engine. Note the flat top pistons, the blade connecting rod (left), and the fork connecting rod (right). (BL)

characteristics of the proposed spherical slipper necessary for transmitting rocker motion to the inclined valve stem.

Combining gears at the front of the engine would connect upper and lower crankshafts. The gears would include one starter drive, two magneto drives, a front oil scavenge pump drive, four camshaft drives, and the main power shaft from the engine to the propeller reduction gearing. There was concern that heat generated by high thrust loads would cause unequal expansion of the gear case and crankcase assemblies.

The rear accessory drive included main oil pressure and scavenging pumps, a coolant pump, and an electric tachometer drive. The contra-rotating gear reduction unit had provisions for the generator, PTO, hydraulic and vacuum pump drives, as well as oil pressure and scavenge pumps to service the gear unit.

The layout for the back-to-back test proposed for the contra-rotating propeller gear reduction unit was examined. In this setup, the inner and outer shafts would be coupled. To provide a load on the reduction gears, a torque shaft would be installed that passed through the reduction gear sets for the inner and outer shafts. The torque shaft would connect the two reduction gear sets via their input shafts. The torque shaft would be twisted the required amount and locked in position to provide the loading on the entire gear train. After applying the load, only the torque required to overcome friction would be required to conduct a full-load test on the reduction gears. This configuration was expected to nearly simulate the operating conditions on an actual aircraft engine. Previous experience with reduction gear tests that were pre-loaded before starting the test equipment indicated extremely high break-away torque loads resulting in initial damage to the bearings and gear teeth. One precautionary measure was recommended: incorporate a device for applying the load after the gear was in operation. This would avoid a lubrication film breakdown when the gear speed passed through the critical lubrication range of the bearings and gear teeth.

In a letter dated 5 May 1945, the Curtiss-Wright Corporation stated that a suitable ground-test propeller for the H-9350 engine would be a SAE #60-80 spline adjustable test propeller incorporating two three-blade contra-rotating propellers. The outboard propeller would have a diameter of 15' 6" and a weight of 515 lb. The inboard propeller would have a diameter of 15' 9" and a weight of 535 lb. Attaching parts would weigh 39 lb, giving a total installed weight of 1,089 lb. These propellers would enable ground tests to be made in one of Studebaker's test cells for the R-1820 engine.

Studebaker revised the cost of three XH-9350-1 engines to $4,303,000. This was only a $75,000 reduction from the estimate made in August 1944. It was recommended that action be taken to ensure Government inspection personnel would be available to inspect and observe future aspects of the MX-232/XH-9350 project. The plant inspection personnel were mainly at the Aviation Division Aircraft Engine Plant (Chippewa Ave) and involved in the production of Wright R-1820s. They would come to the Motor Machining and Assembly Plant (Sample Street) to observe aspects of XH-9350 development as needed. R-1820 production was to stop, and the Aviation Division Aircraft Engine Plant would be closed down around 1 July. The inspection personnel would be transferred to other locations. It was important that some were reassigned to the Motor Machining and Assembly Plant for continuing work on the XH-9350.

June 1945

Single-Cylinder Test Engines
The AF-1 engine had an 8.0" stroke (402.12 in^3) and was fitted with a new cylinder head and barrel. Only the cupped piston and its connecting rod were available at the time. It was noted that this piston did not give the same level of performance with a 7.625" stroke as the other pistons, and detonation was more common. Running 100% ethylene glycol, heavy detonation occurred at 1,600 rpm and 30 inHg MAP. A spacer was installed between the cylinder and test engine to lower the CR to 7.5:1 and eliminate the detonation. Fuel injection tests were completed and revealed the injector's location in any of the six spark plug holes and that the nozzle angle did not affect power or economy. However, there was a very slight performance advantage with cylinder injection versus a spray bar into the intake pipe.

AF-1 was rebuilt with a flat top piston and 8.0:1 CR. Mixture runs up to 2,200 rpm and 40 inHg were planned with the best injector and with standard carburation to compare the performance characteristics of each. However, during a run at 2,200 rpm and 38 inHg MAP, the exhaust valve's outer spring and outer spring damper failed. The cause was under investigation. The engine had 1,464.25 hours.

The AF-3 engine, with its 7.25" stroke (364.42 in^3), completed spark plug combination and location tests. Two spark plugs demonstrated no appreciable loss of power or economy compared to four spark plugs, provided the two spark plugs were in the correct locations. The performance of a single spark plug was also dependent on location, and there was a definite but minor loss of power and economy.

Four spark plugs had little variation (within 1%) at all locations. The best combination was with two vertical and two exhaust spark plugs, but all combinations were tried. At 30 inHg MAP, maximum IMEP was 166 at 1,200 rpm and 189 at 2,200 rpm. The SFC was

.340 lb/hp/hr at 1,200 rpm and .315 lb/hp/hr at 2,200 rpm. Pre-ignition and detonation issues limited testing to 2,200 rpm and 40 inHg MAP.

The performance of the engine with two spark plugs varied by location of the plugs. The worst placement was two spark plugs on the flywheel side, which resulted in decreased performance. The best placement was two spark plugs in the vertical, center position, which resulted in no appreciable loss in power or economy. In the center, vertical location, two spark plugs gave a 0.0–1.6% reduction in power and a 0.0–1.3% reduction in economy. At 30 inHg MAP, maximum IMEP was 166 at 1,200 rpm and 186 at 2,200 rpm. The best SFC was .340 lb/hp/hr at 1,200 rpm and .319 lb/hp/hr at 2,200 rpm. Using just two spark plugs required 5° more spark advance over four spark plugs. Pre-ignition and detonation issues limited testing to 2,200 rpm and 38 inHg MAP.

A comparison of four spark plugs and two spark plugs at 38 inHg MAP showed that two spark plugs had a 1.4% reduction in IMEP at 1,200 rpm and a 1.3% reduction at 2,200 rpm. For economy, two spark plugs had a 1.7% reduction in SFC at 1,200 rpm and a 0.6% improvement at 2,200 rpm.

Six runs were made with a single spark plug, one run for each spark plug location. As with two spark plugs, the performance of the engine depended on the location of the single spark plug. The exhaust spark plug position on the flywheel side was slightly better overall than any other position. Individual test results for this position were never the best nor the worst, which gave it the overall edge. In the exhaust/flywheel location, one spark plug gave a 1.2–4.3% reduction in power and a 2.3–4.1% reduction in economy. At 30 inHg MAP, maximum IMEP was 164 at 1,200 rpm and 181 at 2,200 rpm. The best SFC was .348 lb/hp/hr at 1,200 rpm and .328 lb/hp/hr at 2,200 rpm. One spark plug needed 10° more spark advance over two plugs and 15° over four plugs. Pre-ignition and detonation issues limited testing to 2,200 rpm and 30 inHg MAP.

AF-3 was next used for a spark plug comparison between the then used Champion RP-43S plug and a new AC 439-W plug. The AC plug was a bit hotter, but nearly identical results were obtained with both sets of plugs. However, detonation occurred with AC 439-W plugs but was absent with Champion RP-43S plugs.

Following the spark plug comparison tests, a spark plug hole reducer was tested. The reducer was an

Spark Plug Comparison with AF-3				
8.0" Bore, 7.25" Stroke, 8.0:1 CR, at 30 inHg MAP				
No. of	IMEP at RPM		SFC at RPM	
Plugs	1200	2200	1200	2200
Six	175	193	0.331	0.315
Four	166	189	0.340	0.315
Two	166	186	0.340	0.319
One	164	181	0.348	0.328

aluminum button with a 1/8" orifice which was screwed and staked into the spark plug hole from the combustion chamber side of the head. The spark plug was screwed within 1/16" of the reducer, forming a small cavity around the electrode, with the orifice forming a passage into the combustion chamber. Tests were conducted with only one spark plug firing at 1,200 rpm and 30 inHg MAP. There was a slight increase in IMEP (less than 1%) with the reducer but a corresponding decrease in fuel economy (less than 1%).

Once tests were concluded, the AF-3 engine was placed in storage. The engine had run for 750 hours.

AF-4 completed valve exploration tests using a 7.625" stroke (383.27 in^3) and manifold fuel injection. A cylinder head that blended into the inside diameter of the cylinder barrel was used. The best performance was with the intake valve opening at 25° BTC and closing at 45° ABC (a 250° open duration) and with the exhaust opening at 60° BBC and closing at 20° ATC (a 260° open duration). This combination gave good or better overall performance than any other combination of valve timing. Overall, four intake cams and three exhaust cams were tested through runs up to 30 inHg MAP and 2,200 rpm. The best IMEP achieved at 1,200 rpm was 184, and the best IMEP at 2,200 rpm was 200. The best SFC achieved at 1,200 was .313 lb/hp/hr, and the best SFC at 2,200 rpm was .300 lb/hp/hr.

During a spark plug check, the cylinder head broke off at the intake valve spring boss. This engine was rebuilt with the same XH-cylinder and valve gear used on the twin-cylinder engine so that performance characteristics of the XH-type cylinder and valve gear could be directly compared with those of the original-type cylinder.

Fuel injection tests were completed, and the results mirrored those for AF-1 from the previous month. There was no major difference in injector position,

The AF-6 twin-cylinder test engine in operation. The light-colored barrels on each side of the engine were intake surge tanks that ensured the cylinders were fully charged with pressurized air during their intake stroke. (BL)

angle, or nozzle type. There was slightly higher IMEP with cylinder injection than with manifold injection, but there was no difference in SFC.

The Bendix injector had a spring-loaded poppet valve. Six different closing timings (14° BTC - 190° ATC) were investigated at 1,200 rpm. Three different closing timings (55°, 70°, and 85° ATC) were investigated at 2,200 rpm. Four different injector nozzle spray angles (30°, 45°, 60°, and 90°) were tested. Four different plunger diameters (1/2", 9/16", 5/8", and 41/64") were tested. To deliver the required fuel into the cylinder, the injector's duty cycle increased as the plunger diameter decreased. Test runs were conducted with two and four spark plugs. The best injector combination was a fuel cut-off of 70° ATC, a 30° spray nozzle, and a 5/8" plunger. The best IMEP achieved at 1,200 rpm was 172, and the best at 2,200 rpm was 191. The best SFC achieved at 1,200 rpm was .330 lb/hp/hr, and the best at 2,200 rpm was .304 lb/hp/hr. AF-4 had accumulated 1022 hours.

On average, the newest cylinder heads were now outlasting the previous design. It was reported that heads 12, 13, and 14 had accumulated 369, 122, and 202 hours respectively without a failure. Failures on heads 5, 6, 7, and 8 had occurred at 92.5, 244, 92.5, and 333.5 hours. A 7.75" stroke crankshaft was redesigned to incorporate a cross hole (two outlets) in the crankpin. It was expected that this crankshaft would be completed in July. Valve spring dampers were credited with preventing valve spring failures. Springs in one engine had over 450 hours without a failure. However, the dampers did experience some wear.

For the single-cylinder engines, redesigned valve spring dampers for the older cylinders were detailed and released. Designs were also released and machining begun to rework the domed piston to incorporate a 2.25" diameter piston pin and the corresponding changes to the small end of the connecting rod.

Twin-Cylinder Test Engines

The AF-5 twin-cylinder engine (779.12 in³) was assembled. Its 8.0" bore, 7.75" stroke, and 8.0:1 CR were all representative of the XH-9350's cylinder configuration. Motoring of the engine was started on 22 June, with half hour runs at 600; 700; 800; 900; 1,000; and 1,100 rpm. After three hours of motoring, the right side intake valve roller seized on the roller shaft. Both cams and rocker arm assemblies were removed from the engine. It was found that the cams and rollers were scored for both the left and right cylinder's intake and for the right cylinder's exhaust. In addition, the roller shaft for the left cylinder's intake and both of the right cylinder's rocker arms were scored.

The scored cam and rollers of the AF-5 twin-cylinder test engine. (NARA)

The trouble was apparently started by foreign material leaving the oil distribution hole in the roller shafts. These shafts were flattened longitudinally at the oil hole, and the inner diameter of the rollers were lapped to give a minimum of .003" diametrical clearance. The changes would increase oil flow to the valve train and allow any debris to flow out. New cam followers were modified to include an oil distribution channel to also clear debris. The cams were replaced, and the scuffed cams were reground. The rollers and shafts were also replaced. The same engine run-in was repeated, and the new parts were found to be in satisfactory condition.

Power runs were then conducted up to 1,350 rpm without any issues. Runs up to 2,200 rpm commenced. While running under power at 1,600 rpm, the front main bearing seized to the crankshaft. AF-5 had run 3.25 hours under power.

The AF-6 twin-cylinder engine was being built up. It was identical to AF-5.

Various minor components of the twin-cylinder test engine were designed and released. And some other components, such as snap rings to retain the piston pins and alternative valve lifters, were drawn-up as possible replacements if issues were encountered with the ones in service. The delay in assembling the first twin-cylinder engine was a result of difficulty determining the crankshaft counterweights required. The crankshaft, with counterweights, was delivered on 1 June. Most of the parts for the second engine were on hand, and its assembly was begun.

XH-Engine Development

On 2 June, a request was issued to Studebaker to transfer installation drawings of the XH-9350-1 engine, two-speed propeller gearbox, and the contra-rotating gear reduction unit to Stuart Edleson of the Bell Aircraft Corporation. Studebaker sent the drawings to Bell and also to the Power Plant Laboratory on 17 August.

A meeting was held between Bendix and Studebaker that established the theoretical fuel injector cut-off at 70° ATC on the intake stroke for best power and economy. A 30° spray injector nozzle with 7/16"-20 threads was selected. The selected injector plunger was 5/8" in diameter with a 1/2" stroke. This injector had a capacity of 140 lb of fuel/hr at 1,100 pump rpm. Calculations indicated the complete XH-engine would require 104 lb of fuel/hr/cylinder.

Bendix made a design for a 24-cylinder injector pump, and a meeting was held to discuss designing a combination speed density control unit and fuel transfer pump which would be located on the rear accessory section of the XH-9350 engine. Further work was on hold until results were known of single-cylinder tests that were underway. The American Bosch Corporation reported that it would not be able to work on the Studebaker project anytime soon.

XH-Cylinder

Parts that enabled the XH-cylinder to be installed on the single-cylinder test engines were designed, released, and constructed. These parts would be installed once tests were completed using the older cylinders. Air flow tests of the new cylinder head were completed. The previous month, it was reported that a new XH-cylinder cracked at 1,000 to 1,200 psi during stress testing by ALCOA. It was determined that the crack was pre-existing and most likely a result of the water quench during heat-treatment.

A cam and roller comparison between the 8.0" XH-cylinder and a Wright R-1820 Cyclone cylinder was made. At 2,400 rpm, the XH-cylinder's camshaft was at 1,200 rpm. At 2,500 rpm, the Cyclone's cam ring was at 313 rpm. Even though the cam speed was roughly four times higher on the XH-cylinder, the linear velocity of the roller radius was about 1/2: 684 fpm on the XH-cylinder and 1,171 fpm on the Cyclone cylinder.

XH-Engine Development
Work on the clay crankcase model of the XH-9350 engine continued and incorporated various minor changes suggested by Wright Field Representatives who had viewed it. Studies continued for torsional characteristics of the complete engine including camshafts, gear units, extension shafts, and propellers. Torsional analysis and load diagrams for the camshaft drive system were started. Models of a section of the full-scale camshaft housing were made and installed on a partial engine mockup. A test fixture for the new design valve drive had been completed, and tests began in June.

Work on the two-speed propeller unit was 70% complete. The remaining parts, including the LGS spring clutch, were expected mid-July. Design work for the contra-rotating propeller gear reduction unit continued. This unit's weight was estimated to be 779 lb with 60L-80 shaft ends. Despite the use of a magnesium housing, the weight was up 49 lb from the February estimate. Machining on the gear reduction unit would begin once parts for the two-speed unit were completed.

A weight analysis for the crankshaft combining gear and front-end accessory drive unit indicated an estimated 360 lb with an aluminum housing. If a magnesium housing were used, the weight would be reduced by 35 lb. Detailing of this unit was started. The rear accessory drives were still in the layout phase.

Preliminarily turbosupercharger performance calculations were done for an H-9350 engine at 25,000' cruise altitude. With exhaust pressure equal to intake pressure, the calculations indicated a 5% improvement in minimum SFC with 65% turbine efficiency and a 10% improvement with 80% turbine efficiency. With exhaust pressure 10 inHg in excess of intake pressure, there would be a 10% improvement in

SFC at 65% turbine efficiently and a 16% improvement at 80% turbine efficiency. These estimates were for high cruise power and diminished as the power decreased. GE indicated that turbine efficiencies might be between 70 and 75% if the turbo-compressor speeds were held between 16,000 and 18,000 rpm. More precise estimates were to be calculated.

In a document written in late June (but not dated) by Blackwood of MatCmd, the cost of three complete XH-engines was reduced to $3,904,000 (a $399,000 reduction from the previous month's estimate). The original contract would be amended to include the three XH-9350-1 engines. It was noted that the uniquely large bore of the engine would most likely result in further delays in developing a complete engine. These costs did not include test facilities, which were estimated at $2,002,050. It was believed that the test facilities and the engines would both take about 18 months to complete. An A-1-A priority level was requested for the engine, and the estimated date of completion was 1 March 1947. The total cost of the project was forecasted as $6,833,965.87. Again, this value did not include the $2,002,050 for test facilities and equipment.

July 1945

XH-Engine Cost and Procurement
On 2 July, the expenditure of $3,904,000 to cover the construction of three XH-9350-1 engines was approved. However, the priority was downgraded to 3-A. The estimated date for completing the three engines was given as 1 March 1947. The engines would be built to conform to the XH-9350-1 specifications issued on 1 February 1945.

On 9–10 July, Blackwood and Ford L. Prescott of MatCmd visited Studebaker to discuss facilities to build and test three complete XH-9350 engines. Studebaker was to come up with cost and time estimates for the XH-9350 test facilities at South Bend by 16 July. In addition, a determination of location and extent of such facilities was needed. Studebaker proposed constructing a test building adjoining the Aviation Division Aircraft Engine Plant (for R-1820 production) on Chippewa Ave. Although R-1820 production had just come to an end, the property was still owned by the Defense Plant Corporation. The estimated cost of the building and its test equipment was $2,002,050. R-1820 production stopped on 1 July, and the building was no longer being used. With the war winding down, Studebaker was resuming its automotive activity.

One option for XH-9350 testing was to proceed with the original plan. Some of the Defense Plant Corporation property on Chippewa Ave would be used to house all of the organization and testing facilities currently at the Motor Machining and Assembly Plant on Sample Street. Additionally, some special machine tools required for the construction and testing of the complete XH-engine would be installed. This option would centralize the XH-9350 project and free up space in the Motor Machining and Assembly Plant for new automotive projects, which were Studebaker's main focus.

An alternative option was to leave the XH-9350 project where it was at the Motor Machining and Assembly Plant and build a complete engine test facility on Studebaker property at the proving ground, 10 miles west of South Bend.

Cole stated that Studebaker would not be interested in going beyond the development of the three proposed test engines, not even five or ten additional experimental engines. This was because procuring parts was a slow and costly process, so Studebaker would want to make more parts in-house. However, Studebaker's primary focus was in the automotive field, and it was not currently interested in entering the aircraft engine business.

On 11 July, Studebaker was requested to send the Allison Engine Company the 7.5" cylinder report, without the other cylinder size comparisons.

Single-Cylinder Test Engines
In June, AF-1's outer exhaust valve spring and its damper failed. These parts had run together for 29.25 hours, but the spring had 404.75 hours. It was thought that the new damper had worn the inner diameter of the spring and caused it to fail. Once the spring failed, so did the damper. It was noted that the inner diameter of the outer intake spring was also worn. All springs and dampers were replaced. The new dampers were modified to allow for more clearance. A new cylinder was installed because of the failure of the exhaust valve spring. AF-1 still had an 8.0" stroke (402.12 in^3).

AF-1 completed the manifold versus cylinder fuel injection tests. The manifold injection was 3.375" above the intake port flange. Cylinder fuel injection increased IMEP by 2–6% over manifold fuel injection, with the highest gain at 2,200 rpm and 38 inHg. Here, the maximum IMEP for manifold injection was 205, while cylinder injection was 218. At 1,200 rpm and 40 inHg MAP, the maximum IMEP for manifold injection was 221, while cylinder injection was 229. At 1,600 rpm and 40 inHg the IMEP of manifold and cylinder fuel injection were 230 and 237 respectively.

The SFC results showed the opposite; there was a loss with cylinder fuel injection compared to manifold injection. However, the loss was less than the power gain—1.2% decrease in economy at 1,200 rpm and 2.6% at 1,600 rpm. The decrease in economy with fuel injection was even greater (over 5%) at 2,200 rpm, but this was not much of a concern, because it was above the cruising speed of the engine. Cylinder fuel injection also increased the amount of air consumed by about 3%. The tests took 80.75 engine hours, and the total time on AF-1 was now 1,548 hours.

The AF-4 engine with a 7.625" stroke (383.27 in^3) was conducting mixture ratio runs with the new XH-cylinder head. At 2,200 rpm and 40 inHg MAP, the cylinder (#14) failed at the intake spring housing as a result of the insert cap screws (which had 897 hours) failing. The cap screws held the cylinder-to-crankcase adapter to the crankcase. The cap screws and adapter were replaced, and the engine was reassembled with a new, complete XH-cylinder. Tests would be conducted to compare the old cylinder with the new XH-type. The AF-4 engine had run 1095 hours.

For the single-cylinder test engines, a new valve spring damper design was machined, and the domed piston was reworked for a 2.25" diameter piston pin. The 7.75" crankshaft was completed except for some final machine work. Studebaker stated that single-cylinder testing would be completed under the estimated cost.

Twin-Cylinder Test Engines
The twin-cylinder AF-5 engine (779.12 in^3) was rebuilt following last month's main bearing seizure. The main bearings were modified to increase oil flow by the addition of an oil distribution groove. While disassembled, it was noticed that the pistons had been hitting the oil-cooling jets, and one had been broken off. The oil jets were shortened by .125". During a break-in run at 1,800 rpm, the engine began to vibrate badly and was unsteady. The engine was then motored but was later stopped when the oil pressure did not reach 100 psi. AF-5 was removed from the test stand and disassembled. Inspection revealed the copper-lead surface of the center main bearing had wiped out, and

the bearing journal was scored 0.20" deep radially. The crankcase was distorted at the bearing journal and spread .022" above and below the bearing hole. The holes also closed in as much as .025" (on the diameter) near the parting line. The small section of metal between the bearing bore and through-bolt holes on each side of the bore had been crushed down, causing the gap in the crankcase and the closed-in bearing bore diameter at the parting line. All oil holes were found to be open and clear. The seized bearing overheated the engine's crankcase and forced the two halves to part. The pistons were still hitting the oil jets, so another .125" of each jet was cut off.

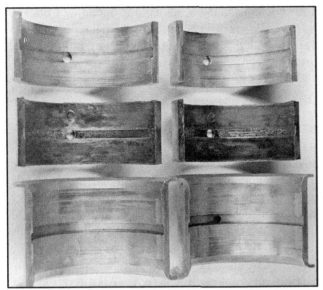

Damaged rear, center, and front crankshaft main bearings of AF-5 caused by a lack of oil. (NARA)

To repair the engine, the crankshaft would be reground .040" undersize. New main bearings .040" undersized were ordered, and the crankcase misalignment would be corrected at the main bearing bore. Steel pins would be installed in the crankcase parting line, parallel to the bearing bore and vertically in line with it. These pins were to maintain a constant gap at the parting face of the crankcase. The bearing bore would then be bored out to its original diameter of 5.0". The extent of the needed repairs meant that AF-5 would not be ready to run for another month. The engine had run 8.25 hours.

The AF-6 twin-cylinder engine's crankcase was built up with only the crankshaft installed to investigate the main bearing trouble experienced with AF-5. The crankshaft was rotated a total of eight minutes and up through 1,000 rpm. The friction load was at 22 lb but then rose quickly and steadily until the test was stopped. Inspection of the bearings indicated

excessive wear, especially considering their eight minutes of use. The wear was caused by inadequate main bearing clearance. The main bearing journals were ground down .003" so that the minimum diametral clearance was .007". The crankshaft was then motored for 10 minutes at each of the following rpms: 1,000; 1,200; 1,350; 1,600; 1,800; and 2,000. The friction load was 1/3 of the prior run at 1,000 rpm and increased only 50% at 2,200 rpm. The main bearings were then inspected and found to be in very good condition. As a result of these tests, AF-5's main bearing clearance was opened up as well. The assembly of AF-6 was then completed using the cylinders and pistons from AF-5.

A coolant leak occurred on the left cylinder during the break-in runs of AF-6. The cylinder was replaced and the runs continued. At 1,800 rpm, the engine began to vibrate. After one hour, speed was increased to 2,200 rpm. After 23 minutes at 2,200 rpm, a connecting rod seized, and the run was halted. The bearing had 19.5 hours of time. Sharp edges of the bearing had worn against the crankpin, creating chips that became lodged between the crankpin and the bearing, resulting in its failure.

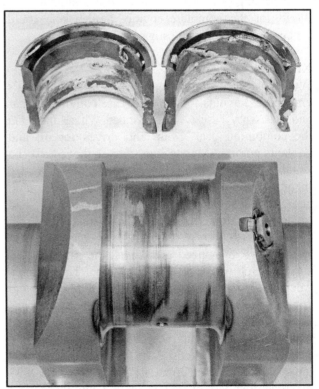

Damaged connecting rod bearing and crankshaft from AF-6. (NARA)

The main bearing was altered to have spreader grooves at the bearing split and a minimum .007" diametral clearance. The bearing was then re-plated and installed in a new fork-and-blade connecting rod assembly. The crankpin was polished and was found to be fine. Further modifications were made to prevent another occurrence of this issue. Oil pressure at the main bearing was 100 psi and 10–15 psi on the cam mechanism. AF-6 had run for 11.25 hours.

XH-Cylinder

The valve action test fixture completed a 50-hour endurance test at 1,200 rpm on the new valve gear for the XH-cylinder. The new valve gear incorporated the spherical slipper that was used on the new cylinder. At the end of the test, the outer spring damper was broken, and the roller pin was badly scuffed and worn. Tests were then conducted to find a more satisfactory pin and outer damper.

The XH-cylinder design was experiencing issues with water jacket cracks and coolant leaks. If the issues continued, a weaker but more flexible alloy (No. 365) would be used, replacing the current alloy (No. 142). New pistons were being designed that incorporated a shorter, 2.0" diameter piston pin and shorter connecting rod bosses. The new design saved 4 lb of reciprocating weight per cylinder, which amounted to 96 lb for the complete engine. Studebaker would proceed with further investigation of this design.

XH-Engine Development

Work continued on clay models of the XH-engine's crankcase. Layouts for the crankcase combining gear and accessory case were continued. These included the combining gear group and drives for oil and coolant pumps. Magnesium was believed to be suitable for the accessory case, which would also incorporate engine supports. The front scavenge pump and magneto drive shafts were evaluated, and torsional vibration studies were being made.

For the two two-speed gear units, the sample LGS spring clutch was received on 29 June. The clutch's calculated maximum torque was 61,300 in-lb, and compressive stress was 71,800 psi. A test fixture was being set up to test the LGS springs. The first tests would be to determine the radial expansion of the springs at various speeds. Parts for the two two-speed units were 95% complete. Only 16 of the 673 manufactured parts were outstanding, and these were 80% complete.

Test fixture designs for the contra-rotating gear reduction unit were completed and released for construction.

Scintilla was asked to clarify its ignition system proposal, whether it was a low-tension or high-frequency system. AC Spark Plug was requested to submit a proposal for a high-frequency ignition system.

The coolant pump was still having issues with air entering the system under simulated altitude conditions. Tests were run to determine the effect of coolant temperature on pump characteristics. Tests were made with water at 100° F with flow rates of 280, 360, and 420 gpm and with an unrestricted flow (in excess of 700 gpm). The test was repeated at 180° F. Constant speed and restriction tests were done with 100° F water and the coolant pump operating from 800 up to 3,300 rpm. The test would be repeated with 180° F water. The coolant pump design, building, and testing was running over cost.

August 1945

XH-Engine Cost and Procurement

At a conference at Wright Field on 8 August, Clark stated that Studebaker was not interested in building the XH-engine. However, the company would build the engine at the AAF's request, provided that there was no financial risk to Studebaker. In other words, if the AAF covered all costs, Studebaker would continue the XH-engine's development. The aircraft engine project would be completely separate from Studebaker's automotive activity. All aircraft engine related activity—design, construction, assembly, testing, and development—would be carried out at one plant. Because of the project changes and the impending post-war budget situation, the request for three engines was reduced to one. This revised procurement had an estimated cost of $1,695,000. Furthermore, one source of a fuel injection system and an ignition system were cancelled, which respectively freed up $107,000 and $32,800 that would be put back into the H-9350 program.

In a letter dated 21 August, Cole reiterated the above and stated that a full-scale engine was part of the developmental work. Cole wrote the following regarding additional engines:

> Frankly, we are not anxious to take on such work. On the contrary, we would prefer to have it performed elsewhere. We are not interested in the commercial possibilities of such an engine and from the standpoint of our own interests the time and energy of our organization devoted to such work could be

much more profitably employed in our own work. However, if this development work is necessary, we feel that we should, purely as a matter of accommodation to the Government, try to assist the Government in working out an arrangement for the performance thereof. With this in mind, we would be willing to undertake the construction of additional engines.

A note from 23 August stated that facilities would take as long to build as the engine itself. The XH-9350 project was getting pushed out of the automotive Motor Machining and Assembly Plant on Sample Street because of increased automotive design activity. Studebaker had requested to move all XH-9350 activity to the Aviation Division Aircraft Engine Plant on Chippewa Ave. The production of R-1820 engines had ceased, and there was some talk of the plant being used as an aircraft engine overhaul facility.

Also on 23 August, supplement number 11 for contract W-535-ac-28386 was signed by the Undersecretary of War (William C. Foster). This allocated an additional $1,223,872.09 to Studebaker. Of that, $970,881.30 was reimbursement for work done prior to 1 January 1945 that exceeded the estimated cost under the fixed-price contract. This included $61,191.75 for Studebaker's existing test facilities and equipment. The total estimated cost of the W-535-ac-28386 contract was now $2,848,249.00. In addition, AAF was interested in obtaining the license and reproduction rights for the engine.

Wright Field requested a cost estimate for one engine and test facilities. A reply was being prepared that included a layout of the Aviation Division Aircraft Engine Plant (on Chippewa) marked off with the proposed space for performing the XH-engine project separated from the Studebaker Automotive Engineering section. A wooden scale mockup of the entire lab and test equipment was being made to determine the best layout for the lab.

Experimental programs were being curtailed as the war ended. It was expected that further delays on the XH-9350 engine would occur. It was recommended that Studebaker should take measures to expedite as many phases of the program as possible.

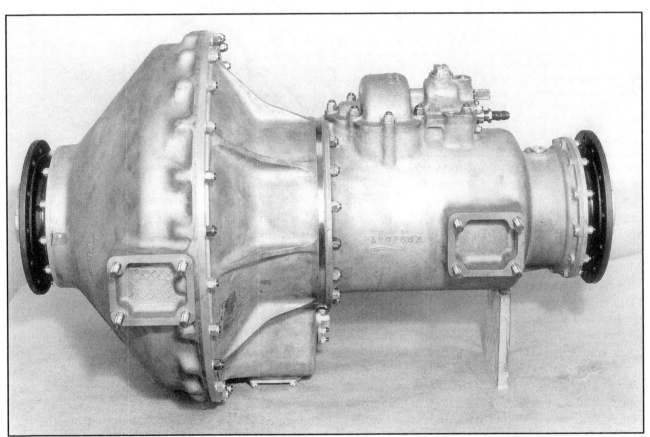

The two-speed gear unit as of 30 August 1945. While it appears to be complete, the LGS spring clutches were not installed in the unit. The internals of the unit can be seen on pages 76 and 77. (BL)

Wooden model layout of the lab for testing the two-speed gear unit and the contra-rotating gear reduction. The gear units would be mounted in their respective cradles and driven by a dynamometer. (AC)

Single-Cylinder Test Engines

AF-1, still with an 8.0" stroke (402.12 in^3), was now involved in additional manifold fuel injection versus cylinder fuel injection tests. Tests were done with different fuel injection cut-offs (20°, 70°, and 120° ATC) and also with a constant-spray fuel bar using a low-pressure pump. During mixture ratio runs with the fuel bar, the cylinder failed by breaking the valve tappet housing at the lower spring seat. Cylinder #15 replaced the broken cylinder, and tests continued. A fuel injector cut-off of 70° ATC remained the superior option. The test results indicated that there was relatively no change in SFC between the fuel delivery methods, but cylinder fuel injection gave 2–5% higher IMEP.

AF-1 then tested timed fuel injection in the cylinder versus timed fuel injection in the intake manifold. Heavy detonation occurred at 2,200 rpm and 38 inHg MAP. The points of the Scintilla timer were adjusted and cleaned, and detonation diminished. However, it was found that the air compressor did not have the capacity to provide enough air for 2,200 rpm and 38 inHg MAP. The most available was 2,200 rpm and 37.6 inHg MAP. A test was run at these settings but was terminated when the fuel injector failed. A replacement injector was made, and the tests continued until the fuel injector comparison was completed. The engine was removed from the test stand to install a modified, older cylinder head. The modified head had an enlarged spark plug hole to test a tangential spray fuel injector.

During disassembly, the flywheel side crankshaft bearing was found to be very worn. A new bearing was installed. There were indications that the piston was hitting the top of the combustion chamber. The head (#15) was stripped off the barrel, and a modified head (#12) was installed. All the piston rings were found to be in good condition. Tests with the new injector were begun. AF-1 had run 1,635.25 hours.

The AF-4 engine retained its 7.625" stroke (383.27 in³) and was comparing the XH-cylinder versus the original-design cylinder. The engine had some issues with worn rockers and rollers. Tests continued once these were replaced. However, difficulties were encountered with the spark plugs fouling in the XH-cylinder. The spark plugs were replaced, but the engine was still unsteady. The XH-cylinder was removed, and new piston rings were installed, but the trouble continued.

At 1,114.5 hours on the engine, the angle drive end of the Bendix fuel injection pump broke. The pump had 119 hours. It was replaced with the pump from AF-1. Bendix planned to improve the design of the shaft. There was excessive backlash in the cam drive gear train from a worn coupling and the upper and lower splined drives.

Oil consumption tests were done with and without oil cooling to the underside of the piston. It was found that oil cooling lessened consumption at rich mixtures but increased consumption at lean mixtures. Comparative cylinder tests were continued.

The new XH-cylinder was indicating practically the same economy as the older cylinder. A SFC of .320 lb/hp/hr was obtained, indicating an estimated .355 lb/hp/hr for a complete XH-9350. It was believed that with turbo-compounding the XH-9350's SFC would be brought back down to .320 lb/hp/hr. Unfortunately, no further information regarding turbo-compounding has been found. Performance of the new XH-cylinder was about 4% lower than the older cylinder at 2,200 rpm and 30 inHg MAP. It was expected that when cams with the best timing were available, the performance would match the older cylinder. The engine had 1,174 total hours.

Twin-Cylinder Test Engines
The AF-5 twin-cylinder was still waiting for parts to repair it from the damage that occurred the previous month. Its operating hours remained unchanged at 8.25.

The AF-6 twin-cylinder engine had been repaired, and break-in runs of 15 minutes each at 1,000; 1,200; 1,350; 1,600; and 1,800 rpm were made. In addition, a 30 minute run at 2,000 rpm and a 27 minute run at 2,200 rpm were made. Considerable spark plug fouling in the right cylinder occurred. The left cylinder was detonating while the right was not. This was believed to be caused by excessive oil in the left cylinder. Adjustments were made, including the installation of hotter spark plugs (Champion C35S). A one hour run at 2,200 rpm and 30 inHg MAP was made, followed by a one hour run at 800 rpm and 30 inHg MAP. The hotter plugs apparently eliminated the oil fouling in the right cylinder. Oil consumption was reported as a very high 15 lb/hr at 2,200 rpm. The engine was removed from the test stand and disassembled for inspection. All parts were found to be in satisfactory condition.

The engine was now built up with XH-cylinders #2 and #5 which were believed to be cracked. The engine was run with these cylinders to open up the cracks so they could be found. No valve spring dampers were used, because satisfactory dampers had still not been developed. At 1,800 rpm, both cylinder heads were badly leaking coolant. The engine was stopped after five hours, and the cylinders were removed and inspected for leaks. AF-6 had run for 39 hours.

XH-Cylinder
On the XH-cylinder, the possibility of using a valve angle of 30° rather than 45° was being explored, and a reduction in the cylinder water jacket thickness from .030" to .018" was being considered. Modifications were made to improve the bearing of the rocker roller to its shaft. A new cam was being designed to allow an intake duration of 250° and an exhaust duration of 270°. Further design work on the cylinder was underway to improve the spark plug and injector nozzle locations and resolve water jacket cracking. The 7.75" stroke crankshaft for the single-cylinder engine was completed.

The valve spring test fixture had been under constant operation. A number of spring dampers were modified to test along with several rocker rollers and shafts. The same valve springs and silver-plated roller pins have been used for all tests. Over 110 hours of testing had been accomplished, but the outer spring damper was still breaking after a few hours, regardless of the modifications tried. The dampers had yet to last 10 hours of operation without cracking. Work was underway to design a better valve spring to eliminate the damping cups without resulting in vibration that

A photograph dated 22 August 1945 of the XH-cylinder undergoing tests mounted to AF-4. Note the camshaft housing mounted above the cylinder. This is the only known image that shows the housing on the single cylinder engine. AF-4 ran approximately 205 hours with the XH-cylinder. (NARA)

would lead to spring failure. Other tests were being run to improve the rocker roller shaft bearing life.

After the latest tests, the pin roller was removed after 62.5 hours of operation and the springs after 53.5 hours. All were found to be in good condition. A new type of springs, rollers, and dampers were installed for testing. Initial results showed the dampening effect to be good.

XH-Engine Development
Bendix was still designing the fuel injection pump and the combination speed density unit and fuel transfer pump. Scintilla was to deliver designs for the high-frequency ignition system. Through the use of clay models, the design for the crankshaft combining gears and front and rear accessories drives were being refined.

Constant-speed restriction tests were done on the coolant pump. Tests with just water were concluded, and tests with ethylene glycol were now underway. Tests were done with a water temperature of 250° F at over 420 gpm at 1,500 rpm (pump). However, below 16 inHg air pressure, the flow dropped, and it was taken as a sign that free boiling was occurring. Two positions at the rear of the engine were being considered for the coolant pump. A vertical position would simplify the outlet but would restrict the inlet. A horizontal position would provide a good inlet, but unequal distribution to the four outlet pipes was a possibility. Further studies were to be made, and the design with the fewest number of drawbacks would be implemented.

The latest intake manifold studies indicated the manifolds should be as close to the crankcase as possible. This arrangement would simplify the four manifolds connecting to a common throttle body at the rear of the engine. Fuel injection studies indicated virtually no difference in performance related to the location of the injector, whether it was in the cylinder head, in the manifold, or a continuous flow through a fuel bar positioned above the intake port. The latest cam box design was being mocked up. It was smaller than the previous design and adapted to the latest angled position of the valves and to the spherical lifter pad on the valve rocker arms. Studies were underway to determine the best engine mount pads.

Preliminary LGS spring clutch studies were completed. A Studebaker auto engine was being used to run tests on two sample LGS spring clutches in a dummy cup fixture. The tests were conducted on the engagement of the clutches for the two-speed unit. One two-speed gear unit was complete except for the intended LGS spring clutches. The second unit and both sets of LGS spring clutches were expected to be ready in November.

There was a newly designed two-speed clutch that replaced the previous LGS spring type clutch. This new unit was 200 lb lighter than the older unit. Careful design and study would precede any attempted use of the new clutch on the engine. The new clutch design was not to supersede the LGS spring clutch, but it would be carried along as a simultaneous development.

Torsional vibration analysis continued on the contra-rotating gear reduction unit. Material for the unit was on hand and undergoing machining. Final assembly drawings for testing both the two-speed and contra-rotating gear reduction units were made.

Test equipment for the propeller drive was being obtained. A 500 hp dyno was ordered and slated for delivery in December. It was expected that all other needed test equipment would be on hand before the dyno. The contra-rotating gear reduction units and their special testing dyno were scheduled to be ready in January 1946.

September 1945

A cost estimated for one XH-9350 engine and test facilities was submitted to the Procurement Division at Wright Field on 20 September.

Single-Cylinder Test Engines
The AF-1 engine was still testing various aspects of fuel injection. A flywheel bearing failed after 1,411.25 hours and was repaired. A special cylinder with a larger hole for injector tests was fitted. A combination fuel injector and spark plug was installed. The best economy was achieved when the injection spray traveled the longest distance in the cylinder. Four combination fuel injectors / spark plugs were on order from AC Spark Plug. Various fuel injector nozzle entrance angle tests, fuel injection nozzle radius and timing tests, and exhaust thermocouple tests were all run. The results of these tests did not yield anything significant. The AF-1 engine had accumulated 1,713 hours

The AF-4 engine was still being used to compare the performance characteristics of the new XH-cylinder's valve gear with the older cylinder's valve gear. After a mixture test at 1,200 rpm and 30 inHg MAP, the cylinder began backfiring. The cylinder was removed from the engine, revealing that the valves were not seating.

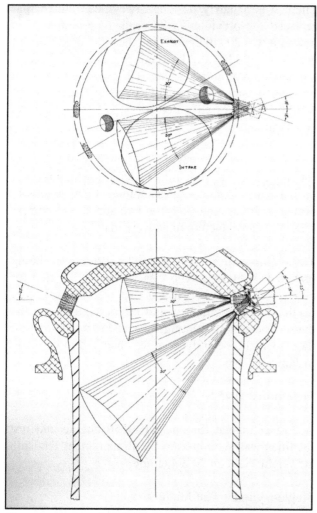

Drawing dated 25 September 1945 illustrating different fuel injection angles for the 8.0" bore and stroke cylinder AF-1. (NARA)

The cylinder tests showed that the best economy was basically the same between the two cylinder designs. However, the XH-cylinder made about 5% less maximum power than the older cylinder. It was believed that different cams could improve performance. The new XH-cylinder also had excessive oil consumption at 2,200 rpm. New rings temporarily decreased consumption, and a new ring with a torsional twist was being designed to further decrease the oil consumption. At 126 hours on the XH-cylinder, a head jacket crack appeared adjacent to the intake flywheel spark plug boss. The crack occurred while the engine was running at 2,200 rpm and 35 inHg MAP. Both inner valve springs were found broken after 154 hours. No dampers had been used.

The AF-4 engine was rebuilt with new camshaft drive shafts and new chrome-faced piston compression rings that had a torsional twist. Oil consumption was reduced with these rings, but spark plug fouling was still occurring at 2,200 rpm. The hotter C-35S spark plugs were used at 2,200 rpm. The new cam drive improved engine operation, and the mixture runs were repeated. The engine was removed from the dyno and would be rebuilt with a 7.75" stroke crankshaft and a new XH-cylinder. The AF-4 engine had 1,227 hours.

Twin-Cylinder Test Engines
AF-5's crankcase was repaired; this included using an undersized main bearing with oil grooves. Assembly of the AF-5 engine was started. A new twin engine crankshaft was being machined, and two others were on order.

The AF-6 engine continued its run-in at 1,800 and 2,000 rpm. Both cylinders had bad external head water jacket leaks. The left cylinder was removed, and coolant was found to have seeped through the pores in the aluminum. The left cylinder (#2) was replaced with another (#6). The cracked heads were originally heat-treated using a water quench process. These heads would be replaced with air quenched heads when they became available. The new heads also had .018" thick water jackets. The silver-plated rocker roller pins did not show any signs of scuffing.

The engine was then reassembled with timed manifold injection. Tests indicated the minimum SFC at 1,350 rpm and 1,600 rpm would be met. Further tests at 2,200 rpm and 820 rpm were to be run next. The engine began to overheat, and the runs were stopped. It was found that the coolant heat exchanger was partially blocked. It was cleared, and tests resumed. During a run, detonation occurred in the left cylinder. A number of tests were run to determine the cause of the detonation, and it was ultimately found that the fuel injector pump was at fault. The injector was running lean for the left cylinder and rich for the right cylinder. It was sent back to Bendix for checking. The pump was returned, and tests continued. Detonation occurred again, and it was determined that this instance was caused by the engine being run at the theoretical maximum power air/fuel ratio. Calibration runs were next for AF-6, followed by endurance tests on piston rings with a torsional twist. The engine had 88 hours.

XH-Engine Development
The valve dampers would still crack or break at under 10 hours. Twelve different designs of valve spring dampers were made and released to fix the issue. The Cleveland Wire Company designed a triple-valve

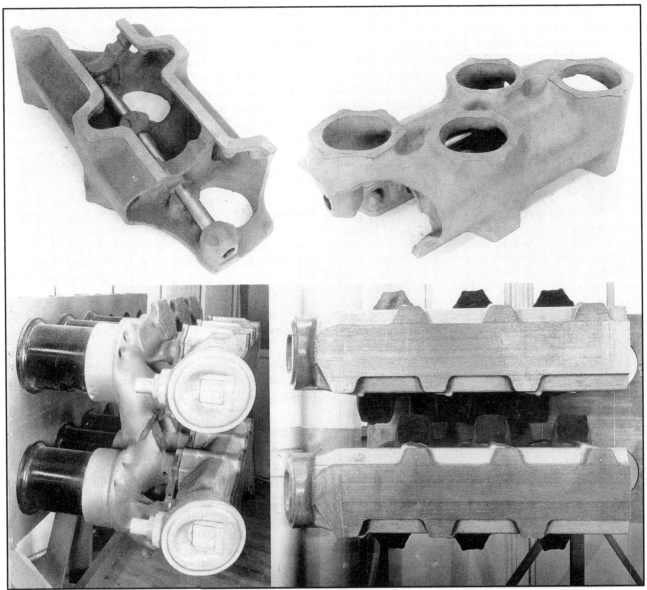

Top—Clay mockup of the cam housing topside (left) and underside (right). The rod represents the centerline of the camshaft. (BL) Bottom—front (left) and side (right) views of the wooden XH-9350-engine-cylinder mockup. Only the first six cylinders are represented. The exhaust ports are between the cylinders, with the intake ports on the outside of the cylinders. All photos are dated 15 October 1945. (BL)

spring that obtained damping by coil rubbing, and a release was made to test this new design in the valve action machine. The valve test machine had run for 230 hours, testing other designs. Some parts continued their endurance tests: 170 hours on the rocker arm, 126.5 hours on the valve springs, 100 hours on the silver-plated pin and roller, and 80 hours on the beryllium bronze bushing roller.

Work continued on clay models and layouts of a section of the full-scale engine's crankcase, including engine supports. A revised camshaft housing mockup was designed, built, and included on the partial engine mockup. This included a tachometer drive and pad at

the drive end. Final analysis reports for the full-scale XH-9350's connecting rod, piston, and cylinder groups were started. Torsional vibration analyses were continued.

A redesign of the combining gear accessory section was completed and included better structure, fastenings, and accessory drive arrangement. Clay modeling of the redesigned housing was started. Detailing and checking of the various drive parts and of the housings were continued. It was expected that these parts would be released for manufacture at the beginning of October. Layout and design of the rear accessory section, including an alternate arrangement with a horizontal drive for the coolant pump, was continued.

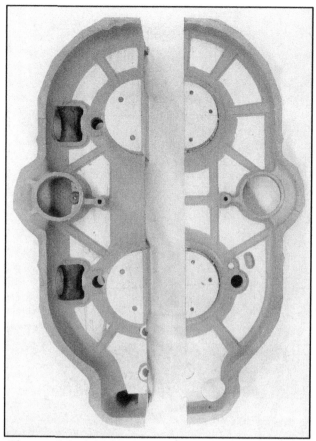

Clay model of the front combining gear housing. (BL)

LGS spring clutch details for the two-speed gear unit were made and released. One unit (without the LGS spring clutches and oil pump) was assembled at Merz Engineering Company in Indianapolis, Indiana and delivered to South Bend. The LGS spring clutches were being machined and would be delivered in late September. The second two-speed unit was being assembled and would be delivered in early October. The weight of the two-speed unit without the LGS spring clutches or oil pump was 500 lb. The estimated weight of the LGS spring clutch was 46 lb. It was estimated that future revisions of the two-speed unit, including the substitution of synchromesh jaw clutches instead of the wrapping spring type, might reduce the unit's weight by 200 lb.

Parts for the two contra-rotating gear reduction units were being machined. Welded cradles, supports, and automatic torque loader housings had been received and were awaiting machine work. In total, the units were 15% complete, and assembly of the units was scheduled for the end of 1945.

The propeller test dyno was now scheduled for a Jan 1946 delivery. Many other parts (oil pumps, potentiometer, weighing scales, oil filters, fast couplings, etc.) required for the test setup were scheduled for delivery in Nov 1945. A scale mockup of the propeller drive test setup was made for location studies in the Automotive Test Lab and in the Aviation Division Aircraft Engine Plant.

4,500 gallons of 28-R (100/130) fuel was received for engine tests.

October 1945

XH-9350 Cancellation
On 11 October 1945, termination of contract W-535-ac-28386 was initiated in order to curtail 1946 expenditures. The action saved $2,550,872 and ended the Studebaker XH-9350. Work on the engine at Studebaker effectively stopped on 15 October.

Construction of at least one of the two-speed gear units would continue, and the Air Technical Service Command would conduct its own tests.

Test Engines
The AF-1 engine was being used for fuel injector spray and nozzle depth tests, thermocouple tests, and heat rejection tests. The engine had run 1,734 hours.

Engines AF-2 and AF-3 were still in storage with 1,024.5 and 750 hours respectively.

The AF-4 engine was being rebuilt with a 7.75" stroke crankshaft and a new XH-cylinder. Due to the program cancellation, this work was never completed. The AF-4 engine had 1,227 hours.

The AF-5 twin-cylinder engine was not fully reassembled at the time of cancellation. The engine had only 8.25 hours.

The AF-6 twin-cylinder engine was reassembled with crankpin bearings having .007 minimum diametral clearance and main bearings with .008 minimum diametral clearance. Machining of a third crankshaft continued, and two additional forgings were still on order. Calibration runs were started with cylinders #5 and #6 and were finished with cylinders #10 and #11. Cylinders #10 and #11 were the latest version, with .018" thick water jackets and air-quenched heads. Also, torsion-type piston rings were fitted.

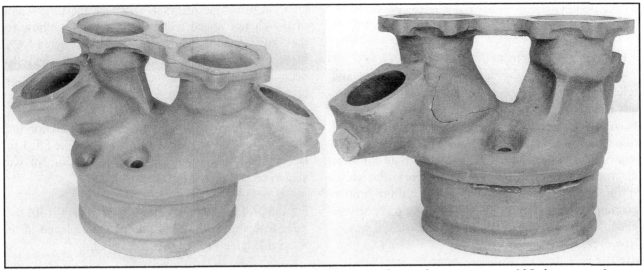

Clay model of the revised XH-cylinder head. The head is very similar to the one on page 135; however, the new head had only two spark plug bosses and one fuel injector. The photos were taken on 15 October 1945. (AC)

After some preliminary performance tests, the cylinders did not exhibit any water jacket leaks. AF-6 recorded a maximum IMEP of 234 at 2,200 rpm and 38 inHg MAP, with a SFC of .45 lb/hp/hr. This represented 506 hp indicated for the twin-cylinder test engine, or 6,077 hp indicated for the 24-cylinder engine. With a 90% mechanical efficiency, the output would be 5,469 hp. The SFC recorded was .310 lb/hp/hr at 1,600 rpm and 33 inHg MAP with an IMEP of 170, and .300 lb/hp/hr at 1,350 rpm and 30 inHg with an IMEP of 140. However, these results were preliminary, and further testing was needed.

AF-6 still exhibited a tendency to detonate, which was to be investigated. The engine was disassembled for inspection, and almost all parts were found to be in very good condition. The piston skirts were scratched, and corresponding marks were found in the cylinder bores. The bottom edge of the piston skirts was found to be very sharp. It was believed that this caused the marks in the cylinder bores which were then transferred to the piston skirts. The piston skirt edges were chamfered to prevent further issues. The cylinder barrel water jacket showed no leaks, but there were leaks in the cylinder head jacket. A change to a 7.1:1 CR was to be made, but the project cancellation put an end to further work. The engine had accumulated 104 hours.

XH-Cylinder

The official report comparing the original cylinder with the XH-cylinder was issued on 5 October. This comparison used AF-4 with a 7.625" stroke (383.27 in³) at an 8.0:1 CR and took 211.5 engine operating hours to complete. For maximum power, the XH-cylinder had an average IMEP reduction at 2,200 rpm of less than 2%. For example, at 38 inHg MAP, the original cylinder had an IMEP of 251, while the XH-cylinder had an IMEP of 246. The IMEP numbers correspond to an indicated 291 and 285 hp respectively.

For maximum economy, the XH-cylinder's SFC averaged less than 3% higher at 1,200 rpm and less than 2% higher at 2,200 rpm. The best SFC at 1,200 rpm and 30 inHg MAP was .322 lb/hp/hr for the original cylinder and .327 lb/hp/hr for the XH-cylinder. At 2,200 rpm and 30 inHg MAP, the original cylinder had a SFC of .308 lb/hp/hr, and the XH-cylinder's SFC was .312 lb/hp/hr.

The XH-cylinder had difficulty with lean mixture operation with direct fuel injection. The cylinder also encountered spark plug fouling with excessive oil consumption (above 5 lb/hr) and occasional detonation at 2,200 rpm and 30 inHg MAP. The spark plug fouling was believed to be a result of their location and the higher oil consumption of the XH-cylinder. When the oil passed the piston, it was thrown directly onto the spark plug. It was recommended that the spark plugs be relocated to a more vertical position.

The XH-cylinder heads had been revised as a result of the tests, and new models were being built. The new design had been released for manufacture. The changes included a thicker head to prevent water jacket cracks, relocated spark plug and injector bosses to improve cylinder performance, and a simplified intake port. This new cylinder head was expected by 1 December 1945.

XH-Engine Development

Two new valve spring dampers were designed and released. Modifications were designed for the valve test fixture to incorporate the three-valve spring setup from the Cleveland Wire Company. A method of testing a full-scale camshaft was devised. The valve test fixture had operated 292 hours. Without failures, the rocker arms had operated 192 hours; the valve springs had operated 150 hours; the beryllium bronze bushing roller had operated 112 hours; and the silver-plated roller pin and roller had operated 100 hours. However, there was still no satisfactory spring damper.

A new twin-cylinder crankshaft with counterweights was designed and released for manufacture. Final design reports on connecting rods and the contra-rotating gear reduction unit were completed. Final reports were being prepared on pistons, cylinders, and crankshaft groups.

Bendix provided preliminary installation drawings of a combination fuel pump and speed density control unit. GE provided an estimate for a high-frequency ignition system. Scintilla proposed two dual 12-cylinder magnetos, and AC Spark Plug was still working on its ignition system proposal.

Coolant pump layouts were completed for a horizontal shaft pump with either two or four outlets and a vertical shaft pump with a banjo type inlet connection. Design work was proceeding on the rear accessory section incorporating the horizontal coolant pump. Final checking of the crankshaft combining gear design and front accessory drives was nearly complete. Weight, load, and stress analyses were started on the combining gear and accessory drives. Torsional vibration analyses continued on the crankshafts, two-speed gear unit, contra-rotating gear reduction unit, extension shafts, and propellers.

The two-speed gear units were complete except for the LGS spring clutches. The stationary helices for both transmission units required finishing to match the spring helix. Two sets of LGS spring clutches were promised for the end of November. A 15' cradle for preliminary and operational testing of the two-speed gear unit was designed and released for manufacture. The cradle permitted mounting one two-speed gear unit with a Studebaker auto engine attached at either end. The cradle's configuration allowed for the creation of torque reversals to check the functioning of the change speed feature. An oil outlet elbow for the two-speed gear unit was designed that incorporated a chip detector. A test fixture had also been designed to permit the application of full torque on an LGS spring clutch.

Machining for the contra-rotating gear reduction unit was 25% complete, and assembly was scheduled for December. The propeller drive test equipment was also to be completed in December.

For the project, 16,000 gallons of 28-R (100/130) fuel were reserved, and 1,500 gallons were placed in the Special Engine Project fuel storage tank.

XH-Engine Cost

Studebaker had spent $483,780.04 on the engine from 1 January to 31 October 1945. Including the $970,881.39 it had spent in the previous years, Studebaker's total expenditure on the MX-232/XH-9350 program was $1,454,661.43 (approximately $20,264,478.50 in 2018 USD). Undoubtedly, the company was fully reimbursed for its efforts. It is believed that all parts of the MX-232 program were eventually scrapped.

November 1945 and Beyond

Wright Aeronautical had expressed an interest in the XH-9350 project. In November 1945, the Air Technical Service Command worked with Wright to determine the company's attitude toward continuing the research. Wright was given a number of MX-232 files, and a rough draft of an untitled report was written by Wright engineers. More work may have been done on the project, but no such work has been found. The report, most likely dated 26 March 1946, compared the older style Studebaker 8.0" bore and stroke cylinder (four hold-down bolts, 402.1 in³) to the Wright C9HD cylinder, used on the latest R-1820 engines. The report indicated some performance advantages of the Studebaker cylinder, but it does not appear that any further action was taken. Wright returned all MX-232 files to Wright Field on 16 April 1946.

On 6 December 1945, thousands of various tracings, drawing, and sketches were sent to the Power Plant Lab at Wright Field. These covered the current engine's design, obsolete designs, other designs that were considered, and the engine test equipment designs. The following are some of the discarded designs considered while developing the XH-9350:

- 8.0" bore and 7.625" stroke X engine with 9.0:1 CR and a four-valve head,
- 7.5" bore and 7.625" stroke X engine, and
- 7.375" bore and 8.5" stroke X engine with four articulating connecting rods.

Work on the two-speed reduction gear continued, and a unit was completed in June 1946. The two-speed gear unit was shipped to Wright Field and arrived on 15 July 1946. Unfortunately, no records have been found regarding the testing or ultimate disposition of this unit. Its completion marked the end of the MX-232/XH-9350 program.

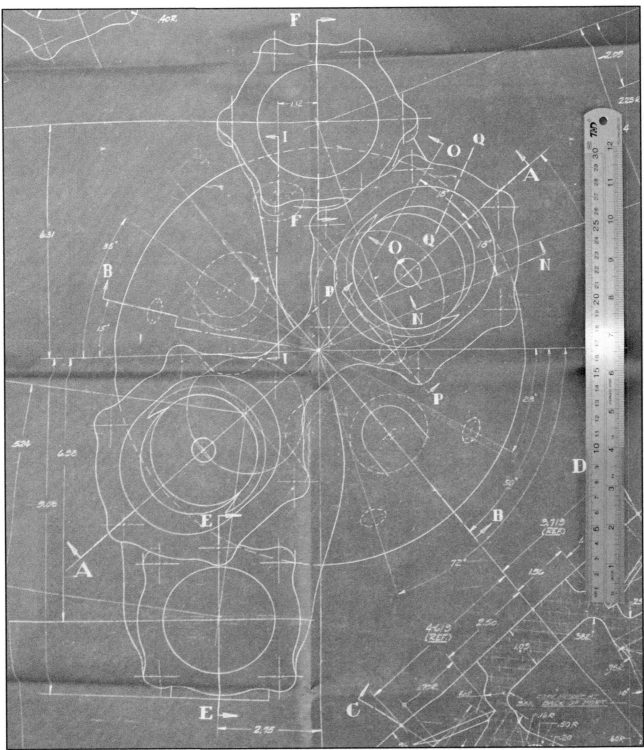

A full-scale drawing of the original XH-cylinder head dated 24 April 1945. A 12" ruler is included on the right for scale. The head was 11.30" in diameter and had a maximum port-to-port width of 17.7". (A)

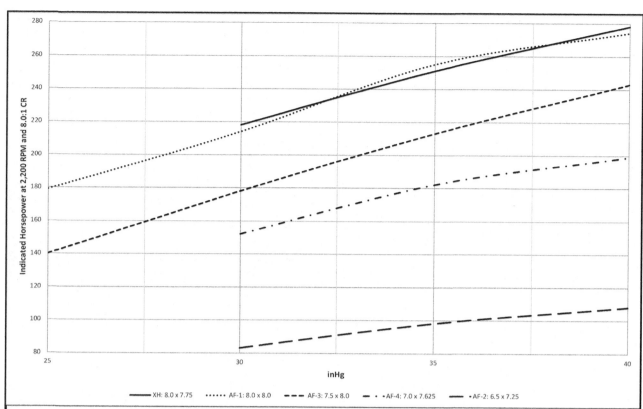

Test Cylinder Indicated Horsepower with 8.0:1 CR

			(Above Chart) At 2,200 RPM and inHg:					(Below Chart) At 40 inHg and RPM:							
			25	30	35	38	40	1000	1200	1400	1600	1800	2000	2200	2400
XH:	8.0 x 7.75	389.6 in^3		218	251	266	278		124	150	177	205	235	266	
AF-1:	8.0 x 8.0	402.1 in^3	179	214	255	267	274	104	133	160	188	218	248	276	301
AF-3:	7.5 x 8.0	353.4 in^3	140	178	213	231	243	98	108	142	180	203	226	243	260
AF-4:	7.0 x 7.625	293.4 in^3		152	182	192	199			138	155	173	199	227	
AF-2:	6.5 x 7.25	205.0 in^3		83	98	104	108			58	75	95	108	122	

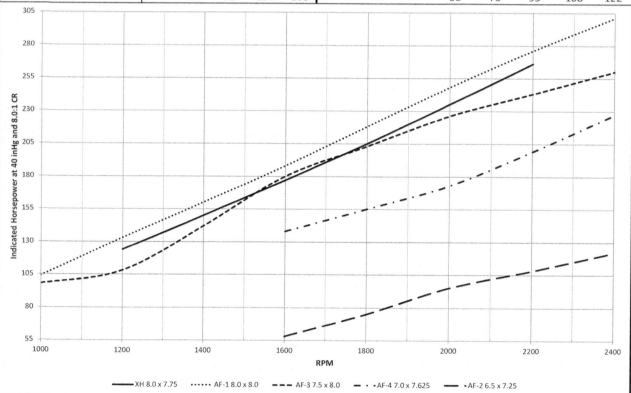

A view of the test cell with the 6.5" cylinder mounted on the test engine. The photo is from a report dated 17 July 1944. The instrument in the foreground is a scale to measure the weight of the oil tank. (NARA)

© 1945 The Studebaker Corporation

What flyers say counts most with us

MEMBERS of the crews of many a Flying Fortress have written Studebaker about the fine performance of that mighty bomber's engines.

Studebaker prizes the comments of those intrepid men far above any of the official commendations its war plants have received.

The senior civilian test pilot at an important army aircraft modification center voluntarily wrote: "I've flown and tested over 200 Studebaker powered Boeing Forts. Nothing could be tougher on engines than the workouts I've given those ships. I've taken them in saw-tooth climbs from sea level up to where the temperature

goes many degrees below zero. Those Wright Cyclones get my vote for smoothness, too."

In proudly fulfilling its wartime assignments, Studebaker has already built over 55,000 Wright Cyclone engines for the Boeing Flying Fortress—over 155,000 heavy-duty military trucks—many thousands of versatile new Weasel personnel and cargo carriers.

Famous for its peacetime motor cars and trucks, Studebaker has but a single purpose right now—to back up our fighting forces with all the military equipment its factories and workers can provide.

Awarded To All   *Studebaker Plants*

The war's "surprise" vehicle—It's the Army's new Weasel personnel and cargo carrier —built by Studebaker and powered by the famous Studebaker Champion engine.

★ ★ ★

Save for the future
WITH
WAR BONDS
THEY'RE THE
BEST INVESTMENT
IN THE WORLD

Studebaker WARTIME BUILDER OF WRIGHT CYCLONE ENGINES FOR BOEING FLYING FORTRESS

158

6. XH-9350 in Perspective

The Misconception

Many people are unaware that any piston aircraft engine larger than the Pratt & Whitney R-4360 Wasp Major ever existed. Given its immense size and complexity, it is easy to understand why many believe the R-4360 is the biggest engine ever built.

For the few that are aware of the Studebaker XH-9350, an engine of over twice the displacement of the R-4360, the impracticality of its size and weight can give the impression that the entire project was nothing more than the dreams of a few mad engineers gone rogue. For an era in which engines were achieving close to 1 hp/in^3, the 5,000 hp output of the XH-9350 seems very low for its displacement. Another common thought is that the cylinders were simply too large, that the flame front could not travel throughout the 8.0" bore with the speed needed for proper combustion. Then there is the question of why the Studebaker Corporation, a company with no aircraft engine experience, would attempt to design an aircraft engine like no other before it. And finally, there is the belief that Studebaker was taking advantage of the government, billing it for work on a hopeless engine at a time when money was being thrown in all directions to find the next great tool that would ensure victory in the war.

The Idea

The concept of separate "fighter" and "bomber" engines was not new. Such was the focus of engine designs during and after World War I. This "bomber engine" mentality inspired engines such as the Napier Cub (3,682 in^3), Argus As 5 (5,742 in^3), Allison X-4520 (4,518 in^3), and many others. Only when engines began to produce more power in the late 1920s did fighters and bombers consistently use the same engines. Even then, and through World War II, water-cooled engines were often used for the "fighter," while air-cooled engines were used for the "bomber."

The Duesenberg Model H was an 800 hp, V-16 engine that displaced 3,393 in^3. The engine was run in 1919, but only a few were built. (AC)

The British Napier Cub (E66) was an X-24 that displaced 3,682 in^3. It was first run in 1920 and was the first aircraft engine to exceed 1,000 hp. (AC)

Since the start of the internal combustion engine era, a larger engine had been synonymous with more power. The saying, "There is no replacement for displacement" is a nearly universal axiom. Since the beginning of aviation, a powerful engine was always desired, as long as it was not too large or too heavy for the intended aircraft. Gigantic and powerful aircraft engines are certainly nothing new.

The German Argus As 5 displaced 5,742 in³ and produced 1,500 hp. The 24-cylinder engine was first run in 1924. (AC)

The Allison X-4520 was a 1,200 hp, air-cooled, 24-cylinder engine completed in 1927. (AEHS)

The chart on the following page lists a sampling of large, piston aircraft engines developed over the years. As can be seen, what was enormous in 1920 became the large side of normal by 1940. Certainly, one would not consider the low-3,000 in³ displacement of the Wright R-3350 or Bristol Centaurus to be pushing the limits of what could be done in 1940, but that same displacement was very much a novelty in 1920 with the Duesenberg H and Napier Cub. As the chart indicates, the size limit was always being pushed to ever-larger engines. While the XH-9350 is still one of the largest on the list, it falls in line with the continued advancement of the piston engine. In fact, it is

somewhat logical to see a split in engine development between compact, high-power engines for fighter aircraft and large, fuel-efficient engines for bombers and transports.

The R-4360 Wasp Major was about the limit of, or perhaps a little beyond, what could be squeezed into a fighter. While it arrived too late for World War II, the engine was installed in the Goodyear F2G Super Corsair, Boeing XF8B, and Republic XP-72 Ultrabolt—all fighters (even if the XF8B had other roles). The engine was also tried in attack aircraft like the Martin AM Mauler and Vultee XA-41. And then there were monstrosities like the Curtiss XBTC and the Douglas XTB2D Skypirate, both torpedo bombers. All of these single-engine aircraft were very large, mostly a result of the enormous R-4360 engine that powered them. If some of the aircraft were any larger, they could lose the ability to complete the task for which they were designed.

However, the large Pratt & Whitney engine really found its home in large aircraft, like the Boeing B-50 and 377 Stratocruiser, Douglas C-124 Globemaster II, Fairchild C-119 Flying Boxcar, and Martin P4M Mercator. R-4360 engines powered the Republic XF-12 Rainbow to over 470 mph, making it one of the fastest multi-engine, piston-powered aircraft. But even the R-4360 seemed small in the Convair B-36 Peacemaker and Hughes H-4 Hercules (Spruce Goose).

The Pratt & Whitney R-4360 was perhaps the only truly successful giant piston aircraft engine. Initially run in 1940 and rated at 2,650 hp, the 28-cylinder engine was eventually developed to produce over 3,800 hp. (AC)

Studebaker and the Army Air Force (AAF) were actively pursuing design work for the installation of four H-9350 engines on the B-36, replacing the six R-4360s. The six R-4360s installed on the B-36

Large Aircraft Engine Comparison											
Year	Cntry	Manufacturer	Designation	Config	Bore	Stroke	in³	hp	lb	lb/hp	hp/in³
1917	Italy	FIAT	A-14	V-12	6.69	8.27	3490	700	1764	2.52	0.20
1918	USA	US Eng Div	Liberty 24	X-24	5.00	7.00	3300	700	1385	1.98	0.21
1919	GB	Sunbeam	Sikh	V-12	7.09	8.27	3913	800	1952	2.44	0.20
1919	USA	Duesenberg	Model H	V-16	6.00	7.50	3393	800	1575	1.97	0.24
1920	GB	Napier	Cub	X-24	6.25	7.50	3682	1000	2450	2.45	0.27
1920	France	Lorraine	24 W	W-24	4.96	7.87	3652	1000	1940	1.94	0.27
1921	USA	Aeromarine	AL 24	DV-24	5.00	7.00	3299	850	1492	1.76	0.26
1922	France	De Dion-Bouton	16 W	DV-16	6.69	7.48	4210	900	2072	2.30	0.21
1922	GB	Beardmore	Cyclone/Typhoon	I-6	8.625	12.00	4207	900	2200	2.44	0.21
1924	France	Lorraine	34 V	V-12	6.89	8.86	3963	850	1874	2.20	0.21
1924	Ger	Argus	As 5	DW-24	6.30	7.68	5742	1500	2425	1.62	0.26
1926	GB	Beardmore	Simoon	I-8	8.56	12.00	5528	1100	2770	2.52	0.20
1927	USA	Allison	X-4520	X-24	5.75	7.25	4518	1200	2800	2.33	0.27
1928	GB	Sunbeam	Sikh III	V-12	7.09	8.27	3913	1000	2760	2.76	0.26
1929	GB	Beardmore	Tornado	I-8 D	8.25	12.00	5132	585	4500	7.69	0.11
1933	USSR	IAM	M-44	V-16	8.74	11.26	8107	1900	3700	1.95	0.23
1934	Ger	Daimler-Benz	DB 602	V-16 D	6.89	9.06	5401	1200	4409	3.67	0.22
1936	Ger	Daimler-Benz	DB 606	InDV-24	5.91	6.30	4141	2700	3175	1.18	0.65
1936	France	Clerget	16H	V-16 D	7.09	7.87	4969	1800	3748	2.08	0.36
1938	France	Hispano-Suiza	24Y	H-24	5.91	6.69	4400	2000	2150	1.08	0.45
1939	USSR	Milkulin	AM-36 (M-36)	Y-18	6.30	7.48	4196	2000	2557	1.28	0.48
1940	Ger	Daimler-Benz	DB 610	InDV-24	6.06	6.30	4365	2950	3461	1.17	0.68
1941	USA	Pratt & Whitney	R-4360	R-28	5.75	6.00	4362	3000	3500	1.17	0.69
1941	Ger	Daimler-Benz	DB 613	InDV-24	6.38	7.09	5434	3500	3902	1.11	0.64
1941	USSR	TsIAM	M-300	IR-36	5.51	6.30	5411	3000	3530	1.18	0.55
1941	Japan	Mitsubishi	Ha-203	H-24	5.91	6.69	4400	2600	unkwn		0.59
1942	Ger	BMW	803	IR-28	6.14	6.14	5095	4000	5922	1.48	0.79
1942	USA	Wright	R-4090	R-22	6.125	6.3125	4092	3000	3230	1.08	0.73
*1942	USA	Studebaker	XH-9350	H-24	8.00	8.25	9350	5000	7000	1.40	0.53
1944	Japan	Aichi	[Ha-70]	InDV-24	5.91	6.30	4141	3100	4458	1.44	0.75
1944	Japan	Mitsubishi	A21 / Ha-50	R-22	5.91	6.69	4033	3100	3395	1.10	0.77
1946	France	Hispano-Suiza	24Z	H-24	5.91	6.69	4400	3600	3197	0.89	0.82
1946	USSR	Shvetsov	Ash-2	R-28	6.12	6.10	5030	3000	4080	1.36	0.60
1946	France	Arsenal	24H	H-24	5.91	6.50	4270	4000	4079	1.02	0.94
1946	USA	Lycoming	XR-7755	IR-36	6.375	6.75	7755	5000	6050	1.21	0.64
1946	USSR	OKB-500-II	Balandin M-127K	X-24	6.30	6.69	5006	8000	7606	0.95	1.60
*1947	France	GEHL SNECMA	32 HL	IR-32 D	7.09	7.87	9938	4000	7716	1.93	0.40
1952	USSR	OKB-500	Yakovlev M-501	IR-42 D	6.30	6.69	8760	6000	6503	1.08	0.68
Engine Configuration: DW = Double W, In = inverted, DV = Double Vee, IR = Inline Radial, "D" after = Diesel											
*A complete engine was not built. The year listed relates to the start of the project.											

represented 168 cylinders, 336 valves, and 672 spark plugs—in short, a maintenance nightmare. In contrast, four H-9350s represented 96 cylinders, 192 valves, and as few as 384 spark plugs. Of course, liquid-cooling and contra-rotating propellers would require more maintenance than air-cooling and single rotation propellers, but the H-9350 engine itself presented fewer parts to be watched and checked. The better fuel economy of the H-9350 and lower installation drag of the four versus six engines would increase the B-36's range or payload capacity over that obtained by the six R-4360 engines.

The B-36 was only the first in a line of long-range aircraft envisioned for a world without jet power. Other giants like the Convair XC-99, Hughes H-4, Bristol Type 167 Brabazon, Saunders-Roe SR.45 Princess, SNCASE SE.200, and Latécoère 631 all could have benefited from large engines designed specifically for long-range fuel efficiency. And with even larger and more ambitious aircraft on the drawing board, engines like the H-9350 could have found success.

The Convair XC-99 was a double-decker transport aircraft based on the B-36. An airliner version of the aircraft was designed but not built. (USAF)

The Hughes H-4 Hercules used eight R-4360 engines producing a combined 24,000 hp to loft its 320' wingspan into the air. (Hughes)

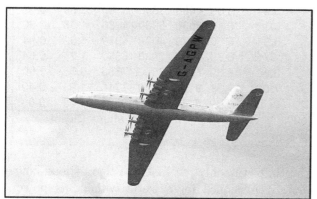

Giant piston-powered aircraft were a world-wide phenomenon following World War II. The Bristol Type 167 Brabazon was designed by the British to fulfill the needs of airliners after the war. It was powered by eight 2,650 hp Bristol Centaurus engines. (AC)

Right—The Canadian Car and Foundry B-2000-B long-range bomber proposal from 1942. The proposed aircraft had a 220' wingspan and was powered by four 5,000 hp (Allison DV-6840) engines. (AC)

Unlike the other aircraft mentioned here, the French Latécoère 631 proceeded beyond the prototype phase and entered service as an airliner. The aircraft first flew in 1942, and all but the prototype were powered by six Wright R-2600 engines. (AC)

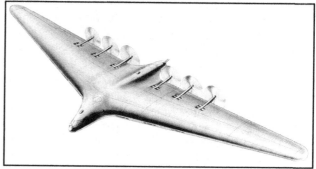

In May 1942, Consolidated proposed a B-36 alternative in the form of a flying wing with a 280' wingspan and powered by six R-4360 engines. This was just one of the many designs for large, piston-powered aircraft on the drawing board during World War II. (AC)

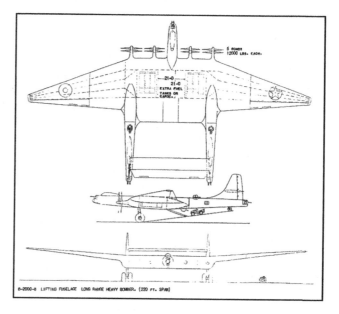

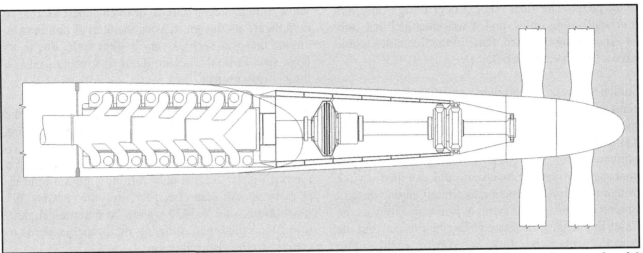

The XH-9350 shown installed in the leading edge of an aircraft's wing. Reproduced from a drawing dated 2 June 1943, the remote two-speed unit and contra-rotating propeller gear reduction are depicted. The distance from the tip of the propeller's spinner to the rear of the engine is around 25'. (A)

The Reality

The 5,000 hp output of the XH-9350 seems low because fuel-efficient cruise took priority over nearly all aspects of the engine's design; the goal was a low specific fuel consumption (SFC) figure, not a high power figure. Working toward that goal, a low SFC of .292 lb/hp/hr was obtained during single cylinder testing. This was with an 8.0" bore, 8.0"stroke, and 8.0:1 compression ratio (CR). While the SFC number was sure to rise for the complete XH-9350 engine, notes regarding the twin 8.0" bore 7.75" stroke engine indicate a SFC of .300 lb/hp/hr was achieved. The XH-9350 was guaranteed to have a SFC of .370 lb/hp/hr, but calculations based on late-development tests projected a SFC of .355 lb/hp/hr, dropping to .320 lb/hp/hr with turbo-compounding.

During single cylinder tests, the highest indicated mean effective pressure (IMEP) recorded was 277 psi. This was with an 8.0" bore, 8.0"stroke, and 6.8:1 CR. Higher power should have been obtained with 8.0:1 CR, but the tests were limited because of detonation. Still, an IMEP of 277 psi converts to 357.5 indicated hp for the 402 in^3 cylinder. Not accounting for friction losses, that output would result in 8,100 indicated hp for a complete 24-cylinder engine (of 9,651 in^3). If 10% of that power were lost to friction, 7,290 hp would be the output. Of course, a complete XH-9350 would produce less power, but output does indicate the basic cylinder design was capable of more power.

Monobloc construction of cylinder banks for liquid-cooled aircraft engines gained traction in the 1920s. Such construction, in which a number of cylinders are

one integral unit, drastically increases the engine's rigidity, especially in longer engines like V-12s. However, the AAF had become somewhat fixated on utilizing individual cylinders and even listed this as a design requirement for the high-performance engines. Although no such requirement has been noted for the MX-232 project, given Tilley's involvement and knowledge of various high-performance programs and his long history with individual cylinder construction, it is not surprising that individual cylinders were chosen for the MX-232 project. The individual cylinder design could be readily adapted from the single cylinder test engines to a full-scale, multi-cylinder engine. However, with the XH-9350 forecasted at 109" long, it is likely that the engine's overall rigidity would have been a concern, and individual cylinder construction certainly would not help.

Originally, the XH-9350 cylinders had six spark plugs. For the 8.0" cylinder, power and economy tests revealed very little performance degradation with only four spark plugs firing when compared to six plugs. In fact, some tests showed a slight increase in performance with just four spark plugs. Further testing showed a small decrease in performance of 1% to no more than 2% with only two spark plugs. There was a 2–4% decrease in performance with just one spark plug, but the test engine still ran without difficulty. From the test results, one can surmise that there were no issues with flame front propagation throughout the large 8.0" cylinder. The shape of the cylinder head, with the spark plugs positioned near its center, and the relatively low rpm of the engine combined to maintain an efficient combustion cycle, even with only two spark plugs. The final XH-cylinder design only had four spark plug holes, and it was intended that only two spark plugs be used. (One of the free holes would have a fuel injector installed.)

Studebaker was in the unique position of having idle plant space and design staff at the moment when the special engine project, which would become the XH-9350, moved forward. Other companies were evaluated, but they were preoccupied with other important projects. Studebaker did not just switch from automobile production to aircraft engine design; support was brought in, with Norman N. Tilley as the Chief Engineer of the Special Engine Project, and the Power Plant Laboratory at Wright Field, Ohio provided assistance. The project was under continuous guidance and supervision, with numerous onsite visits by various military personnel and a steady stream of reports to indicate the project's progress, or lack thereof.

There was nothing revolutionary about the XH-9350 engine design. With the engine proper, everything had been done before, just not on the scale of the XH-9350. The remote, two-speed gear unit and contra-rotating gear reduction unit were unique, along with the fuel injection, but everything else was fairly conventional. The engine was always kept as flat as possible for submerged installation in the wings of large aircraft. The engine did not possess any variable

valve timing, sleeve-valves, or even supercharging to complicate its design. It was an internal combustion engine that was seen as very experimental due to its large size. From the beginning, it was recognized as a long, costly project.

Another engine concept that was conceived along the same lines was Allison's DV-6840 proposal. This 5,200 hp and 6,300 lb engine consisted of two V-3420s with two propeller shafts each, attached to a remote gear reduction turning contra-rotating propellers. As can be seen in the MCD 392 illustrations, one V-3420 was to be mounted slightly lower than the other, allowing the propeller shafts to connect to the gear reduction.

While Authority for Purchase No. 224892, dated 10 April 1942, sought to initiate development of the Studebaker long-range engine, Col. Franklin O. Carroll also included the DV-6840, stating the following:

> [T]he [DV-6840] design was further studied and a wooden model constructed. As a result of conference between General [Oliver P.] Echols and Colonel Carroll on April 4, 1942, the Allison Division will be asked to submit a proposal on continuation of this development as an engine in the same general power class as the Studebaker project.

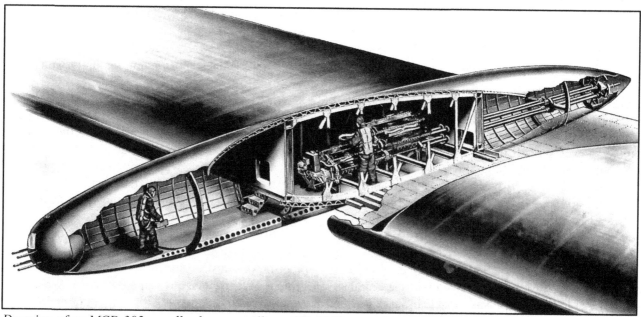

Drawing of an MCD 392 nacelle shows an Allison DV-6840 powering a remote, contra-rotating propeller gear reduction. Each of the two V-3420 engines that made up the DV-6840 powered one set of the contra-rotating propellers via two extension shafts connected to the gear reduction. (AC)

The 36-cylinder Lycoming XR-7755 was capable of 5,000 hp. The engine was built with both single rotation and contra-rotating propeller shafts. Reportedly, running the engine on the test stand at high power caused canned goods to vibrate off the shelves of a nearby grocery store. Lycoming representatives visited the store and installed strips on the shelf edges to keep the cans from falling. (AC)

It is not clear just how much developmental work was expended on the DV-6840; Allison had its hands full with the V-1710 throughout the war, which left even the V-3420 underdeveloped. A reduction gearbox for the DV-6840 was built and ready for testing in November 1946, but it is not known if it was ever tested.

Although they had different AAF origins, the XH-9350's development and purpose ran in parallel with the Lycoming XR-7755, and both engines were in the 5,000 hp class. Development on the XR-7755 began in 1943, and it was given Materiel Experimental Number MX-434. The XR-7755 was a liquid-cooled, inline-radial with nine banks of four cylinders, for a total of 36 cylinders. Like the XH-9350, the Lycoming engine used individual cylinders that had a bore of 6.375" and a stroke of 6.75". The XR-7755 was slated for possible use in the B-36, but with a diameter of over 5' and a length of 12', it is hard to image how it would have been installed into a streamlined wing nacelle. The engine was first run in July 1946, and three examples were built. Like with the XH-9350, as events played out, there was no need for the XR-7755.

An issue that continued to plague XH-9350 testing was the formation of cracks in the water jacket. The cracks in the cylinder water jacket had mostly been solved by redesigning the cylinder to have solely a flange hold-down rather than long hold-down bolts passing through the cylinder head. Tension on the through-bolts created additional stresses that caused the water jacket surrounding the cylinder to crack. But even the final cylinder still had leaks in the cylinder head.

It is interesting that none of the documentation found indicates any concern regarding the water jacket cracks. Cracks are mentioned as the reason a cylinder was replaced or a test halted or an engine repaired, but no mention is made about the implications leaking cylinders would have on a complete engine or how it was still an issue after three years of development. The issue was not hidden, nor were the involved parties blind to it. Most likely, the cracks were seen as an issue that would be resolved as development progressed.

165

Another issue was with detonation occurring above 40 inHg MAP and 2,200 rpm when the test engine had an 8.0:1 CR. To avoid detonation, the test engine was not run above those parameters. It should be noted that there was no intercooler installed on the test engine—just a straight pipe feeding air under pressure at a relatively low 100° F. The induction air for the complete XH-9350 was to be intercooled after it left the CH-5 turbosuperchargers, but no specific information has been found regarding this configuration. It is doubtful that an intercooler would reduce the charge temperature below 100° F, improving the detonation limit and allowing more power to be made.

Even at 350 mph, a 10,000-mile journey would take close to 29 hours to complete. One can only speculate as to whether or not the H-9350's cylinders would have achieved the level of reliability needed for such a long and continuous operation. If a cylinder were to leak mid-flight, the other cylinders of that engine would be called upon to take up the slack. This would increase the stress placed on the other cylinders and perhaps make them more prone to leaking, thus multiplying the issue. While it was fairly common for the B-36 to return with one of its six engines shut down (a 17% power loss), it would be a bit different with one of four engines shut down (a 25% power loss).

Another issue was weight. Keeping with the R-4360 versus H-9350 in the B-36 comparison, the early R-4360s as installed in the B-36 weighed around 3,800 lb. This would give a total engine weight of 22,800 lb for the six R-4360 engines in the B-36. With a complete H-9350 engine weighing 6,870 lb, which includes both remote gear units, the total engine weight of four H-9350s in the B-36 would be 27,480 lb. A B-36 with H-9350 engines would have an advantage of increased fuel economy but would also have a 4,680 lb (1,170 lb per engine) penalty in engine weight alone—not counting the weight of the liquid-cooling system needed to cool the engines.

Studebaker was not interested in making a profit on the MX-232/XH-9350 program. The initial phase of the contract was a fixed price amount, and Studebaker lost around $600,000 in the course of fulfilling its obligations. Studebaker brought this loss to the government's attention to stress why it wanted a new contract arrangement. The government made it clear that it would reimburse Studebaker because it did not want any contractor losing money on legitimate work

requested. Studebaker sought, and was granted, a cost-plus fixed fee contract and made it clear on multiple occasions that the company felt the fee should be only $1.00.

Unlike most government contracts, the XH-9350 was not cancelled immediately after World War II. The AAF showed continued interested in the project, and it was Studebaker whose interest waned. As the war wound down, Studebaker made it clear that it was interested in building a complete engine only on an experimental basis. It was not interested in building many experimental engines, and it had no interest in entering the aircraft engine field. Studebaker was looking forward to resuming automotive production and felt the engine would only be a military product, not for commercial aviation.

With that knowledge, the Power Plant Laboratory ordered three XH-9350-1 engines on 2 July 1945. Even when faced with budget issues, the number of engines on order was reduced and not cancelled. One can only wonder how long the XH-9350 would have continued if Studebaker had been more enthusiastic about the project and if the AAF had not experienced budgetary constraints with the end of World War II. With enthusiasm and funds, a complete engine would most likely have been built. The XH-9350 contract was ultimately cancelled in October 1945, months after Japan had surrendered and the war was over.

Amongst the documents obtained from the Tilley Estate was a rough draft of an untitled Wright Aeronautical report. The report compared the older style Studebaker 8.0" bore and stroke cylinder (four hold-down bolts, 402.1 in^3) to the Wright C9HD cylinder. The C9HD was one of the final developments of the R-1820 engine and was in production from 1945 until 1961. The engine still had a 6.125" bore and a 6.875" stroke, with each cylinder displacing 202.6 in^3, but power output had risen to 1,425 hp, or 0.78 hp/in^3. The report was written by H. W. Welsh and E. F. Pierce and was dated 26 March 1945. However, Tilley had circled the "45" and written "46?" above. A date of 1946 fits better into the historical timeline. Regardless, the conclusions from the report were as follows:

- The Studebaker cylinder had a minimum SFC 9% lower than the Wright cylinder.
- The Studebaker cylinder had an indicated thermal efficiency of 44.5%, the highest ever in recorded literature at the time.

- The volumetric efficiency and specific power of the Wright and Studebaker cylinders was found to be comparable.
- SFC versus displacement was as important as SFC versus compression ratio.
- Cylinder displacement had no effect on detonation.
- Exhaust temperature increased as displacement increased, which would provide more energy for a blowdown turbine (turbo-compounding).

It is interesting to note the reference to a blowdown turbine. Wright was experimenting with turbo-compounding, and Welsh and Pierce wrote a report on the process in 1948 titled *Engine Compounding for Power and Efficiency*. Overall, the Wright report seems to validate the Studebaker test reports and the MX-232 engine concept. Wright's interest in the XH-9350 did not lead to it continuing any development of the engine.

The Recollections

Robert E. Bourke worked directly for Studebaker as a designer from 1940 to 1953. In a 1985 interview for the Edsel Ford Design History Center at the Henry Ford Museum, he recalled the MX-232 engine project:

[A]t Studebaker … they needed [extra] hands, and they couldn't get 'em. So, they swung me into the chassis division at Studebaker, which, in turn, had been cordoned off, and that became part of the U.S. Air Corps contract to develop a new internal combustion engine for the Air Corps. This was a very interesting thing to me, getting back to aircraft, and it was just a delight to see how these fellows went about it. A man by the name of Tilley was in charge of this, and he was a very well-known internal combustion aircraft designer. There was quite a group, and Frank Alhroth was swung in from doing clay modeling automobiles to do clay modeling for internal combustions chambers.

To make a long story short, the idea was to develop a large engine—intercooled—which, in turn, would be situated in the center of a large bomber fuselage with the powertrains going out to the wings and driving four propellers. An 8.0" bore was about as big as we got with a single cylinder, and we

developed, with twin turbo chargers, close to 300 hp with one 8.0" bore single cylinder.

Then we went from a single to doubles … they were huge, and they had to be run in on dynamometer tests in special rooms where, in turn, the components were so darned big that the coefficient of expansion in the aluminum with the crank and a piston were such that it was very difficult to keep the engine together at high rpms. But they finally got that whipped.

But they were in cages, so that when they did break loose, it didn't blow the room out. They had .5" steel bar meshes on 1.0" centers that air was coming in. Then they had a secondary mesh in case something got through, it would be stopped. They'd build these engines one after the other with modifications and changes. Money was no object, but, boy, they needed manpower. Then we'd set them up, and then we'd run them in. Then we'd have bets on how long this engine would last and run 'em 'till they broke. Literally blew them all up. Some of them would [only] fracture, and we'd take them down, save the components, and make a change, or have a change ready for it.

When it was obvious that the jet engine was going to replace the internal combustion engine, that slowed down the Tilley project.

There is no indication that the power delivery configuration described by Bourke was ever considered for a bomber. Most likely, it was a simply a misunderstanding, given the buried wing and shafting installations that were planned for the engine. While the XH-9350 was to have two turbo-superchargers, and the induction air was forced into the test engines at up to 45 inHg, the test engines were never turbocharged. Even with time possibly clouding memory, Mr. Bourke's account of the Studebaker long-range engine program is very insightful.

In a letter dated 7 May 1947 to Gid Herreshoff, Chief Engineer of Development Design at the Chrysler Corporation, Norman Tilley stated the following regarding the XH-9350:

A .30 lbs/bph/hr. cruise consumption was in sight which apparently was not good enough to warrant continuation of a nearly one lb/hp

5000 – 8000 hp reciprocating engine power plant, with jet jobs sprouting all around.

Whether or not Tilley believed that "his" complete engine was truly capable of such numbers will never be known. While such figures were achieved during testing, it is hard to imagine that there would be no variations in the results when another 23 cylinders were added to the mix. However, with continued development, further refinement, and the inclusion of two CH-5 turbosuperchargers and intercooling, perhaps an H-9350 would have been capable of such performance.

The Comparison

The XH-9350 was a very unique engine developed during a time of war by a company unfamiliar with aircraft engines. XH-9350 single- and twin-cylinder test engines accumulated a total of 4,847.75 hours. A complete engine was never built. The program ran for about three and a half years at a cost of $1,454,661.43. There are no truly similar programs to which the XH-9350 engine and Studebaker's performance can be directly compared. However, a few other engine programs can provide some perspective to Studebaker's efforts.

Like Studebaker, Ford and Chrysler designed their own aircraft engines for World War II. None of these automotive companies had previously built a powerful aircraft engine. While the engines were very different, the companies were in essentially the same position as they worked to expand in a new design direction.

Ford initiated its own unique engine design in June 1940 after reviewing design documents for the Rolls-Royce Merlin. The Ford GGA engine had the same 1,650 in^3 displacement as the Merlin and was a private venture without government financial support. Twin-cylinder test engines were run for over 300 hours. At least three complete engines were built and run for a total of more than 100 hours. After two and a half years and spending $2,000,000 of its own money, Ford abandoned the V-12 aircraft engine and focused on a V-8 version (GAA) for tanks.

Chrysler's development of its XI-2220 engine spanned about five years, but no aircraft was ever designed specifically for the 2,500 hp, V-16 engine. Single- and twin-cylinder test engines accumulated 22,265 hours. Six complete XI-2220 engines were built and run a cumulative total of 2,619 hours. Two engines were test-flown in Republic XP-47H

Thunderbolts, but all flight activity occurred after development on the Chrysler engine had stopped. The XI-2220 program cost $13,760,623.48.

Lycoming was an experienced aircraft engine manufacturer. Outside of a few experimental developments, Lycoming focused on smaller, general aviation aircraft engines. As mentioned earlier, one of the company's experimental engines was roughly the same size and power as the XH-9350. The Lycoming XR-7755 provides a unique example of how a company with aircraft engine experience can tackle a large-engine program. The 5,000 hp XR-7755 engine was developed over the course of three years (1943–1946). Single-cylinder test engines had accumulated over 10,000 hours before the first complete XR-7755 had run in 1946. Two (or possibly three) complete 36-cylinder engines were built. Program cost for the XR-7755 was over $2,000,000. The XR-7755 engine was not a success, and its cylinder design did not break new ground, but Lycoming managed to build and run a complete 5,000 hp engine while Studebaker was still years away from that achievement.

Smaller and less powerful than the XH-9350, the Pratt & Whitney R-4360 was an engine that used proven components and was built by an experienced aircraft engine manufacturer. As history unfolded, the R-4360 was the largest mass-produced piston aircraft engine ever built. Utilizing production R-2800 cylinders, a proof of concept R-4360 engine was run just six months after serious design work began. It took around four and a half years of development before the first production R-4360 engine (of 3,000 hp) was shipped in January 1945. In that time, over 12,000 hours of complete engine test stand operation had occurred, and $15,300,000 had been spent. Development of the R-4360 continued through 1949. Ultimately, over 40,000 hours of single-cylinder and 2,000 hours of single-row testing were completed; 23 complete engines accumulated 25,000 hours on the test stand, and $42,900,000 was spent on development of this successful engine. As the R-4360 shows, even with knowledge, experience, and proven components, developing a large aircraft engine was a monumental task requiring massive amounts of money and extensive resources.

Reviewing the Ford GGA, Chrysler XI-2220, Lycoming XR-7755, and Pratt & Whitney R-4360 programs, it is apparent that Studebaker had a long way to go and a lot more money to spend before the XH-9350 would have been a viable, reliable engine. At the same time, the company's position was

Engine Program Comparison										
	Project Start	Test Engine 1st Run	Test Engine Hours	Complete Engine 1st Run	Complete Engine Test Hours	Engine's 1st Flight	Start of Production	Project Cancellation	Project Cost
Studebaker XH-9350	Mar 1942	Feb 1943 (11 Months)	4,848	Est. Mar 1947 (Est. > 5 Years)	0	None	None	Oct 1945 (3.5 Years)	$1,454,661.43
Ford GGA (V-1650)	Jun 1940	Nov 1940 (6 Months)	300	Aug 1941 (1.25 Years)	100	None	None	Dec 1942 (2.5 Years)	$2,000,000.00
Chrysler XI-2220	May 1940	May 1941 (1 Year)	22,265	Jul 1942 (2.25 Years)	2,619	Jul 1945 (5.25 Years)	None	Apr 1945 (5 Years)	$13,760,623.48
Lycoming XR-7755	Mid- 1943	Not Known	10,000+	Jul 1946 (3 Years)	Not Known	None	None	1946 (3 Years)	>$2,000,000.00
Pratt & Whitney R-4360*	Nov 1940	Mid-1941 (~8 Months)	24,000	Apr 1941 (6 Months)	12,000	May 1942 (1.5 Years)	Jan 1945 (4 Years)		$15,300,000.00
* Engine hours and cost for the R-4360 are up until production and not the grand total for all development.										

somewhat in line with other automotive manufacturers endeavoring for the first time into the field of aircraft engines.

The Companions

In the quest for fuel efficiency, few engines can approach the results obtained during the Studebaker tests. However, Studebaker's results were achieved with just single- and twin-cylinder engines, not a complete engine. While the complete H-9350 had a SFC guarantee of .370 lb/hp/hr, it seems Tilley thought numbers of .355 lb/hp/hr were obtainable; a SFC of .320 lb/hp/hr or even lower was mentioned with turbo-compounding. Had these numbers actually been achieved, the H-9350 engine would have set the standard for fuel efficiency by which all other piston aircraft engines were judged.

For large aircraft engines that went into production, the low SFC leader is the 3,400 hp Wright R-3350 turbo-compound built in the 1950s. With three blowdown turbines recovering energy from the exhaust and feeding it back to the crankshaft, this 18-cylinder radial engine achieved a SFC of .378 lb/hp/hr. On the experimental side, the Lycoming XR-7755, an engine of the same vintage and scale as the XH-9350, reportedly achieved a SFC of .430 lb/hp/hr. The Allison V-3420, representing half of a DV-6840, achieved a SFC of .410 lb/hp/hr.

Also, from the same time as the XH-9350 was the German Klöckner-Humboldt-Deutz Dz 720. The Dz 720 was a two-stroke, diesel, H-32 engine that was intended to produce a maximum of 5,900 hp. It consisted of two 16-cylinder Dz 710 engines coupled together. The Dz 710 had a minimum SFC of .342

lb/hp/hr. The Dz 720 was very tall, never completed development, and never flew.

The KHD Dz 720 held some promise as a high-power, fuel efficient diesel, but it was never completed. (AC)

The experimental engine with the lowest SFC was the exotic, half jet / half two-stroke diesel Napier Nomad II developed in the 1950s. It may be an apples-to-oranges comparison with other pure-piston engines, but the British Nomad II obtained a minimum SFC of .327 lb/hp/hr at 2,025 ehp (equivalent hp combining the engine and turbine), 1,750 rpm, and 25,000' altitude. However, the engine operated with a SFC of less than .350 lb/hp/hr throughout all of its power and rpm ranges, including 3,135 ehp takeoff power at

The Wright R-3350 Turbo Compound was the most advanced large piston aircraft engine produced in quantity. Three power recovery turbines were geared to the crankshaft and fed power from the exhaust back to the engine. Late models produced as much as 3,700 hp. A total of 11,954 R-3350 Turbo Compound engines were built. (AC)

The Napier Nomad II (E145) was a 12-cylinder, two-stroke, diesel engine compounded with a three-stage turbine. The turbine drove an axial compressor and fed power back to the crankshaft. The engine displaced 2,502 in³ and produced up to 3,580 eshp, which included 250 lb of thrust from the turbine. The Nomad II was first run in December 1952. With the exception of fuel economy, the engine was outclassed by turboprops and jet engines. (AC)

2,250 rpm. The Nomad II was a horizontally opposed 12-cylinder with a small turbine situated under the engine. The turbine was geared directly to the crankshaft—feeding power to the propeller. While the Nomad did not enter production, it did fly in the nose of an Avro Lincoln test bed in 1955.

Neither the R-3350 nor the Nomad II ever approached the maximum power output projected for a complete H-9350. The XR-7755 and Dz 720 did have power (and SFC for the Dz 720) on par with what was projected for the H-9350. But the size of these engines, a height of 66.25" for the XR-7755 and a height of approximately 79" for the DZ 720, precluded their installation submerged in the wing as proposed for the 40" tall H-9350. The H-9350 was not a compact engine; it was just designed for installation in the wing of a very large aircraft.

As already stated, the chart on page 161 consists of engines that were considered large for their time. All the engines listed on the chart were built except two: the Studebaker XH-9350 and the GEHL SNECMA 32 HL. The XH-9350 is on the list because it is the main subject of this work. The 32 HL is listed because, being some 600 in³ larger that the XH-9350, it is the largest aircraft engine ever seriously pursued. In 1946, SNECMA's GEHL (*Groupe d'étude des moteurs à huile lourde*, or study group of heavy oil engines) endeavored to build a large diesel aircraft engine to be in transport service in 1953. This design effort led to the 32 HL, which was a four-row radial with eight liquid-cooled cylinders per row (32 cylinders total). The bore was 7.09" (180 mm) and the stroke was 7.87" (200 mm), giving a total displacement of 9,938 cu in (162.86 L). The engine was to produce 4,000 hp and weigh 7,716 lb (3,500 kg). As designed, the 32 HL had two fuel injectors per cylinder and was turbocharged. Some cylinder testing (probably only single) and crankcase construction was underway when the project was cancelled in 1948. The 32 HL was cancelled because the ATAR 201 turboprop SNECMA was developing would have produced the same hp but at one sixth the weight.

The chart does not include a number of other large aircraft engines that were halted at the design or early developmental stage. Also excluded are completely separate engines geared to a common, remote gear reduction.

Harnessing the power of two separate engines in a common installation was a way to make due with

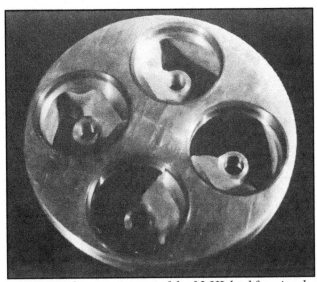

The 7.09" diameter piston of the 32 HL had four intake valves. The engine's cylinder head had four exhaust valves. A complete 32 HL was never built. (AC)

existing engines rather than create an entirely new, large, powerful engine. To power the Bristol Brabazon, two Centaurus 18 engines were coupled to a common gear reduction to create the Centaurus 20 (XX), a 6,543 in³ power unit capable of 5,000 hp. This was the same concept that led to the Allison DV-6840 (two V-3420s) design.

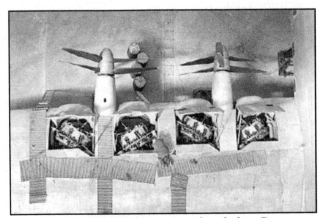

For the Bristol Brabazon, each of the Centaurus engines was installed in the wing at a 32° angle. Each of the four Centaurs 20 engine installations weighed 8,390 lb. (AC)

In France, the question of how to power the next generation of large aircraft was answered by the Hispano-Suiza 48Z (Type 96) and the Arsenal 24H Tandem. Both engines were a pair of H-24s coupled in tandem. The Hispano-Suiza 48Z displaced 8,800 in³ and was rated at 7,200 hp. The Arsenal 24H Tandem displaced 8,541 in³ and was also rated at 7,200 hp. These engines were never completed, and the giant

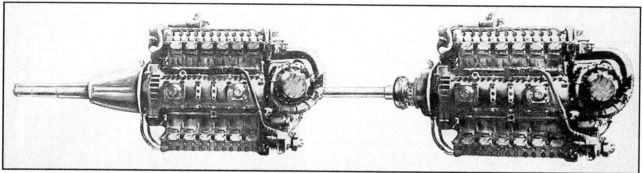

The Arsenal 24H Tandem offered 7,200 hp but weighed 9,039 lb and was around 20' long. It is unlikely that a complete engine was ever built. (AC)

aircraft they were to selected to power never materialized. Fortunately, the jet engine moved aircraft development in a different direction.

Of the 38 engines listed on the chart, perhaps only one, the Pratt & Whitney R-4360, can be considered a true success. The FIAT A.14 had a limited production run of around 500 units. The Daimler-Benz "double-Vees" did reach production, and the DB 606 did not create too much difficulty in the experimental Heinkel He 119, but the DB 610's installation in the Heinkel He 177 *Greif* bomber left much to be desired. The engines caught fire so often that Luftwaffe aircrews nicknamed the He 177 *Luftwaffenfeuerzeug*, meaning *Luftwaffe's lighter*.

Rear view of the DB 610 illustrates how the 24-cylinder engine consisted of two inverted V-12 DB 605 engines coupled together. (AC)

Although far from trouble-free, the Pratt & Whitney R-4360 was well-mannered in contrast to the Daimler-Benz engines. With 18,697 engines built, the R-4360 served for many years, and a few are still regularly flown. This makes the R-4360 the most successful of the large aircraft engines; this achievement was realized in part through a tried and tested design and in part due to the end of the large piston engine era.

The Conclusion

Many of the developmental issues encountered by Studebaker with the XH-9350 were not necessarily unique to that engine. The issues were a fairly common part of designing high-performance, liquid-cooled, piston aircraft engines. To develop the engine, the manufacturer tenaciously pushed through the issues, redesigning parts along the way, until a reliable engine resulted.

To truly understand the XH-9350, it is essential to consider the particular time in history that the engine was envisioned and developed. In the era before mid-air refueling and powerful jet engines, the only option to carry a payload of bombs or passengers over a distance of 10,000 miles was to use a very large aircraft. The power required to propel an aircraft increases as the aircraft grows in size and weight. Using four or six 5,000 hp engines is simpler and much more desirable than using eight, ten, or twelve 2,500 hp engines. While not the most powerful or the largest aircraft engine ever designed, the Studebaker XH-9350 was conceived to propel the next generation of very large aircraft over very long distances.

In 1941, the fate of Britain was in question against the German onslaught. With this threat at hand, the concept of developing the H-9350 engine to power B-36 bombers capable of taking off from the United States and Canada to bomb targets in Germany was well within reason. As events played out, the H-9350 and B-36 were not needed. But no one knew that in 1941. At that time, no one could see how the war would evolve or how jet engines would change everything. The XH-9350 was developed and moved forward because it was the next logical step for piston aircraft engine technology in 1941. It was an engine that was needed to power the large aircraft that were then being built and others that were still on the drawing board—aircraft like the Hughes H-4 Hercules (320' wingspan), the Conviar XC-99 (230' wingspan) and its commercial derivatives, and the Bristol Brabazon (230' wingspan). Although its development was seriously delayed, the test-cylinder engines gave every indication that an H-9350 engine would have met the requested design goals for a high-power, fuel-efficient engine.

But between 1941 and 1945, aviation changed, and it continued to change. The B-36 was the last of the line; such large aircraft and aircraft engines were not practical. The jet engine continued to gain momentum and redefined large aircraft design. Not only was there no place for engines like the H-9350 and R-7755, there was no place for aircraft like the C-99 or Brabazon. All of these projects on which so many worked so diligently became just a footnote in the history of aviation.

SUMMARY COMPARISON
GENERAL DESIGN DATA

	M.C.D. 392	A	B	C
SPAN (FT.)	280	280	259	321
WING AREA (SQ.FT.)	7140	7140	6100	9355
ASPECT RATIO	11	11	11	11
TAPER RATIO	4	4	4	4
ROOT SECTION (IN.)	520	520	452	576
TIP SECTION (IN.)	130	130	113	144
HORIZONTAL TAIL AREA (SQ.FT.)	1570	1570	1345	2060
VERTICAL TAIL AREA (SQ.FT.)	785	785	670	1030
OVER-ALL LENGTH (FT.)	129	129	120	160

PERFORMANCE AT DESIGNED GROSS WEIGHT

	M.C.D. 392	A	B	C
NUMBER OF ENGINES	8	12	8	12
DESIGN GROSS WEIGHT (LBS.)	500,000	500,000	427,000	655,000
WING LOADING	70	70	70	70
POWER LOADING (NORMAL)	24	16	20.5	21
WEIGHT EMPTY (LBS.)	216,610	242,610	195,600	295,000
USEFUL LOAD (LBS.)	283,390	257,390	231,400	360,000
HIGH SPEED (MPH/ALT)	342/20,000	420/35,000	376/25,000	381/25,000
RATE OF CLIMB (FPM/S.L.)*	330	870	500	500
RANGE (MI./16,000 LBS. BOMBS)	11,250	10,000	10,450	11,700
RANGE (MI./120,000 LBS. BOMBS)	6,100	5,450	4,700	7,550
RANGE (MI./NO BOMBS)	12,000	10,700	11,400	12,400
SERVICE CEILING (FT.)	20,000	35,500	25,000	25,000
TAKE-OFF DISTANCE (FT.)	9,200	6,100	7,800	8,000

PERFORMANCE AT .3 RANGE.

	M.C.D. 392	A	B	C
WEIGHT (LBS.)	385,000	402,000	342,000	513,000
HIGH SPEED (MPH.)	386	430	402	410
SERVICE CEILING (FT.)	36,250	39,750	37,000	37,000

*BASED ON NORMAL RATED POWER.

Ambitious aircraft projects in the early and mid-1940s needed ambitious engines to power them. In a world without jets, piston engines like the H-9350, R-7755, and DV-6840 were the next logical step of aircraft propulsion: massive, powerful, fuel-efficient engines to power huge aircraft over very long distances. The designers of these engines set out to solve anticipated problems that did not come to pass as the future unfolded. (AC)

© 1944. The Studebaker Corporation

When the Marines got Lukavich they took a good man

But his team-mate father still builds Cyclone engines at Studebaker

Studebaker-built Cyclone engines keep swarms of Flying Fortresses flying—And Studebaker craftsmen build much other vital war matériel, including vast quantities of heavy-duty war trucks. Studebaker is proud of its part in our country's war production program.

TWENTY-ONE years ago last January, a mechanic named Paul Lukavich signed his first pay voucher as a Studebaker employee.

His son, Steve, now in the Marine Corps, was then a chubby baby two years old.

In September, 1940, in keeping with a custom that's generations-old in South Bend, the Lukaviches became a Studebaker father-and-son team. And not long after that, the two moved over from the automotive shops to the great modern aircraft engine plant where huge quantities of Studebaker-built Cyclones that power the Flying Fortress are being produced. A year ago this March, Steve Lukavich joined the Marines.

Today, the record shows that Studebaker is one of the world's largest builders of engines for warplanes—one of the largest manufacturers, too, of big multiple-drive

military trucks, tens upon tens of thousands of which are in the far-flung transport service of the United Nations.

Many Studebaker fathers and sons have parted company for the duration—but the solid principles of Studebaker craftsmanship endure.

When peace comes, that craftsmanship, tested and proved anew in the flaming crucible of war, will give the world the highest quality motor cars and motor trucks ever manufactured.

BUY U. S. WAR BONDS

STUDEBAKER

Builder of Wright Cyclone engines for the Boeing Flying Fortress — big multiple-drive military trucks — and other vital war matériel

7. Studebaker-Built GE J47 Turbojet

Fewer than five years after the end of World War II, the United States found itself drawn into another war. This time, the Chinese and Soviet Union-backed communists of North Korea were the focus of the United States military. With sales slumping, Studebaker was desperate for any type of work. Late in 1950, Studebaker was contracted to build General Electric J47-25 turbojet engines under license. These engines were for the Boeing B-47 Stratojet bomber. Studebaker quickly moved forward to construct a new plant in New Brunswick, New Jersey to accommodate J47 production.

As jet engines began to emerge early in 1941, their true potential was still unknown. At the time, the United States lagged behind Germany and Britain in the development of jet engines. In March 1941, the Special Committee on Jet Propulsion was created to instigate and expedite the development of jet engines in the United States. Because of the jet engine's uncertain future, General Hap Arnold ordered existing aircraft engine manufacturers to focus on piston engines and be excluded from jet engine development. This meant that companies like Pratt & Whitney, Wright, and Allison would continue to develop and build only piston engines. Despite the fact that Pratt & Whitney, Wright, Northrop, and Lockheed had all begun studies of gas turbine engines around this time, the accelerated development of jet engines was turned over to other industrial firms that had experience with steam turbines. These companies were General Electric, Westinghouse, and Allis-Chalmers.

General Electric (GE) was particularly well suited for the development of gas turbines; it had two separate divisions with experience in the general principles of turbine technology. GE's Steam Turbine Division focused on industrial turbines and was located in Schenectady, New York. GE's Supercharger Division specialized in both superchargers and turbosuperchargers and was located in Lynn, Massachusetts.

GE's history with steam turbines began at Schenectady in 1897. The first GE industrial steam turbine was installed in Chicago, Illinois in 1903 to generate power. At the time, it was the most powerful steam turbine generator in the world. Over the years, the Schenectady Steam Turbine Division had solved many problems associated with turbines, particularly with vibrations and bucket and axial-flow compressor development.

The Supercharger Division at Lynn really came into its own through the work of Sanford A. Moss. Moss began working for GE in 1903 and was engaged in turbine experimentation. In 1917, spurred on by World War I, Moss focused on creating turbosuperchargers—devices that used the piston aircraft engine's exhaust gases to spin a turbine connected to a centrifugal compressor that forced more air into the engine's induction. A Moss-developed turbosupercharger was installed on a Liberty V-12 engine and tested at Pikes Peak, Colorado from September through October 1918. Tests at the 14,109' elevation of Pikes Peak indicated that the turbosupercharger engine produced 377 hp—an increase of over 60% compared to 230 hp for the normally aspirated engine.

The Moss-designed turbosupercharger attached to a Liberty engine. The engine installed in a LUSAC-11 reached 33,113' on 27 February 1920. (AEHS)

Moss continued his research, but his work was often put on hold because metal alloys did not exist that could withstand the heat created in the turbosupercharger's turbine. Suitable materials were eventually developed, but little effort was expended on developing an entire aircraft engine based on the turbine principle. However, the turbosupercharger endeavor proved quite successful, and many US aircraft that fought in World War II—such as the Boeing B-17 Flying Fortress, Consolidated B-24 Liberator, Lockheed P-38 Lightning, Republic P-47 Thunderbolt, and more—were equipped with GE turbosuperchargers (also called turbochargers).

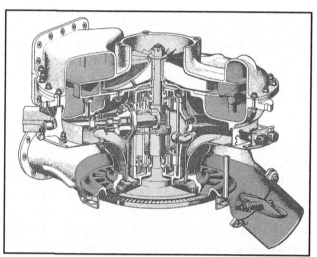

Cutaway view of a GE B-series turbosupercharger. The type was used on the B-17, B-24, B-29, and P-38. (AC)

Starting in 1939, GE's interest in gas turbines increased, and various studies were undertaken, including trips to the United Kingdom to see the work of Frank Whittle. The Schenectady Steam Turbine Division had also done some experimental work on gas turbines to power locomotives and ships. Building on its previous turbine experience and work with the Special Committee on Jet Propulsion, the National Advisory Committee for Aeronautics (NACA) endorsed the development of the GE Schenectady Steam Turbine Division's TG-100 axial-flow turboprop engine in July 1941. Later, the US Army Air Corps provided a contract for the development of the TG-100.

During The TG-100's development, GE's Lynn Supercharger Division was involved in building an engine closely based on the Frank Whittle-designed Power Jets W.2B centrifugal-flow turbojet engine. The GE jet engine was called the Type I (later designated I-A) and was first run on 18 March 1942,

becoming the first US-built jet engine. Almost immediately, additional engines based on the I-A were developed by GE. Still of the centrifugal-flow design, these engines were the I-14 and I-16 (later designated J31). The I-14 was first run in February 1943, and the I-16 followed two months later, in April. This developmental line continued with the I-18 (first run in January 1944), I-20 (first run in April 1944), and I-40 (also run in January 1944). The I-40 was the most successful of these early jet engines and was later designated J33. It represented the last of the centrifugal-flow jet engines based on the original Whittle design, which yielded to the more promising axial-flow design.

Meanwhile, GE's TG-100 (later designated T31) turboprop from the Schenectady Steam Turbine Division was run on 15 May 1943, becoming the first US turboprop engine. It produced 1,200 hp and weighed 800 lb. All of these jet engine projects were developed under the strictest security, and the work done at Lynn Supercharger Division was, for the most part, completely separate from the work done at Schenectady Steam Turbine Division. As the projects developed, there was occasional movement of personnel and information from one division to another, but the groups were still separate.

The GE TG-100 (T31) turboprop that formed the basis for the TG-180 (J35) axial turbojet. (USAF)

The same month the T31 first ran, the Schenectady Steam Turbine Division began developing an axial-flow turbojet based on the T31. This engine was designated TG-180 (later J35) and had a target of 4,000 lb static thrust. The J35 had an 11-stage axial-flow compressor, giving an air mass flow of 75 lb per second at a pressure ratio of 4 to 1. The compressor was driven by a single turbine, and the engine weighed 2,400 lb. The J35 was first run on 21 April 1944. Initial tests indicated 3,620 lb of thrust, and no issues with the engine were encountered. The J35 saw service in the North American FJ-1 Fury, Republic F-84 Thunderjet, Northrop F-89 Scorpion, and many prototypes, including the Northrop YB-49 flying wing and first Boeing XB-47 Stratojet. The US Military

The GE TG-180 (J35) was the first axial-flow engine adopted by the USAF. (AEHS)

gave the J35 production contract to Allison to keep the company's ample workforce engaged, and the engine's thrust was eventually upped to 6,000 lb on some models.

With the war nearly over, a realignment of efforts and resources occurred at GE on 31 July 1945. The Schenectady Steam Turbine Division focused on land and sea applications for turbines, and all aircraft engine development was transferred to the Lynn Supercharger Division. The Lynn division was renamed the Aircraft Gas Turbine Division and took over the development of the J35 and future axial-flow engines.

GE and the Aircraft Gas Turbine Division decided to produce another jet engine based directly on the J35. The new engine would be the same size as the J35 but with a new compressor and turbine. This new engine was to initially produce at least 5,000 lb of thrust. Development began on 19 March 1946 with Neil Burgess in charge, and the new engine was designated TG-190 (later J47). The J47 had a 12-stage axial compressor, giving an air mass flow of 90 lb per second at a pressure ratio of 5 to 1 at 7,950 rpm. The compressor casing was made up of two aluminum alloy halves bolted together, and it included one row of steel inlet guide vanes. The compressor rotor was made up of 12 aluminum alloy discs, each with a row of steel blades. Each disc was shrunk onto the hollow steel rotor shaft. The rotor shaft was connected to the turbine shaft by a splined coupling. As in the J35, the compressor was driven by a single-stage turbine. Between the rotor and the turbine were eight stainless-steel combustion chambers. A stainless-steel casing surrounded the turbine and led to the exhaust nozzle.

The J47 was first run on 21 June 1947 and produced around 4,850 lb of static thrust. Some developmental issues were encountered, and the engine was slightly

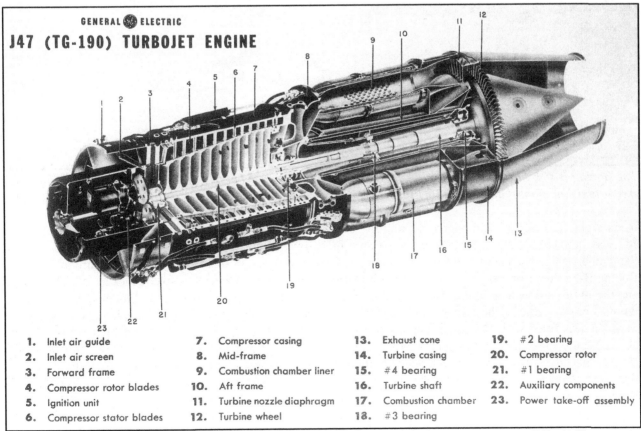

1.	Inlet air guide	**7.**	Compressor casing	**13.**	Exhaust cone	**19.**	#2 bearing
2.	Inlet air screen	**8.**	Mid-frame	**14.**	Turbine casing	**20.**	Compressor rotor
3.	Forward frame	**9.**	Combustion chamber liner	**15.**	#4 bearing	**21.**	#1 bearing
4.	Compressor rotor blades	**10.**	Aft frame	**16.**	Turbine shaft	**22.**	Auxiliary components
5.	Ignition unit	**11.**	Turbine nozzle diaphragm	**17.**	Combustion chamber	**23.**	Power take-off assembly
6.	Compressor stator blades	**12.**	Turbine wheel	**18.**	#3 bearing		

Cutaway drawing of a GE J47 engine. Note the 12 stages attached to the compressor rotor (20). (AC)

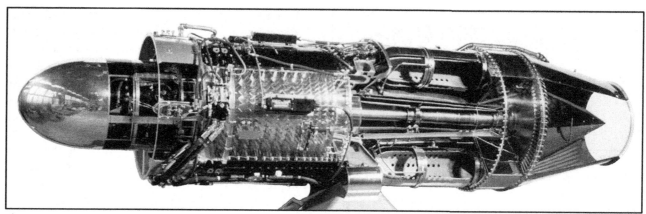

A cutaway J47 engine illustrates the amazing advancement in aircraft propulsion over just a few years. The J47 was first run only five years after the Studebaker XH-9350 project was started. For additional power in the B-36, four J47 engines were added to supplement the six 3,800 hp R-4360s. (AC)

The Boeing B-47E Stratojet used six J47 engines and had a top speed of 606 mph. The first B-47 took to the air a year and four months after the B-36, illustrating again what a revolution the jet engine was to aviation. (USAF)

overweight. The issues were overcome, and the first J47 was delivered to the United States Air Force in September 1947. The engine first took to the air in a Boeing B-29 Superfortress test bed on 20 April 1948, and the J47 first flew in a fighter (F-86) the following month, on 18 May. The second Boeing XB-47 Stratojet was fitted with J47 engines and took to the air on 21 July 1948. The GE J47 entered production in the summer of 1948 and was the intended engine for the B-47, North American F-86 Sabre, FJ-2 Fury, B-45 Tornado, and other aircraft.

Back in late 1943, Boeing initiated design studies on a jet-powered reconnaissance bomber known as the Model 424. The fall of Germany provided data on swept wing aircraft performance. This information led to a redesign of Boeing's proposed aircraft—from a straight wing to a wing swept back at 35°. The refined bomber design, known as the Model 450, was to have a maximum speed of 550 mph, cruise speed of 450 mph, range of 3,500 mi, ceiling of 45,000 ft, and be capable of carrying a nuclear bomb. In April 1946, the Air Force ordered two prototypes of the six-engine Model 450 bomber, and the aircraft became the B-47 Stratojet. The first example was completed by 12 September 1947 and first flew on 17 December 1947. Flight testing went well, and the B-47 quickly entered production.

The definitive variant of the B-47 was the E model. This aircraft was equipped for in-flight refueling, had a 606 mph top speed, 557 mph cruise speed, could carry up to 20,000 lb of bombs, and had a 4,640 mi ferry range. The B-47E used six GE J47-25 engines. The compressor rotor for the J47-25 was made up of one steel disc at the front, nine aluminum alloy discs, and three steel discs at the rear. Air mass flow and the pressure ratio were respectively increased to 100 lb per second and 5.5 to 1 at 7,950 rpm. The J47-25 produced 6,000 lb of static thrust that could be increased to 7,200 lb with water-alcohol injection. The J47-25 was 39.5" in diameter, 144.0" long, and weighed 2,650 lb.

In late 1950, Studebaker was contracted to produce 3,000 J47-25 engines for the B-47 bomber. These engines carried the designation J47-ST-25; the "ST" identified Studebaker as the manufacturer. The General Electric-built engines carried "GE" in their designation. The Packard Motor Car Company received an order similar to Studebaker's, and its J47 engines were identified with "PM" for Packard Motors. The Studebaker and Packard orders were later increased to 6,000 engines each.

A J47 engine positioned vertically to ease assembly at Studebaker's Chippewa Avenue plant. (AC)

Studebaker had been planning to construct a plant in New Brunswick, New Jersey, and used the J47 engine contract as a reason to proceed. Once the engine contract was fulfilled, the plant would be converted for vehicle production, supplying Studebaker automobiles to East Coast dealerships. The New Brunswick plant opened on 19 November 1951 and employed about 300 workers (far below the 2,500

expected) making components for the J47. However, complete J47s were never built there. Some 100 components for each engine were made in New Brunswick and sent to the Chippewa Avenue plant in South Bend, where complete J47s were assembled and tested. The Chippewa plant was the same location that had produced Studebaker-built Wright R-1820s engines during World War II. Another plant in Chicago also manufactured some components and sent them to South Bend.

Each J47 was comprised of some 8,859 parts and required 87 skills to manufacture. To ease engine assembly, the J47 was positioned vertically over a pit, with the front of the engine down (a technique pioneered by GE). The engine could be raised and lowered as needed during the assembly process. The upright assembly increased worker efficiency and conserved factory space.

Studebaker produced 3,129 of the 6,000 contracted J47 engines. Here, completed engines are lined up to be tested. (AC)

For engine testing, each assembled J47 was taken to one of 22 test cells Studebaker had built behind the Chippewa plant. In the test cell, the J47 was run up to full power. Air would enter the engine at around 100 mph and exit with a velocity up to 2,000 mph. The engine's exhaust would flow from the test cell through concrete baffles to deaden the noise and then exit through an exhaust stack. After the engine completed its test run, it was disassembled and inspected. The J47 was then reassembled and test run again before being crated for delivery.

Studebaker and Packard experienced cost overruns in their production of the J47 engine. Early in 1953, J47 production outpaced demand, and the budget was cut for Studebaker and Packard engine production.

A Studebaker-built J47 engine in one of the 22 test cells at the Studebaker plant. (AC)

As a result, J47 engine production slowly coasted to a halt at Studebaker and Packard. Of the 6,000 engines for which Studebaker was originally contracted, only 3,129 were produced. The remaining order for 2,871 additional engines was cancelled. Packard had a similar experience, producing 3,025 of the 6,000 engines ordered.

Studebaker was in a bad financial position at the time of the J47 engine cancellation. The company merged with Packard (which had slightly better financials) in 1954 to create the Studebaker-Packard Corporation. The New Brunswick plant was sold to Volkswagen of America in 1955, never having produced a single Studebaker vehicle or even a part destined for a Studebaker automobile.

The J47 was the most produced jet engine in history; around 35,832 examples were built by various manufacturers over 10 years. As impressive as that number may be, it represents roughly 56% of the 30-month R-1820 engine production from Studebaker—a definite sign of changing times.

In July 1956, Studebaker-Packard and Curtiss-Wright embarked on a three-year joint program intended to help both companies. Studebaker-Packard was to focus on automobile manufacturing, and Curtiss-Wright was to focus on defense contracts. This three-year agreement was a test-merger of sorts, and Curtiss-Wright was in control, with 52% of the Studebaker-Packard stock. Through the agreement, Curtiss-Wright purchased the remaining inventory of J47 parts and tooling, thus ending Studebaker's involvement with aircraft engines. At the end of the unsuccessful three-year merger, Curtiss-Wright withdrew from the agreement. Studebaker-Packard was left to continue its slow decline.

An impressive view of an RB-47E. The B-47 handled well and was liked by pilots. The aircraft remained in service as a bomber until 1965 and in the recon role until 1969. The aircraft's basic layout was repeated with the B-52. (USAF)

8. Conclusion

The work Studebaker accomplished in the field of aircraft engines is wide-ranging. The company converted an auto engine into an aircraft engine, mass produced a radial engine, designed and developed a huge, liquid-cooled experimental piston engine, and even manufactured a jet engine.

Yet, the only project those at Studebaker were truly passionate about was the 218 in^3 engine for the Waterman Arrowbile. In the 218 in^3 engine, Studebaker saw the opportunity to take a product it was already producing and use it to diversify into a new market. Selling Arrowbiles in dealerships ended up being impractical, but the concept required little investment and no special manufacturing from Studebaker.

Before producing the Wright R-1820 engine, the largest engine built by Studebaker was a 354 in^3 straight six-cylinder. This 75 hp engine had a 3.875" bore, 5.0" stroke, and was used in the 1919–1927 Commander and President models. The most powerful Studebaker engine was the 200 hp straight eight-cylinder engine used in the 1932 and 1933 Indianapolis 500 racers. This 337 in^3 engine had a 3.5" bore and 4.375" stroke. It was originally used in the President, in which it produced 122 hp. Compared to Studebaker's previous experience with engine production, manufacturing the R-1820 represented a quantum leap in terms of numbers produced and the engine's size and power.

R-1820 production was a much-needed war-time effort undertaken when automobile manufacturing in the United States had stopped. Studebaker did an incredible job of producing the engine in huge numbers and was able to purchase the government-funded Aircraft Engine Plant at a good price once R-1820 production ceased. Never-used Studebaker parts are still finding their way into R-1820 engines, which indicates the massive number of parts made and that their quality is still second to none.

The XH-9350 engine was an Army Air Force idea designed by an outside engineer. As the war moved toward its conclusion, Studebaker's interest in the project declined. The government urged Studebaker on despite the project being delayed and over budget. When the government was ready to order a complete engine, Studebaker made it clear that it did not want to enter the aircraft engine business but wanted to return to vehicle production. Neither Studebaker nor the engine's designer saw any commercial possibilities for the engine.

When the need for jet engines arose, Studebaker saw production of the GE J47 as an opportunity to build a new factory through which it could expand its empire. Studebaker wanted to challenge the "Big Three" auto makers by elevating itself to the level of Ford, General Motors, and Dodge to become the "Big Four." Weak Studebaker vehicle sales in the 1950s derailed these plans, necessitated Studebaker's merge with other firms, and ultimately led to its decline.

With two unsuccessful original projects, the Arrowbile engine and the XH-9350, and two mass-produced engines designed by other companies, the R-1820 and GE47, it is easy to see why Studebaker's aircraft engine history is often overlooked. It was scarcely mentioned in the company's centennial publication from 1952, *100 Years on the Road*. Books detailing Studebaker's history mention aircraft engine production only in passing. However, Studebaker's involvement with aircraft engines is a unique aspect of the company and demonstrates that Studebaker had the technological ability to produce whatever it needed and in whatever quantity it wanted. The fact that Studebaker parts are still being used in R-1820 aircraft engines over 75 years after they were made is a testament to their impeccable quality.

Although the Studebaker Corporation ceased to exist long ago, the machines they built will continue to be used for years to come, keeping the memory of the company, its founders, and its employees alive.

Studebaker craftsmen again give "more than they promise"

The devastating bombing power and matchless fighting power of the Boeing Flying Fortress make comforting daily items in the war news. Much of the flying power for this invincible dreadnaught of the skies comes from Studebaker, which has long been regarded as one of the foremost builders of motor car engines in the world.

Studebaker, America's oldest manufacturer of highway transportation, is privileged to collaborate with Wright,

America's oldest producer of airplane engines, in this vital assignment. And Studebaker is also building much other war matériel including tens of thousands of big, multiple-drive military trucks for the United Nations.

Today, as for generations past, Studebaker craftsmen make their watchword— *"give more than you promise."* Every Studebaker employee is justly proud of his organization's achievements in the arming of our Nation and its Allies.

BUY U.S. WAR BONDS

War Trucks for the United Nations!
Studebaker, famed for years for dependable transportation, has now become one of the largest producers of big, multiple-drive military trucks for the fighting forces of the United Nations.

Studebaker BUILDS WRIGHT CYCLONE ENGINES FOR THE *Flying Fortress*

Appendix:

MX-232 / XH-9350 Documents

MDAC-312-WF-6-27-41-100M

ADDRESS REPLY TO
ASS'T. CHIEF, MATERIEL DIVISION

WAR DEPARTMENT
AIR CORPS
MATERIEL DIVISION
OFFICE OF THE ASSISTANT CHIEF OF DIVISION

WRIGHT FIELD, DAYTON, OHIO

January 15, 1942.

Mr. N. N. Tilley,
Lawrence Engineering & Research Corporation,
Linden, New Jersey.

Dear Norm:

     This is in reply to your letter of January 14th,
saying it will be satisfactory for Opie to visit you at the
Lawrence Engineering Company's plant.

     He will be there sometime Monday and discuss the
project that I have in mind. You understand Norm, this is a
discussion with you and does not involve the Lawrence Engineering and Research Corporation, and if when Opie arrives you
prefer to have him see you in the evening to discuss the matter,
that will be entirely satisfactory, as it is only necessary for
him to catch a night train from New York to be in Washington
the next morning.

     Very sincerely yours,

E. R. PAGE,
Colonel, A. C.

THE STUDEBAKER CORPORATION
SOUTH BEND, INDIANA

April 24, 1942

Mr. N. N. Tilley
511 Springfield Avenue
Cranford, New Jersey

Dear Mr. Tilley:

Thought you would like to know that we have
just received from Wright Field a notice of
award of contract; this contract being designated as W 535 ac-28386, covering the
development of Long Range Engine, and an A-1-A
priority rating has been assigned to this contract.

Very truly yours

Vice President

R.E.Cole
hs

THE STUDEBAKER CORPORATION
SOUTH BEND, INDIANA

April 30, 1942

Mr. N. N. Tilley
511 Springfield Avenue
Cranford, New Jersey

Dear Tilley:

Enclosed is copy of telegram just received from
Wright Field. The other day I just did not understand the letter we received on award of contract,
so I called Col. Page and told him about it and he
had not even heard of the letter or sent it, so he
said he would investigate it right away and wire us
back. The enclosed is a copy of his wire. Am giving you this just to let you know just how the situation stands.

However, I think if possible you should come out
here Monday and you and I, and Bill, can sit down
and sort of map out a tentative program as to how
we will start; that is, which size cylinder shall
we build first - 6-1/2, 7-1/2, or 8. Personally,
don't think it will make a whole lot of difference,
because I think all three types will come thru very
close together. However, think we should have some
sort of tentative plan set up to be working on.

If it is not convenient for you to be here Monday or
Tuesday, almost any other day will be satisfactory
except Wednesday. I expect to be out of town on
that day.

Best regards

Ray E. Cole
Vice President

R.E.Cole
hs

THE STUDEBAKER CORPORATION
SOUTH BEND, INDIANA

March 3, 1942

E. R. Page, Col, Air Corps
Chief Power Plant Section
Material Division, Wright Field
Dayton, Ohio

SUBJECT: LONG RANGE ENGINE DEVELOPMENT

Dear Sir:

The following proposals for development of the Long Range Aircraft Engine are submitted for your consideration.

Studebaker Corporation Aircraft Engine Specification No.1 of March 1942, for the engine is enclosed. The various items of this proposal are to be conducted as concurrently as practical.

It is also understood that upon failure of parts of multicylinder engine construction in preliminary test engines, component parts tests or multicylinder tests, that the government will buy replacement parts, redesigned or corrected against the particular failure at prices to be negotiated and that labor for replacement is without charge to the government.

It is understood that title to the design will remain with The Studebaker Corporation but that the Air Corps would have full shop rights.

It is proposed that payment for items, except 5, be made upon acceptance of reports and for item 5 after assembly of first engine ready for test, the other engines after production acceptance test. It is presumed that partial payments can be arranged.

1. Design, construct and conduct performance investigations of at
    least four sizes of cylinder bores in the range of 6 to 8
    inches diameter and several stroke bore ratios, to determine the
    best design combination for low fuel consumption of the multi-
    cylinder engine -- 30% - Not on the 5 h/cyl   531,800.00

    A report will be submitted in ten months from contract date,
    but testing will be continued for a period of at least twelve
    additional months to be covered by additional reports, as
    agreed between contractor and government after delivery of
    the first report.

APR 18 1946

-2-   3-2-42

2. Design, construct two complete twin-cylinder test engines and
    conduct endurance tests of most desirable cylinder size and
    construction determined in item 1, together with connecting rods
    and pistons suitable for the multicylinder aircraft engine - -   245,000.00

    A report of tests of first endurance runs will be submitted
    within five months after completion of item 1, but endurance
    testing will be continued for a period of at least twelve
    additional months to be covered by additional reports as
    agreed between contractor and government after delivery of
    the first report.

3. Design studies of multicylinder engine to be made concurrently
    with items one and two - -   50,000.00

    This work to be completed in ten months from date of contract.

4. Design and development with suitable component sub-assemblies
    of multicylinder engine including reduction gears, (co-axial
    two-speed propeller drive with torque meter); fuel injection;
    ignition; coolant pump, supercharger; accessory section;
    special controls; multicylinder valve and cam drive; oil pumps;
    and evaluation of various structures not included above. This
    work to be completed prior to complete release and construction
    of item 5 - -   700,000.00

5. Design and complete detail drawings including installation and
    assemblies, construct and assemble six multicylinder engines
    as required for items 6, 7, 8 and 9 - -   1,837,000.00

Completion of first engine eight months after completion of item one,
others as required for items 7, 8 and 9.

6. Development runs and calibration of one multicylinder engine - -   170,000.00

    Completion six to twelve months after completion of item 5.

7. Fifty-hour development test of one multicylinder engine - -   270,000.00

    Completion six to twelve months after completion of item 6.

8. Fifty-hour military test of one multicylinder engine - -   125,000.00

    Completion six to twelve months after completion of item 7.

9. Deliver three engines to the government, one for type test and
    two for flight test.

    Completion to be within three months of completion of item 8.

                                                                         _____

    Total of Items 1 to 8 inclusive - -   3,928,800.00

(3-2- 2)   -3-

The above program will be expedited to the best of the contractor's ability
and will be in close cooperation with the Government at all times. Consulta-
tion will be held with the best authorities obtainable. A high priority rating will be necessary to meet the proposed schedule. It must be understood
that this project is one which has never been attempted and is reaching out
into a field in which there has been very little research. Therefore, while
every effort will be made to attain the objective as proposed, there is no
guarantee that these specifications can be met.

Very truly yours

THE STUDEBAKER CORPORATION

Roy E. Cole

Vice President

R.E.Cole
hs

MDAC-265-WF-6-28-41-200M

CONFIDENTIAL

INTER-OFFICE MEMORANDUM

WAR DEPARTMENT, AIR CORPS
Office, Assistant Chief
Materiel Division

OC:rwy:57.

MX-232

Wright Field, Dayton, Ohio

Date ....APR 1 0 1942

TO: Commanding General, A.A.F. Materiel Center, Wright Field.

SUBJECT: Authority for Purchase No. 224892.   Early Phases of an
Engine Specifically Built for Long Range Bombardment
Applications.

1.   <u>General</u>:- The long range bombardment airplane presents some
difficult engineering problems in attaining the desired range. When
an airplane has been built with minimum drag and maximum propeller
efficiency the only method of increasing the range is to reduce the
fuel consumed per mile of flight. An engine has never been built
wherein the first consideration in its design has been fuel consumption.

2.   <u>Historical</u>:- As early as 1935 studies were made by the
Engineering Section which indicated the desirability of recommending
two separate and distinct classes of engines instead of an all purpose
engine as had been previously built by all manufacturers. The first
class was the engine for pursuit, light bombardment and all other
applications except long range bombardment, and for this group high
output and low engine weight are of supreme importance. The second
class would be specifically constructed for long range aircraft with
fuel consumption of maximum importance. Of course durability under
cruising conditions is important, as well as sufficient take-off
power to get the long range bomber in the air without an excessive
ground run. Obviously this engine would be heavier per horsepower
than an engine of the first class because the only known practical
means of obtaining the required fuel consumption is by high compression
ratio, and to simultaneously obtain the large take-off power an engine
of large piston displacement would be indicated. Many engines of the
first class for pursuit and light bombardment are available, but the
engine visualized for the second class of application has not been
built.

Early in 1940 Request for Data R40-D for a 4000-5500 horse-
power aircraft engine was sent to Wright Aeronautical Corp., Pratt
and Whitney Aircraft Div., United Aircraft Corp., Allison Division,
General Motors Corp., Continental Aviation & Engineering Corp. and
Lycoming Div., Aviation Mfg. Corp., and on April 17, 1940, a Technical
Committee was appointed for the evaluation of the data submitted.
Because of important production work some of the manufacturers sub-
mitted bids on gearing together existing engines to obtain the horse-

Signature ....

CONFIDENTIAL

Project MX-232

t-639

190

Commanding General, A.A.F. Materiel Center, Wright Field.
Authority for Purchase No. 224892. Early Phases of an
Engine Specifically Built for Long Range Bombardment Applications.
APR 10 1942

power instead of attempting to design an engine specifically for the
purpose. As a result, the report of July 25, 1940, to the Chief of
the Air Corps recommended as follows:

a. Cancellation of Request for Data R-40D.
b. Hold the subject in abeyance until the aircraft
engine industry is in a better position to
judge the effects of the expansion program and
can undertake new developments with less risk
of interference with production.

However, studies in this Section still were continued which more and
more convinced the engineers of the necessity of an engine specifically
built for long range operation, but no concrete action was taken until
December, 1941.

3. Recent action on engines specifically for long range bombardment aircraft. A survey was made of the companies building or undertaking the construction of aircraft engines and all except one had an
engine of their own under development or were affiliated with a company
having an aircraft engine under development or production. The larger
established aircraft engine manufacturers had engines of the 2500 to
3000 horsepower type under development and were extremely busy with
their own problems. As stated above, the automotive industry, except
for one case, had affiliations which would prevent their undertaking
such a program. The one corporation that had constructed a large aircraft engine production plant, without an aircraft engine of its own
and without any affiliations, was the Studebaker Corporation. This
corporation has an engineering staff composed of two men from the
National Bureau of Standards who had considerable experience with aircraft engines, Mr. W. S. James, the Chief Engineer, and Mr. Stanwood W.
Sparrow. This corporation likewise has a good automotive laboratory
wherein the early single and twin cylinder tests could be undertaken
with a minimum of modification, and an engineering department composed
of approximately 250 engineers, draftsmen, experimental machinists and
dynamometer operators. However, the corporation did not have available
a designer thoroughly familiar with modern aircraft engine practice and
it was realized that men of the ability required for this pioneering
project would be extremely difficult to obtain. There was, however,
one qualified aircraft engine designer, Mr. N. N. Tilley, who has been
employed for some time with the Lawrence Engineering and Research
Corporation and acting as consultant for the Chrysler Corporation on
their engine project, who would be of greater usefulness in the
National Defense effort on a larger engine development. The auxiliary
engines being built by the Lawrence Corporation had been sufficiently
developed to be placed in the production stage and the Chrysler engine

t-639

CONFIDENTIAL

Commanding General, A.A.F. Materiel Center, Wright Field.
Authority for Purchase No. 224892. Early Phases of an
Engine Specifically Built for Long Range Bombardment Applications.
APR 1 0 1942

design was nearing its completion. In addition, the present war had
emphasized to this Section the extreme necessity for long range
bombardment aircraft with the forceful realization that engines of
much improved fuel consumption and higher output are urgently needed.
Mr. Tilley and the Studebaker Corporation were contacted as to their
interest in such a project, with an explanation that it was a pioneering project which would require a great deal of engineering effort.
Studebaker Corporation representatives, Mr. Cole, Vice President of
Engineering, and Mr. James, the Chief Engineer, stated that their
corporation had frequently discussed the future possibility of entering into some phase of aircraft engine development. Since the war had
stopped automotive production, their engineering department would be
free to undertake such a development. As a result, the Studebaker Corp.
has had numerous conferences with Mr. Tilley and has submitted a
proposal on the early phases of this important development with options
for six of the full scale engines, as described in the subject Authority
for Purchase.

4. _Scope of present proposed procurement._ As stated above, the
only known means in the present state of the art of obtaining the low
fuel consumption desired for the 5000 horsepower for take-off and
military operation is to incorporate in the engine a very large cubic
displacement. To obtain this very large displacement by a large number
of small cylinders complicates the engine unduly, adds to its weight
and probably increases mechanical losses. Therefore, the largest
possible cylinder should be used, bearing in mind the balance between
minimum fuel consumption and the required 5000 horsepower. There are
no data available on cylinder bores in the range of 6 to 8 inches which
indicate the cylinder size that would be optimum for this specialized
condition. It is necessary, therefore, to build at least four sizes of
cylinders to determine this very important factor before the exact
arrangement of the engine can be determined. Concurrently, two twin
cylinder engines should be constructed for durability tests of the
cylinder finally selected and component parts of the multi cylinder
engine should be performance and durability tested. At the same time
design studies of the complete engine can be undertaken which will
indicate the best general arrangement of cylinders and other parts.
To proceed to this extent it was necessary that a specification be
prepared by Studebaker Corporation which designates the principal
features of the engine and they propose that it be a liquid cooled
engine with fuel injection, a two speed co-axial propeller system,
with the altitude rating obtained by an exhaust driven supercharger.

CONFIDENTIAL

Project MX-232

- 3 -

t-639

CONFIDENTIAL

Commanding General, A.A.F. Materiel Center, Wright Field.
Authority for Purchase No. 224892. Early Phases of an
Engine Specifically Built for Long Range Bombardment Applications.

The exact displacement cannot be designated, but it will probably be
in the range of 6500 to 8000 cubic inches, with every consideration
given to obtaining the lowest possible fuel consumption. This engine
would certainly be extremely valuable following the war for intercontinental air transportation.

5. A pioneering project of this magnitude will be costly and
will require several years to accomplish. Experimental funds are
available at this time for work of this nature, which may not be
available following the war. There is no known means of saving time
by bypassing the many preliminary tests which should be undertaken
prior to the building of the full scale engine. It is therefore
urgently recommended that the early phases of this project be undertaken while the money and the Studebaker engineering organization
are available and interested in undertaking a development which will
have outstanding military applications.

6. At the time the Allison Division initiated development of
the V-3420 engine there was some consideration given to building this
as a double engine, making thereby an R-6840 type. Subsequently the
design was further studied and a wooden model constructed. As a result
of conference between General Echols and Colonel Carroll on April 4, 1942,
the Allison Division will be asked to submit a proposal on continuation
of this development as an engine in the same general power class as the
Studebaker project.

F. O. CARROLL,
Colonel, Air Corps,
Chief, Experimental
Engineering Section.

CONFIDENTIAL

Project MX-232

-4-

- 1 -

Specification No. 10
February 1, 1945

MODEL SPECIFICATION
ENGINE, AIRCRAFT XH-9350-1

The Studebaker Corporation, South Bend, Indiana
Studebaker XH-9350-1 Aircraft Engine.

- 2 -

RESTRICTED

A. APPLICABLE SPECIFICATIONS

A-1. The following specification listed on page 2 shall form a part of this specification:

A-1a. Army-Navy Specification.-

AN-9500c Engines, Aircraft; General Specification and all applicable AN specifications and drawings in effect as of 1 February 1945.

B. TYPE AND MODEL

B-1. This specification covers the requirements for the Army Air Force XH-9350-1 engine.

B-1a. The Army Air Force XH-9350-1 engine for aircraft is a liquid cooled, flat "H", or twin horizontally opposed engine equipped with extension shafts and with provision for two-speed drive of two co-axial propellers. Take-off and altitude power is obtained with turbo superchargers, which also may be used for compound operation of this power plant. It is especially designed for low specific fuel consumption over a wide range of power in the cruising range to facilitate long range operation of aircraft (30 hours or more non-stop). The overall dimensions are such as to facilitate submerged type installation in aircraft. It is equipped with extension drive shafts for either pusher or tractor installations.

C. MATERIAL AND WORKMANSHIP

C-1. The requirements for material and workmanship shall be as specified in Specification AN-9500.

D. GENERAL REQUIREMENTS

D-1. See Section E.

This document contains information affecting the National Defense of the United States within the meaning of the Espionage Act, 50 U.S.C., 31 and 32, as amended. Its transmission or the revelation of its contents in any manner to an unauthorized person is prohibited by law.

RESTRICTED

- 3 -

E. DETAIL REQUIREMENTS

E-2. Drawings and Data.-The following of The Studebaker Corporation drawings and photographs form a part of this specification:

Dwg. No.	Title
A-909100	Engine Assembly, Complete
A-909101	Installation Drawing
A-909102	Priming System Assembly
A-909103	Fuel Injector
A-909104	Spark Plug Assembly
A-909105	Terminal Spark Plug
A-909106	Lubrication System Diagram
A-909107	Shielding Assembly
A-909108	Complete list of AN Standard Parts Used on Engine

E-6. Engine Weight.-

E-6a. Dry weight of the complete engine shall not exceed that specified in the Model Specification. It shall include the following parts and shall be recorded in the following form:

Basic Engine, including coolant pumps and piping on the engine, engine lubrication system oil pumps, starter connection including starter dog, tachometer drives, fuel pump drive, and all piping and controls between engine parts

. . . . 5357 lbs.

Fuel Injector, Including Speed Density Controls, Air Valve, Injectors, and Fuel Pipes . . . . 120 lbs.

Carburetor Screens and Gaskets . . . . None

Ignition System . . . . 100 lbs.

Priming System on Engine . . . . Not established

Cooling Air Deflectors and Baffles . . . . . None

RESTRICTED

Accessory Drive Covers . . . . 3 lbs.

Supercharger Pressure Regulator (on geared engine
  driven supercharger only) . . . . None

Propeller Extension Shaft (Length __) . . . . Not established

Bearings; Propeller Extension Shaft . . . . Not established

Propeller Gear Reduction Unit, Including
  Generator Drive, Power Take-off Drive,
  Vacuum and Hydraulic Pump Drives, and
  Propeller Governor Drive . . . . 730 lbs.

Propeller Change Speed Unit . . . . 560 lbs.

After Coolers . . . . None

Independent Mechanical Drive Auxiliary Engine
  Supercharger . . . . None

TOTAL DRY WEIGHT OF ENGINE . . . . .6870 lbs. plus
                                          items not established

E-7. Performance Characteristics.-The ratings, curves, and guarantees specified herein are based on the terms and standard conditions defined in Specification AN-9502 or AN-9503.

E-7a. Guarantees.-

E-7a(1). The performance guarantees shall be as listed in the following table. These data are based on the use of fuel conforming to Specification AN-F-28 and oil conforming to Specification AN-VV-O-446, Grade 1120.

RESTRICTED

- 5 -

TABLE I

Ratings and Specific Fuel Consumptions

Ratings	BHP	RPM	Altitude (feet)	Spec. Fuel Cons.	Max.Temp. Allowable Coolant (°C)	Max. Static Exhaust Pressure (In.Hg.Abs.)	Min. Dry Static Air Pres. at Air Valve Inlet (In. Hg. Abs.)
Take-off	5000	2200	Sea Level	0.50	121	37	36
Military							
(a) Sea Level	5000	2200	Sea Level	0.50	121	37	36
(b) 1st Crit.	5000	2200	25,000	0.50	121	37	36
Normal (Max. Power Mixtures)							
(a) Sea Level	4000	2000	--	0.48	121	33	32
(b) 1st Crit.	4000	2000	30,000	0.48	121	33	32
(c) 90% Normal	3600	1930	30,000	0.47	121	33	32
(d) 80% Normal	3200	1860	30,000	0.47	121	33	32
(70% Normal	2800	1775	30,000	0.47	121	32	31
Cruise Power Operation Schedule (Max. Economy Mixtures)							
	3000	1600	30,000	0.37		38	38
	2500	1600	30,000	0.37		31	31
	2000	1350	30,000	0.37		30	30
	1500	1100	30,000	0.33		28	28
	1000	900	30,000	0.33		24	24

E-7a(1)a. Maximum power on normal rated power and speed propeller load to which operation with best economy mixture strength is permissible shall be furnished when available. The minimum power and speed for best economy mixture strength shall also be furnished when available.

E-7a(1)b. The take-off rating shall be with manifold air temperature of 120° F.

E-7a(2). Ratings.- Values of specific fuel consumption on normal rated power and speed propeller load shall be supplied for each specified simulated altitude test condition and for the condition of 100 percent normal rated power and 110 percent normal rated speed when available.

E-7a(3). Curves.- Not applicable.

E-7b. Estimated Curves.- Curves shall be furnished as part of this specification upon completion of investigations of certain cylinders upon which this engine is based.

E-7d. Specific Oil Consumption.- The specific oil consumption shall not exceed .025 pounds per B.H.P.-hour at military power and speed and .025 pounds per B.H.P.-hour at normal rated power and speed and .025 pounds per B.H.P.-hour at 70 percent normal rated power and 89 percent normal rated speed with the lowest degree of supercharging used at sea level.

E-7e. Cylinder Head Temperatures (Air Cooled Engines) - Not applicable.

E-7f. Cylinder Barrel Temperatures (Air Cooled Engines) - Not applicable.

E-7g. Coolant Flow and Heat Rejection.

E-7g(1). Normal Rated Power and Speed.- When operating with a coolant outlet temperature of 121° C. (250° F.) at normal rated power and speed and guaranteed fuel consumption, the coolant flow is estimated as 640 gallons per minute and the estimated heat rejection is 47,000 B.T.U. per minute (1110 horsepower).

E-7g(2). Military Rated Power and Speed.- When operating with a coolant outlet temperature of 121° C. (250° F.) at military rated power and speed and guaranteed specific fuel consumption, the coolant flow is estimated to be 700 gallons per minute and the estimated heat rejection is 56,000 B.T.U. per minute (1320 horsepower).

- 7 -

E-7g(3). Data on coolant pump characteristics shall be furnished upon completion of tests not yet accomplished.

E-7i. Oil Flow and Heat Rejection.

E-7i(1). Normal Rated Power and Speed.- When operating on a rigid test stand at normal rated power and speed, with an oil inlet temperature of 85° C. (185° F.) for Grade 1120 and with an oil pressure to be determined from test, and with other conditions as specified for liquid cooled engines for Normal Rated Power and Speed under section entitled "Coolant Flow and Heat Rejection", the estimated oil flow in the engine is 580 pounds per minute and the estimated heat rejection to the oil from the engine is 22,000 B.T.U. per minute (520 horsepower).

The estimated oil flow in the change speed gear set is 87 pounds per minute and the estimated heat rejection to the oil from this gear set is 920 B.T.U. per minute (22 horsepower).

The estimated oil flow in the final reduction and dual propeller drive set is 290 pounds per minute and the estimated heat rejection to the oil from this gear set is 3080 B.T.U. per minute (73 horsepower).

E-7i(2). Military Rated Power and Speed.- When operating on a rigid test stand at military rated power and speed, with an oil inlet temperature of 95° C. (203° F.) for Grade 1120, and with an oil pressure to be determined from test, and with other conditions as specified for liquid cooled engines for Military Rated Power and Speed under section entitled "Coolant Flow and Heat Rejection", the estimated oil flow is 640 pounds per minute and the estimated heat rejection to the oil is 27,000 B.T.U. per minute (646 horsepower) in the engine.

The estimated oil flow in the change speed gear set is 120 pounds per minute and the estimated heat rejection to the oil from this gear set is 1270 B.T.U. per minute (30 horsepower).

- 8 -

The estimated oil flow in the final reduction and dual propeller drive set is 400 pounds per minute and the estimated heat rejection to the oil flow from this gear set is 4250 B.T.U. per minute (100 horsepower).

E-8. Engine Performance.- The complete engine shall function satisfactorily up to and including an altitude of 40,000 feet.

E-9. Torquemeter.- The engine shall be equipped with torquemeter.

E-11. Overall Dimensions.- The overall dimensions of the engine shall not exceed the following:

Length

Co-axial final reduction propeller drive unit	65 inches
Two-speed transmission unit	37 inches
Engine length overall, fuel injector to power-out shaft	102 inches
Engine length overall, fuel injector to magneto	106 inches
Engine length overall, fuel injector to starter	109 inches

Propellers approximately 15 feet from engine for tractor installation require about 9 1/2 feet of extension shafts and couplings.

Width

Except manifolds, at gear end drive of cam housings	80 inches
Overall approximately, including manifolds	105 inches

Height

Except at oil sumps	36 inches
Overall at oil sumps	40 inches

E-14. Pistons.- The engine shall be fitted with pistons of not less than 8.00 to 1 compression ratio.

- 9 -

E-15. Propeller.- Provision shall be incorporated for a system without oil transfer provisions to propellers. A shift rod requiring longitudinal motion shall be provided on the change speed gear set to select the reduction gear ratio. A plunger shall be provided in the engine thrust cover plate, in accordance with Army Air Forces Drawing No. X45G12188. The engine shall have No. 60L-80 shafts for dual rotation propeller shafts. The direction of rotation when viewed from the anti-propeller end shall be counter-clockwise for the inboard shaft, and clockwise for the outboard shaft.

E-16. Propeller Drive.- The propeller drive shall be equipped with a reduction gear ratio of 2.400 to 1 for cruise powers and 3.427 to 1 for take-off and military power. The change speed gear ratio is 1.428 to 1.

E-18. Impeller Gear.- Not applicable.

E-25. Coolant Temperature (Liquid-Cooled Engines).- The cooling liquid outlet temperature for liquid-cooled engines shall be 121° C. (250° F.). The coolant used shall be ethylene glycol or water-glycol mixtures as found desirable as result of test. The engine shall operate satisfactorily at all of its ratings with 70% ethylene glycol and 30% water by volume as a coolant.

E-25a. Coolant Pressure.- The maximum inlet pressure to the cooling liquid pump on liquid cooled engines shall be as determined from tests.

E-27. Fuel Metering System.- The engine shall be equipped with one Bendix 24 cylinder type fuel injector system for cylinder injection, or some other method of fuel injection if found more satisfactory.

E-27a. Following flight tests conducted by the aircraft manufacturers, sufficient data shall be submitted to the engine manufacturer to enable him to check the performance of the intake air scoops with any approved setting and to submit his recommendations to the Procuring Agency. Approval by the Government of any reference carburetor or equivalent or required metering curve established therefrom shall not relieve the engine manufacturer of the responsibility for proper functioning of that carburetor or equivalent and setting in various models of aircraft providing the recommendations of the engine manufacturers regarding scoop design changes are placed in effect.

E-30. Engine Starting.- Provision shall be made for starting the engine with an electric starter. The engine shall start with the fuel specified in the engine model specification at a minimum temperature of minus 30°C.

E-31e. Scavenging System.- When using an oil or diluted oil as specified in AN-9500, inlet temperature shall be maintained at values as established by test.

E-31h. Oil Pressure.- The main engine oil pressure at normal rated power and speed and the oil pressure in the various reduction gear and other units shall be established as a result of tests.

E-32a(1). Spark Plugs.- The engine shall be fitted with spark plugs of type and models to be established by certain cylinder developments upon which this engine is predicated.

E-32d. Magnetos.- The engine shall be equipped with low tension magneto ignition and ignition timing as determined by test.

E-33. Accessory Pads and Drives.- Accessories required for normal functioning of the engine, including the starter, shall be located on the engine. Other accessory drives, as for propeller governor, power take-off, generators, vacuum or hydraulic pumps, shall be located at the final drive of the propellers to permit minimum speed range during flight. Ratios of these units are specified relative to propeller shaft rather than to crankshaft.

The type of each accessory drive, the number used, and the gear ratio to the engine crankshaft, the maximum permissible torque in pound-inches for continuous operation, the maximum permissible static torque in pound-inches, and the direction of rotation when looking at the end of the accessory drive shaft in the engine, shall be as follows:

Accessory	Type	No. Used	Ratios	Continuous Torque	Static Torque	Direction of Rotation
Magnetos and Distributors	High Freq.	2	0.500	(Not Established)		Clockwise
Fuel Charger	Bendix	1	0.500	(Not Established)		---
Starter	IV	1	3.000	9,600	9,600	Counter clockwise
Coolant Pump	Centrifugal	1	1.5 approx.	(Not Established)		---
Pressure Oil Pump	Gear	1	(Not Established)	---		---
Engine Scavenge Pumps	Gear	4	(Not Established)	---		---
Speed Change Transmission Oil Pump	Gear	1	1.947	---	---	Counter clockwise
Fuel Pump	---	1	1.000	50	600	Counter clockwise
Tachometer Drives	II	2	.500	7	50	---
Generator	IIIA	1	*12.830	1,700	7,200	Clockwise
Final Transmission Oil Pump	Gear	1	*5.009	---	---	Counter clockwise
Vacuum and Hydraulic Pumps	II	2	*5.283	250	2,250	Clockwise
Propeller Governor	---	1	*4.007	125	2,300	Clockwise
Power Take-off	IIIA	1	*12.830	1,700	7,200	Clockwise

* Ratio to propeller shafts

E-34. In view of the size and special requirements of this engine beyond the scope of Specification AN-9500, it may be necessary to take exceptions or make additions not noted herein, as found desirable after completion of design studies and further engine laboratory investigations.

F. METHODS OF SAMPLING, INSPECTION, AND TESTS

F-1. The requirements for sampling, inspection, and tests shall be as shown in Specification AN-9500.

G. PACKAGING, PACKING, AND MARKING FOR SHIPMENT

G-1. The requirements for packaging, packing, and marking for shipment shall be as shown in Specification AN-9500.

H. REQUIREMENTS APPLICABLE TO INDIVIDUAL DEPARTMENTS

H-1. There are no requirements applicable to the individual departments.

I. NOTES

I-1. Deviations.- No deviation from this specification permitted except as a war emergency measure and then only after formal authorization from the Air Technical Service Command, or the Bureau of Aeronautics through the Procuring Service's District Representative.

© The Studebaker Corporation

The Connells of South Bend are traveling...

They've left the job of building Flying Fortress engines at Studebaker to their Dad

GEORGE CONNELL is in the Marine Corps. His brother Francis is in the Navy. Both are in the air service.

Only a little while ago they were one of numerous family groups in the Studebaker factories—headed by a father who has seen active service as a Studebaker man for over 28 years.

War has separated many of the famous father-and-son teams that have long made fine craftsmanship one of the great traditions of Studebaker's home community.

Boys who worked with their fathers on the Studebaker production lines are now seeing military equipment bearing the Studebaker nameplate in grim action in far-off places. Some write home to tell how heartening the quality of Studebaker craftsmanship is to the men-at-arms of our Nation and its Allies.

Steadily, off to the fighting fronts, from the Studebaker factories, move ever-increasing quantities of Wright Cyclone engines for the mighty Boeing Flying Fortress—tens upon tens of thousands of big multiple-drive military trucks—as well as other vital war matériel.

It's reassuring to every Studebaker man—on the production line or the firing line—to know that each shipment Studebaker makes today is helping to hasten the dawn of a safe, new tomorrow. After victory comes, still finer Studebaker motor cars and motor trucks than ever will be built.

BUY U.S. WAR BONDS

STUDEBAKER

Builder of Wright Cyclone engines for the Boeing Flying Fortress, big multiple-drive military trucks and other vital war matériel

On his Studebaker job over 28 years

Charles R. Connell began his Studebaker career before either of his air-crew sons was born. From early boyhood, their ambition was to follow in their father's footsteps in the Studebaker plants. That has been a typical family experience in Studebaker's home community for over 92 years.

Bibliography

1: Studebaker History

100 Years on the Road. The Studebaker Corporation, 1952.

Bonsall, Thomas E. *More Than They Promised: The Studebaker Story*. Stanford University Press, 2000.

Donnelly, Jim. "South Bend Stalwarts." *Hemmings*, December 2005, http://www.hemmings.com/hcc/stories/2005/12/01/hmn_feature19.html.

Erskine, Albert Russel. *History of the Studebaker Corporation*. The Studebaker Corporation, 1918.

Gibney, Morgan W., "30,000 Miles in 26,326 Minutes," *The Studebaker Wheel*, October 1928. (reprinted at http://www.studebakerclassics.com/30000.html)

Harper, Marilyn M. *World War II & the American Home Front*. National Historic Landmarks Program, 2007.

Longstreet, Stephen. *A Century on Wheels: The Story of Studebaker*. Henry Holt and Company, 1952.

2: Waldo Waterman and the Arrowbile

"The Curtiss Autoplane." *Aerial Age Weekly*. 19 February 1917.

"'Flying Automobile' Christened in So. Bend." *The Westfield Leader*. 14 October 1937.

Grey, C.G. *Jane's All the World's Aircraft 1935*. Sampson Low, 1935.

Grey, C.G., and Leonard Bridgman. *Jane's All the World's Aircraft 1937*. Sampson Low, 1937.

Gyger, Patrick J. *Flying Cars*. Haynes Publishing, 2011.

Schmid S.H., and Truman C. Weaver. *Golden Age of Air Racing Pre-1940*. EAA Foundation, Inc, 1991.

True, Ernest L. "The Wings of Waldo Waterman." *American Aviation Historical Society Journal*. Volume 11, Number 4, Winter, 1966.

Waterman, Waldo Dean, with Jack Carpenter. *Waldo: Pioneer Aviator*. Arsdalen, Bosch & Co., Publishers, 1988.

3: Studebaker-Built Wright R-1820 Cyclone

100 Years on the Road. The Studebaker Corporation, 1952.

Bonsall, Thomas E. *More Than They Promised: The Studebaker Story*. Stanford University Press, 2000.

Engines Shipped (on an invoice basis) by Wright Aeronautical Division and Licensees From 1920 to January 1, 1964. Wright Aeronautical, September 1960, Revised June 1964.

Lilley, Tom, and et. al. *Problems of Accelerating Aircraft Production During World War II*. Harvard University, 1947.

McCutcheon, Kimble D. "Wright R-1820 Cyclone." *Aircraft Engine Historical Society*. http://www.enginehistory.org/Wright/Wright%20R-1820.pdf.

McFarland, Stephen L. *A Concise History of the U.S. Air Force*. Air Force History and Museum Program, 1997.

Mead, Cary Hoge. *Wings Over the World: The Life of George Jackson Mead*. Swannet Press, 1971.

Roosevelt, Franklin D. *Message to Congress on Appropriations for National Defense*. 16 May 1940.

Roosevelt, Franklin D. *State of the Union Address*. 6 January 1941.

White, Graham. *Allied Piston Aircraft Engines of World War II*. Society of Automotive Engineers, 1995.

The Wright Cyclones. Wright Aeronautical Corporation, 1942.

4: XH-9350 in Context

Numerous reports and documents held by the U.S. National Archives and Records Administration at College Park, Maryland under Records of U.S. Air Force Commands, Activities, and Organizations (Record Group 342) - Air Force Engineering Division Records RD 1685 and 1686 - Boxes 1924–1928, 1930, 1931, and 1934.

Numerous reports and documents acquired secondhand from the estate of N. N. Tilley Jr.

Balzer, Gerald H. *American Secret Pusher Fighters of World War II*. Specialty Press, 2008.

Conn, Stetson, and Byron Fairchild. *The Framework of Hemisphere Defense*. Center of Military History, 1960.

Jenkins, Dennis R. *Magnesium Overcast: The story of the Convair B-36*. Specialty Press, 2001.

Mathews, Birch. *Cobra! Bell Aircraft Corporation 1934-1946*. Schiffer Publishing, 1996.

Norton, Bill. *American Bomber Development in World War 2*. Midland Publishing, 2012.

Request for Data R40-D. Army Air Corps, 6 March 1940.

USAF Historical Division. *The Development of the Heavy Bomber 1918-1944*. Air Force Historical Research Agency, 1951.

Wagner, Ray. *American Combat Planes of the 20th Century*. Jack Bacon & Company, 2004.

Whitney, Daniel D. *Vee's For Victory! The Story of the Allison V-1710 Aircraft Engine 1929-1948*. Schiffer Publishing, 1998.

5: XH-9350 in Development

Numerous reports and documents held by the U.S. National Archives and Records Administration at College Park, Maryland under Records of U.S. Air Force Commands, Activities, and Organizations (Record Group 342) - Air Force Engineering Division Records RD 1685 and 1686 - Boxes 1924–1928, 1930, 1931, and 1934.

Numerous reports and documents acquired secondhand from the estate of N. N. Tilley Jr.

6: XH-9350 in Perspective

Numerous reports and documents held by the U.S. National Archives and Records Administration at College Park, Maryland under Records of U.S. Air Force Commands, Activities, and Organizations (Record Group 342) - Air Force Engineering Division Records RD 1685 and 1686 - Boxes 1924–1928, 1930, 1931, and 1934.

Numerous reports and documents acquired secondhand from the estate of N. N. Tilley Jr.

Angle, Glenn D. *Aeroshpere 1939*. Aircraft Publications, 1940.

Brew, Alec. *Sunbeam Aero-Engines*. Airlife, 1998.

Bodemer, Alfred and Robert Laugier. *Les Moteurs a Pistons Aeronautiques Francais (1900/1960) Tome I and II*. Dovica, 1987.

Bourke, Robert E. "The Reminiscences of Robert E. Bourke. Dave Crippen interview with Robert E. Bourke." *Automotive Design Oral History, Accession 1673*. Benson Ford Research Center at The Henry Ford, 23 October 1986. http://www.autolife.umd.umich.edu/Design/Bourke_interview.htm.

Chatterton, E. E. "Napier Nomad: An Engine of Outstanding Efficiency." *Flight*. 30 April 1954.

Gersdoff, Kyrill von, and et. al. *Flugmotoren und Strahltriebwerke*. Bernard & Graefe Verlag Bonn, 2007.

Hartmann, Gérard. "Naissance d'un géant." *Dossiers historiques et techniques aéronautique française*, 19 January 2005. http://www.hydroretro.net/etudegh/naissance_d_un_geant.pdf.

Kotelnikov, Vladimir. *Russian Piston Aero Engines*. Crowood, 2005

Marchi, Oscar. *Aeronautica Militare Museo Storico Catalogo Motori*. Casa Editrice Pàtron, 1980.

McCutcheon, Kimble D. *Chrysler Aircraft Engines*. Weak Force Press, 2012.

McCutcheon, Kimble D. "Ford's Aircraft Engines." *Aircraft Engine Historical Society*, 19 March 2014. http://www.enginehistory.org/members/FordGGx.php.

Neal, Robert J. *A Technical & Operational History of the Liberty Engine*. Specialty Press, 2009.

Pearce, William. "Argus As 5 Aircraft Engine." *Old Machine Press*, 22 September 2012. http://oldmachinepress.wordpress.com/2012/09/22/argus-as-5-aircraft-engine.

Pearce, William. "Beardmore Cyclone, Typhoon, and Simoon." *Old Machine Press*, 23 January 2013. http://oldmachinepress.wordpress.com/2013/01/23/beardmore-cyclone-typhoon-and-simoon.

Pearce, William. *Duesenberg Aircraft Engines: A Technical Description*. Old Machine Press, 2012.

Pearce, William. "Klöckner-Humboldt-Deutz (KHD) Dz 700, Dz 710, and Dz 720." *Old Machine Press*, 17 August 2013. http://oldmachinepress.wordpress.com/2013/08/17/klockner-humboldt-deutz-khd-dz-700-dz-710-and-dz-720/.

Pearce, William. "Lycoming XR-7755 36-Cylinder Aircraft Engine." *Old Machine Press*, 20 May 2018. http://oldmachinepress.com/2018/05/20/lycoming-xr-7755-35-cylinder-aircraft-engine/.

Pearce, William. "Napier Cub (E66) – First 1,000 hp Aircraft Engine." *Old Machine Press*, 22 December 2012. http://oldmachinepress.wordpress.com/2012/12/22/napier-cub-e66-first-1000-hp-aircraft-engine.

White, Graham. *Allied Piston Aircraft Engines of World War II*. Society of Automotive Engineers, 1995.

White, Graham. *R-4360: Pratt & Whitney's Major Miracle*. Specialty Press, 2006.

Whitney, Daniel D. *Vee's For Victory! The Story of the Allison V-1710 Aircraft Engine 1929-1948*. Schiffer Publishing, 1998.

Welsh H. W. and Pierce E. F. *Wright Aeronautical Report 1052* (unpublished and possibly never completed). 26 March 1945 (possibly 1946).

7: Studebaker-Built GE J47 Turbojet

100 Years on the Road. The Studebaker Corporation, 1952.

Bowers, Peter M. *Boeing Aircraft since 1916*. Naval Institute Press, 1989.

Eltscher, Louis R. and Edward M. Young. *Curtiss-Wright: Greatness and Decline*. Twayne Publishers, 1998.

GE Aircraft Engines. *Eight Decades of Progress*. General Electric Company, 1990.

Kay, Antony L. *Turbojet: History and Development 1930-1960 Volume 2*. The Crowood Press, 2007.

Leyes, Richard A., and William A. Fleming. *The History of North American Small Gas Turbine Aircraft Engines*. American Institute of Aeronautics and Astronautics, 1999.

Morris, Leigh E. "Studebaker has come to New Brunswick to stay…," *Turning Wheels* Vol. 27, No. 1 January 1995.

Simmons, W. F. and H. J. Wagner. *Current and Future Usage of Materials in Aircraft Gas Turbine Engines.* Defense Metals Information Center, 1 February 1970.

St. Peter, James. *The History of Aircraft Gas Turbine Engine Development in the United States.* International Gas Turbine Institute of the American Society of Mechanical Engineers, 1999.

Wilkinson, Paul H. *Aircraft Engines of the World 1947.* Paul H Wilkinson, 1947.

Wilkinson, Paul H. *Aircraft Engines of the World 1954.* Paul H Wilkinson, 1954.

Index

National Advisory Committee for Aeronautics (NACA), 18, 92, 176
P.R. Mallory, 123
Packard Motor Company, 8–10, 30, 49, 107, 110, 179, 180
Pierce-Arrow, 5, 6
Pratt & Whitney Aircraft Company, 7, 29, 30, 43–49, 97, 159, 160, 168, 172, 175
Rolls-Royce, 30, 168
Scintilla Magneto, 134, 144, 146, 149, 154
Studebaker Aviation Division, 30, 33, 34, 113, 137, 141, 145, 152
Studebaker Brothers Manufacturing Company, 3, 4
Studebaker Corporation, 4–6, 10, 81
Studebaker-Garford, 4
Studebaker-Packard, 8–10, 180
Tucker Corporation, 27
United States Aircraft Corporation, 15
Volkswagen, 8, 180
Waterman Aircraft Manufacturing Company, 15
Waterman Arrowplane Corporation, 19, 25, 26
Wright Aeronautical, 9, 30, 31, 39, 43, 49, 78, 154, 166, 167, 175
White Motor Company, 6
Willys-Overland, 5, 22

Concepts/Programs
Hemisphere Defense, 44–46
MX-232, 1, 52, 62, 66, 77, 78, 81–83, 163, 166, 167
MX-434, 165
Project A, 43, 44, 50, 77
Project D, 43, 50
RFD R40-B, 45, 46
RFD R40-C, 46
RFD R40-D, 46–48, 50

Contracts
W-535-ac-17399 (R-1820), 33
W-535-ac-28386 (MX-232), 52, 84, 145, 152

Engines, Aircraft
Allison DV-6840, 47, 162, 164, 165, 169, 171, 173
V-1710, 43, 44, 165
V-3420, 45–47, 164, 165, 169, 171
X-3420, 44, 45
X-4520, 159, 160
Argus As 5, 159, 160
Arsenal 24H Tandem, 171, 172
Bristol Centaurus, 160, 162, 171
Chrysler I-2220, 168
Continental GSV-750A, 50
Hyper cylinder, 43, 50
I-1430, 46, 50
O-1430, 50
Curtiss OXX, 13
Daimler-Benz, 172
Duesenberg Model H, 159
Engineering Division W-1, 50
GEHL SNECMA 32 HL, 171

General Electric J47, 8, 11, 181
Various jet engines, 176, 177
FIAT A.14, 172
Franklin O-335, 26, 27
Ford GGA, 168
Hispano-Suiza 48Z, 171
Junkers Jumo 211, 107, 110, 118
Kinner K-5, 16
Klöckner-Humboldt-Deutz Dz 720, 169, 171
Liberty V-12, 175
Lycoming H-2470, 46, 47, 50
H-4940, 47, 51
O-1230, 50
R-7755, 165, 168, 169, 171, 173
Menasco B-4 Pirate, 18
Napier Cub, 159, 160
Nomad II, 169–171
Packard 1A-2500, 107, 110
2A-2500, 107
Power Jets W.2B, 176
Pratt & Whitney H-2600 (X-1800), 45, 46
H-3130 / H-3730, 46
R-1830, 30, 43, 44
R-2800, 7, 30, 168
R-4360, 47, 48, 97, 159–162, 166, 168, 172
Rolls-Royce Merlin, 168
Studebaker-Waterman S-1, 22
Wright Gipsy L-320, 17 18
R-1750, 31
R-1820, 7, 11, 51, 52, 78, 88, 101, 137, 141, 145, 154, 166, 177–181
R-2160, 45, 46
R-2600, 30, 162
R-3350, 30, 45, 46, 160, 169–171

Engines, Automotive
Franklin/Tucker six-cylinder, 26, 27
Studebaker 164 in³ six-cylinder, 82, 83
190 in³ six-cylinder, 20
205 in³ six-cylinder, 20
218 in³ six-cylinder, 20, 22, 181
226 in³ six-cylinder, 20
245 in³ six-cylinder, 20
337 in³ eight-cylinder, 6, 181
354 in³ six-cylinder, 181

Events
Boer War, 4
Cleveland National Air Races, 15, 24
Great Depression, 5, 16, 25
Korean War, 7, 8, 175
World War I, 5, 15, 159
World War II, 1, 5–9, 26, 29, 30, 159, 160

People
Alhroth, Frank, 167
Altman, Nathan D., 11
Arnold, Henry (Hap), 175
Blackwood, J. G., 127, 128, 141

© 1943, The Studebaker Corporation

More and more Flying Fortresses are powered by Studebaker-built Cyclone engines

Clear-eyed, clean-hearted young Americans are up there in those Flying Fortresses—writing new chapters of a free world's destiny. Many of them were carefree school boys only yesterday. Today, they're pouring cringing fear into the souls of once boastful "supermen." To these gallant youngsters—and to their expert crews below that keep them flying—we of Studebaker pledge ourselves to go on producing more and still more of the mighty Wright Cyclone engines

for these devastating Boeing bombers. We recognize and respect the responsibility for maintaining quality that the Army-Navy "E" Award has placed upon the Studebaker Aviation Division plants. We'll "give more than we promise" in the best Studebaker tradition. Meanwhile, civilian needs must and will wait . . . until Studebaker completes this wartime assignment . . . until the finer Studebaker cars and trucks of a brighter day can be built.

Awarded to Aviation Division *of The Studebaker Corporation*

Big Studebaker military trucks stand out in all the major war zones—Studebaker is now one of the world's largest builders of multiple-drive military trucks. The Studebaker factories also produce much other war matériel, including big quantities of Flying Fortress engines. We are proud of our assignments in arming our Nation and Allies.

★ BUY U. S. WAR BONDS ★

Studebaker BUILDS WRIGHT CYCLONE ENGINES FOR THE BOEING *Flying Fortress*

Made in the USA
Middletown, DE
30 September 2023

39840781R00124